Diagnoses of Our Time
Six Views on Our Social Condition

Diagnoses of Our Time

Six Views on Our Social Condition

John A. Hall

HEINEMANN EDUCATIONAL BOOKS

Heinemann Educational Books Ltd
22 Bedford Square, London WC1B 3HH

LONDON EDINBURGH MELBOURNE AUCKLAND
HONG KONG SINGAPORE KUALA LUMPUR NEW DELHI
IBADAN NAIROBI JOHANNESBURG
EXETER (NH) KINGSTON PORT OF SPAIN

British Library Cataloguing in Publication Data

Hall, John A.
    Diagnoses of our time.
    1. Sociology
    I. Title
    301.092'4   HM51

    ISBN 0-435-82402-3

Photosetting by Thomson Press (India) Limited,
New Delhi, India

Printed in Great Britain by
Biddles Ltd, Guildford, Surrey

Contents

Acknowledgements

Daniel Bell, Ralf Dahrendorf, Raymond Aron, Jürgen Habermas and Ernest Gellner discussed their work with me at some length, and I am grateful for questions answered and encouragement received. Special thanks are due to Gellner and Habermas for sending me unpublished material. Tom McCarthy has let me use some of his translations from Habermas that appear in his *The Critical Theory of Jürgen Habermas*, published by MIT Press and Hutchinson, and I am grateful for this. Various chapters have been improved by comments received from Chris Bryant, Robert Colquhoun, Gordon Causer, Donald MacRae, Ian Jarvie and Mick Mann. My thanks go, too, to the University of Frankfurt for allowing me to teach there in the Sommersemester 1978. I cannot praise enough the highly developed decoding skills developed by those who typed my manuscript: sincere thanks to Doreen Davies, Susan Sidgwick and Gill Harley. And, finally, I am more grateful than I can say for the support and forbearance of my family.

John A. Hall
October 1980

The author and the publishers would like to thank the following for kind permission to reproduce extracts from their material in this book (the numbers in brackets give the pages on which these extracts appear in this book): Cambridge University Press (212, 233); Collier Macmillan, New York (97, 98–9); Trustees of Columbia University in the City of New York (167); Professor Miriam B. Conant (157); Doubleday and Joan Daves, New York and Piper Verlag, Munich (134); The Free Press, New York (167); Hutchinson, London and MIT Press, Cambridge, Massachusetts (56–7); Telos Press Ltd (14).

1 Introduction

The Current State of the Philosophy of History

It is possible to make out two separate and distinct concerns housed under the single rubric 'philosophy of history'. On the one hand, this subject comprises the *formal* analysis of the limits and character of historical—and therefore of sociological—knowledge. On the other hand, however, the philosophy of history attempts the *substantive* mapping of the broadest possible sweep of historical development; the central interests here are the establishment of typologies of societies and the specification of mechanisms that explain movements between particular types. The most celebrated examples of the formal approach are the attempts of Dilthey and Sartre to propound an historical or dialectical reason to complement 'analytic' reason; and the best-known example of the latter approach probably remains the idea of progress born of the Enlightenment.

But if it is *possible* to make this distinction, it is, nevertheless, very mistaken to do so. Historically, the classical sociologists combined the approaches mentioned. Their desire to understand the social changes brought about by the creation of industrial societies went hand in hand with, or—more accurately—gave rise to, reflections on the proper way in which to study social life. And even this does not describe the range of their preoccupations fully. For, intimately linked with historical awareness and methodological reflection, was a more or less self-conscious attempt to produce moral philosophies or, perhaps better, conceptions of the sort of social identity that men could expect from modern society. This stands in very marked contrast to the situation of modern sociology, which has witnessed extreme exuberance in formal questions at the expense of the understanding of patterns of history. The point to be made is that abstract methodological analysis has produced little of value. (Indeed, in my opinion, it never will: methodological advance is born of attempting to explain social life.) This is perhaps especially true of the debates, to be discussed, over idealism—materialism and positivism. In the latter case, the jejune discovery that there are well-known weaknesses to classical positivism has occasionally led to the nihilistic argument that the very enterprise of understanding society is impossible. This turning-of-the-back on 'the facts' may be a merciful release for some, but it is surely a dereliction of professional duty. For our times have obviously not been without their own measure of drama—world wars, fascism, the attempt to industrialise the third world, the emergence of socialist societies in Eastern Europe, the spread of nationalism, the brief efflorescence of student rebellions, and so on. And the fact that current sociology has not fulfilled the promise of its classic antecedents to produce a plausible philosophy of history for our time is probably responsible both for the terrible self-doubt afflicting the subject and for the hostility shown to it by the general public.

The aim of this book is to contribute to the encouraging signs already apparent, of a renewed interest in the substantive philosophy of history[1] by examining the work of six thinkers, some of whom have not received the critical attention they deserve, who have retained something of the range of their forebears. In each case, I suspect that this range was occasioned by personal circumstances such as Jewish family background (Marcuse, Bell, Aron and Gellner), experience of exile (Marcuse, Aron and Gellner) and the attempt to come to terms with Germany's past (Marcuse, Habermas and Dahrendorf). But I am concerned less with the sociology of knowledge than with a description and assessment of different views on our social order. The expression 'our social order' is carefully chosen and represents the first of two caveats to be borne in mind. The principal interest of the thinkers concerned lies in their diagnoses of our own time and, although this sometimes involves commenting on history as a whole, the focus is less on all human societies than on the character of those of the present. Secondly, all these thinkers may be considered post-Marxist, i.e. I have not chosen to discuss a 'mainstream' Marxist, if any still exist. Of course, this is not to say that no interest is shown in Marx. On the contrary, Habermas and Marcuse see it as their task to improve on Marx, whilst the remaining thinkers all wish to point out his weaknesses.

A part of the interest in considering this set of thinkers together is that they treat substantially similar themes. Naturally, however, very different conclusions are reached, since we are offered, roughly speaking, three rather different general views of modern society. The first such approach is that of Habermas and Marcuse, who are both critics of what they consider to be 'one-dimensional' or 'technological', modern, and especially Western, society. Both are post-Marxist in the specific senses that they have reservations about the role of science in society and believe that the working class is no longer capable of creating a socialist society. This part of their argument, of course, owes much to the Frankfurt School, but it must be emphasised that Marcuse and Habermas are not being treated here as representatives of that school. Nor could they be, for their relations with the orthodoxies of that school are very tenuous. Martin Jay, in his brilliant account of the Frankfurt School, insists time and again on how resistant Horkheimer and Adorno were to 'positive', i.e. constructive, social theory. Problems arose from this:

> Reality had to be judged by the 'tribunal of reason', but reason was not to be taken as a transcendent ideal, existing outside history. Truth, Horkheimer and his colleagues always insisted, was not immutable. And yet, to deny the absoluteness of truth was not to succumb to relativism, epistemological, ethical or otherwise. The dichotomy of absolutism and relativism was in fact a false one. Each period of time has its own truth, Horkheimer argued, although there is none above time. What is true is whatever fosters social change in the direction of a rational society. This of course once again raised the question of what was meant by reason, which Critical Theory never attempted to define explicitly. Dialectics was superb at attacking other systems' pretensions to truth, but when it came to articulating the ground of its own assumptions and values, it fared less well.[2]

Habermas and Marcuse are atypical of the Frankfurt School as a whole because they systematically try to spell out their own standards of rationality. Although the hagiographers of the Frankfurt School often lament this, it seems to me very much to be preferred to the insinuation so often practised by Adorno. And Marcuse and Habermas can be seen as 'positive' thinkers in a way additional to their desire to produce constructive political philosophy. Both of them offer us very full-blooded defences of 'positive' freedom; in other words, both are deeply critical, on theoretical and empirical grounds, of the limited, neo-Schumpeterian view of democracy as allowing for a circulation of elites. In this matter, Marcuse and Habermas differ completely from the remaining thinkers who endorse precisely some such revisionist theory of democracy.

Bell and Dahrendorf see modern Western society in rather different terms: they describe it as 'post-capitalist'. Curiously, this means that there are many points of overlap with the views of Habermas and Marcuse. The most important of these is the insistence that class conflict is no longer likely to destroy Western society. But this overlap, of course, hides a very different assessment: Habermas and Marcuse regard one-dimensional society as incorporating and stabilising class privileges, whilst Dahrendorf and Bell consider that various social changes since Marx's own time have turned Western society along the path of social justice, i.e. insofar as there are classes, they result from the division of labour and are no longer essentially the result of privilege.

A third approach is offered by Aron and Gellner. Most obviously, these thinkers have little time for the argument presented (with the partial exception of Dahrendorf) by the other thinkers that the impact of science on society is such as to create a new social 'stage', variously described as 'technological' or 'post-industrial'; such developments as have taken place are seen, instead, as fulfilling the basic logic of industrialism. Perhaps more important, however, is the insistence on the fragility of Western society. Aron and Gellner are rather sceptical as to whether the working class was *ever* a revolutionary class, and they argue that piecemeal pressure in certain circumstances can cause a crisis for Western society. This is not to say that they do not recognise and welcome some of the social changes that have taken place since Marx, although they are not completely rosy-eyed about them. But the point they make is that there are different regimes supported by industrialism, that an understanding of political factors is necessary to understand crises in the West.

These are but preliminary remarks, since interesting overlaps between all these thinkers exist, whilst there are noteworthy differences between the pairs of thinkers identified. But before considering these questions in detail, something should be said about methodology.

A Controlled Methodological Excursus

After some of the earlier criticisms made, it may seem almost hypocritical to consider methodology at all. But this is necessary so that certain issues that concern the thinkers are identified, and in order that one or two points of terminology may be clarified. But the excursus is short: I only wish to say something about certain issues derived from the debates over idealism—materialism and positivism.

Perhaps the key insight of all modern social thought is that behaviour which seems strange from the 'outside' can make sense, or be meaningful and rational, from the 'inside'. This insight has been variously applied to understand 'the savage mind' and the behaviour of schizophrenics. But it has recently been systematised so as to produce a demand for nothing less than 'sociology by meaning'. The central tenets of 'sociology by meaning' are: that humans, unlike atoms, make meanings; that the social world is made up of such meanings; that the authorities on such *Weltan-*

schauungen are those who participate in them; and that sociology has no choice but to accept the accounts offered by such experts. Roughly speaking, there are two sources of this extreme idealist doctrine which, given its emphasis on social behaviour as the product of the available conceptual apparatus, I shall term Platonism.

On the one hand, certain currents in modern philosophy have led to a particularly rigorous formulation of this doctrine. The most important of these currents are Wittgensteinianism, with its demand that we approach life by means of our language or concepts, and the *Geisteswissenschaften* tradition, with its emphasis on meaning as the central characteristic of social life. Both of these and the difference between them are discussed later. On the other hand, however, a more directly political source can be detected. Both Parsons and Durkheim felt that unfettered Hobbesian individualism would lead to anarchy, and they consequently argued that shared social values were a precondition for social life. As is well known, there has been a lengthy debate between conflict and consensus theorists which is still largely unresolved. For our purpose, however, it will prove useful to describe this argument as about an 'ideal consensus'. And—curiously—these debates are by no means over; the theories of Althusser and Gramsci are a form of Platonism in so far as they argue that capitalism is held together by 'hegemony' or by 'ideological state apparatuses'.

Whether this approach offers us a false method, a mistaken view of the nature of belief-systems and a poor guide to their role in society, are questions that will be discussed later. However, one striking criticism of Platonism concerns us now since it allows us to see other issues raised by the idealism-materialism debate. Martin Hollis argues that Platonism has a 'plastic' image of man that is vitiated by its failure to take into account the manner in which individuals manipulate their circumstances to their own ends.[3] In a nutshell, Platonism does not take account of the wily deviousness of social actors as portrayed by, say, Erving Goffman. Interestingly, Hollis makes a commendable and forthright attempt to introduce some concept of the 'ends' which human beings try to maximise. He begins by considering such ends, or 'interests', as purely economic, but rapidly comes to the conclusion that ideational interests are quite as real. Personally, I have some sympathy for the more limited and instrumental version of 'rational man theory', but I am well aware that this theory can easily degenerate into mere cynicism. More importantly, Hollis is surely right to insist that 'interest' be interpreted generously so that we are able to recognise men's attempts to manipulate both received belief and economic institutions in order to create a way of life that makes sense to them. No better description for this process has yet been found than Max Weber's notion of an 'elective affinity' between circumstance and way of life.

These points could be summarised by saying that there is no merit in the crude opposition between 'ideas' and 'economic circumstances'.[4] But what sort of method results from seeing all social actors as having ideational and economic interests? Is Martin Hollis right to fear that such a view of man disallows any sense of social structure?[5] After all, treating all spheres of society—ideological, political and economic—as having their own interests, does introduce a degree of freedom into social analysis.[6] One example of this is literature. The naive Marxist hope that every literary text could somehow be reduced to class interests ignores the fact that the literary sphere, in part, runs along its own autonomous lines.[7]

The fact, however, that there is no one-to-one correspondence between the economy and intellectual spheres does not mean that sociologists can do without a strong sense of social structure. On the contrary, the sociologist must engage in 'power-accounting' if he is to understand the chances that particular spheres have of dominating their society, i.e. he must estimate the size and functional importance of different groups—the latter point being understood widely so as to allow the Weberian insistence that power has sources other than the economic. This sense of social structure is likely to lead to a very different view of the way in which societies gain sufficient 'consensus' to operate. There is, of course, nothing in this approach to deny the presence of ruling ideologies, and of attempts made to socialise members of a society into them. However, a 'group' conception of society strives to determine whether the stick of coercion or the carrot of economic advantage is being used to ensure social stability, and will seek for what can be called a 'material consensus'.

These observations about structure are intended to avoid the stark contrast between idealism and materialism, as does, for the most part, it has been claimed, the work of Weber and Marx. But there remains a substantial difference between these two thinkers concerning ideology and history. Most immediately, Weber argued that history could be disrupted by the emergence of charisma, and this made him reluctant to endorse Marx's view of the essential rationality of the historical process. This contrast can usefully be borne in mind when recalling that modern society has witnessed the predominance of the great ideologies of nationalism, fascism and socialism.

This then gives us two points that are important in allowing us to understand the different approaches of the thinkers discussed here, namely, whether such ideologies are part of a rational logic of history, and whether their historical prominence and character can be explained in social structural terms. These two points—abstractly—can give four possibilities, and something can be said about each of them. So Bell, despite his awareness of, and indeed attachment to, the 'logic' of the economy, sees ideology as the bearer of the irrational; and as ideology disrupted European society in the 1930s so it may do again, thus ruling out any conception of a rational course to history. Habermas argues, perhaps incorrectly, that Marx failed to complement his analysis of developing economic contradictions with an understanding of the ideological developments that would lead to men reacting to crisis in a revolutionary manner. If Habermas were simply to describe how structural change bred various ideologies he could properly be understood as complementing an account that was perhaps deficient. But he posits—albeit with qualifications that should be borne in mind—an independent 'logic' of moral development that is the pacemaker of historical change.

The accounts offered of ideology by Bell and Habermas must be considered idealist since it is the eruption of, or rational developments within, ideology that makes history. This must be contrasted to accounts which recognise the force of ideology but seek to explain its character and emergence. None of the thinkers discussed below is a traditional Marxist, believing that a single mechanism (class conflict), always brought into play by the economy lends rationality to the historical process. But Gellner does argue that we should conceive of the industrial revolution as a structural transformation sufficient to explain the prevalence and character of modern ideology. The fact that the origins of this revolution were more accidental than rationally determined does not lead him to see history as completely formless and unpatterned. On the contrary, he is currently seeking to replace the concept of evolution with that of 'episodes' in human history caused by the neolithic and industrial revolutions which, themselves the product of accident, thereafter determined various patterns in history.

So much misunderstanding has been created by the idealism-materialism debate that the discussion of the two issues raised—Platonism and ideology—has been somewhat laboured. Although positivism raises equally difficult issues, it can be discussed here more succinctly. It must be remembered initially that positivism has become a somewhat vague creature. Specifically, 'positivism' is no longer considered to be the secularised religion proposed by Comte, but a much more general attitude, which Comte also shared, as to the proper way of gaining human knowledge. Kolakowski has argued that positivism, in this loose sense, rests upon four assumptions: that facts exist; that they are separable from one another; that human values do not have the status of facts; and that all knowledge is of a single type.[8]

Three issues follow from this. Firstly, we can see that there is a strong link between Platonism and the rejection of the positivist insistence on the unity of all knowledge. For if human life is determined by meaning, and if such meanings are different in each society, it becomes impossible to have sociological knowledge modelled after the natural sciences. This is a very complex matter but we can say, roughly, that the less Platonist a thinker the more he will seek for generalisations about social behaviour. Secondly, Kolakowski's first two tenets, nominalism and phenomenalism, have been much criticised ever since Kant insisted that it was our mental equipment that allowed us to apprehend facts in the first place. This line of argument has been extended in well known attacks, particularly that of Thomas Kuhn, who insists that facts are so 'theory-laden' as to vitiate the positivist philosophy of science. We shall see Habermas trying to avoid the relativistic implications of Kuhnian analysis, i.e. he refuses to accept any old paradigm, whilst Gellner offers a sophisticated defence of positivism as a cognitive ethic. And we need to remember, in this connection, Max Weber's insistence that modern science, by making the world less homo-centric, 'disenchants' modern man. Again, Gellner and Habermas take different sides on this issue. Finally, there is the question as to whether values can be rationally justified. If knowledge derives *only* from facts, it is often held to be impossible to justify values, which then become adopted in some sort of existentialist moment of faith or commitment. This Nietzschean sort of ethic is opposed by those who think that values can themselves be justified rationally, a debate related to arguments in the philosophy of science. And something follows from this. A political thinker deserves to be judged not just on the plausibility of a particular set of values, but also on whether he can specify a means by which these values will be realised. This is what most people understand as the question of theory and practice. However, we must note that this expression can have a slightly more technical meaning to those who stress strongly that the understanding of man can never take on the character of natural science.

Such thinkers, above all Habermas, condemn as dangerous theories that treat men as objects; these should be replaced, he holds, by a systematic addressing of theory to active, 'practising' human agents. It must be stressed that this linking of theory and practice, i.e. the desire to produce theory to enlighten a particular clientele, does not rule out the more traditional use of these terms to describe the difficulty of translating political plans into reality. On the contrary, it is hoped that the right sort of theory may itself play a crucial role in social change. Perhaps the very writing of books would become impossible if authors felt that nobody would ever be influenced by them, and it is certainly the case that the thinkers discussed who do seek for something like natural science generalisations are well aware that social life is not without options; but for all that, this doctrine is implausible since it tends, as we shall see Habermas having to admit, to lack any moderately realistic sense of social structure.

Rousseau's Problem

Herbert Marcuse was born in 1898, and served briefly in the army at the end of the First World War. On his return, he was involved with the Spartacists; he left in 1919 because he felt that the emergence of directing officers in the workers' councils represented a betrayal of socialist ideals.[1] His extreme radicalism naturally kept him out of the Social Democrats (SPD) but he was much influenced by the two characteristic cultural products that filled the vacuum of defeat in war, namely expressionism and existentialism.[2] His early writings speak of 'total' and 'authentic' man, and it was not surprising that he chose to go to Freiburg to study with Heidegger in 1928. In 1932 Marcuse's very Heideggerian book on Hegel (*Hegel's Ontologie und die Grundlegung einer Theorie der Geschichtlichkeit*) appeared. This begins by describing how the young Hegel felt that the modern world was out of joint, divided and bereft of 'totality'. Hegel consequently tried to create and realise a new total vision that would allow us to feel whole and at one with the world once again.[3] Marcuse writes warmly of this project, as well he might, for it is his own.

This chapter describes how the elements of Marcuse's moral vision were assembled from his early Heideggerian Marxism, from the curious and by no means entirely 'negative' materialism of the period between 1932 and 1941, when he was closely associated with the Frankfurt School in exile, and from the important encounter with Freud. Roughly speaking, this vision comprises three elements. Firstly, he envisages fraternal community based upon full realisation of individual authenticity. That is to say, that his marriage of existentialism and Marxism is unlike that of Sartre in refusing to create an opposition between individual and society: the individual can only realise himself *through* others, in Marcuse's eyes. Secondly, he insists that freedom must be 'real' freedom, and more is meant by this than a traditional Marxist attack on mere 'formal' freedoms. Marcuse attacks German Idealism because freedom is so much a mental, spiritual matter. Freedom cannot, in Marcuse's vision, be separated from happiness in normal life, and so must include sexual happiness as well. Thirdly, Marcuse eventually accepted the view famously expressed by Adorno and Horkheimer, that a social world free of domination depended upon adopting a non-dominating approach to nature.[4] Marcuse's version of this idea derives from Hegel and is characterised by his advocacy of 'dialectical logic'. This moral vision is fantastically ambitious and generous and, for once, a Freudian category helps us: Marcuse's vision is clearly an example of that 'oceanic feeling' characterising those desperate to have the world make sense.[5]

Any thinker who offers us this sort of moral utopia will condemn out of hand the fallen and inauthentic world of the present. Marcuse certainly does this, and in doing so he reminds us very much of Rousseau. And we can structure the discussion of Marcuse by noting that his thought faces a problem familiar to us from Rousseau. All political thinkers must be judged both in terms of their ideals and of their ability to realise them. This problem of theory and practice is especially acute for those who, like Marcuse and Rousseau, consider their society bereft of any saving grace. Rousseau never overcame the simple contradiction that follows from this: the social contract was required in order to take men from a false and insincere existence to the civil virtues—but how can such a move be made unless the makers of the contract are *already* morally whole? And the problem of strategy is compounded for Marcuse by the emphasis of political theory, since Rousseau, on epistemology. In a sense, things were easy for Rousseau who felt sure that a mere examination of his soul would provide universal standards. But once we adopt, as we surely must, a more realistic view, stressing that beliefs are social and historical products, it becomes necessary to be much more rigorous in describing how universal standards are to be achieved. Marcuse is certainly aware of this dilemma and, as early as 1930, criticised Lukács's concept of 'correct class consciousness' on this account:

> This notion is (as the conception of class consciousness has been on the whole) a violation of the dimension of historicity, a fixation 'outside' of what happens from whence an artificially abstract connection with history must be produced.[6]

If thought is historical, in other words, why should we believe that any particular political recommendation is universally true? And this problem is, of course, immensely important since the question of how to achieve a political strategy scarcely arises until some set of values is specified in a way that allows us to consider them universal. Marcuse's attempts to find a reliable way of specifying universal standards are highly idiosyncratic, as we shall see.

Heidegger + Marx = The Historicity of Labour

The attraction that Heidegger had for Marcuse is clearly outlined in his first article, 'Contribution to a Phenomenology of Historical Materialism'. Existentialism is held to be an advance on traditional philosophy because it is more concrete:

> .... the constitution of being involving existence appears as 'being-in-the-world'. As such, being and world exist together. The problems of transcendence, reality, and the demonstrability of the world in their traditional contexts turn out to be pseudo-problems. Existence is always 'being-in-the-world'. This is because the world and its existence is already given, and it is given in its accessibility.[7]

This is a fairly high-handed way of dealing with whole traditions of philosophy, and it is open to the objection that some social situations are highly objectionable and must not be accepted. Marcuse is aware of this for he notes that men always search for authenticity:

> Existence is always concerned for its own being, and this existentially conceived 'concern' is regarded as the actual existential essence. In spite of all dejectedness and forfeiture, the potential to realise its essence lies in this concern. It can thus reach its own authentic existence.[8]

However, Marcuse rejects Heidegger insofar as this search is said to be simple, i.e. timeless and somehow spiritual. Marx is applauded on account of his realisation that man's condition is historical, and therefore that authenticity depends upon particular social arrangements. Marcuse suggests that placing Marx and Heidegger together leads to a crucial question:

> ...we demand that Heidegger's phenomenology of human existence be driven to dialectical concreteness so that it can be fulfilled in a phenomenology of concrete existence and of the historically concrete act demanded of it. And, on the other hand, the dialectical method of knowing must go the other way and become phenomenological so to incorporate concreteness in a complete account of its object. In the analysis of the given, it must not simply locate it historically, or indicate its roots in an historical existential situation. It must also ask whether the given is thereby exhausted, or whether it contains an authentic meaning which, although not ahistorical, it endures through all historicity. Although this question may seem superfluous in relation to actual historical action, it becomes unavoidable if it is to actually arise out of knowledge.[9]

This is indeed crucial. For only if such an element in historicity can be discovered will it be possible to know what the authentic life is and only then will Marxism be sure of its own aims.

The search for such an element in historicity is not, Marcuse insists, a simple discovery of a universal, non-changing human character. That would, of course, be the pure ontology which is anathema to any historical thinker. Marcuse argues that the element of historicity he discovers—labour—is not itself ontological but merely an ontological category in human life, i.e. all men labour, but labour takes different forms. Labour is described in another essay in terms reminiscent of the Sartrian 'pour-soi', always incomplete, always searching for new experiences:

> The essential factual content of labour is not grounded in the scarcity of goods, nor in a discontinuity between the world of disposable and utilizable goods and human needs, but, on the contrary, in an essential excess of human existence beyond every possible situation in which it finds itself and the world. Being human is always *more* than its present existence. It goes beyond every possible situation and precisely because of this there is always an ineliminable discrepancy between the two: a discrepancy that demands constant labour for its overcoming, even though human existence can never rest in possession of itself and its world.[10]

As noted, Marcuse does not regard this constant searching as in any way tragic. But the general analysis is used to criticise capitalism mercilessly. It is men's very nature to change and develop or, in other words, to seek to mould their world via new forms of labour. Capitalism is appalling because it creates a static, one-dimensional world in which this essential character of historicity is arrested. This is made clear in an essay in which Marcuse enthusiastically argued that Marx's *Economic and Philosopic Manuscripts of 1844* confirmed his own argument:

> It is precisely the unerring contemplation of the essence of man that becomes the inexorable impulse for the initiation of radical revolution. The factual situation of capitalism is characterised not merely by economic or political crisis but by a catastrophe affecting the human essence....[11]

Before assessing this argument it is as well to spell it out by noting that it is derived from Hegel. *Hegel's Ontologie* is a highly technical interpretation of Hegel, and of very Heideggerian tone. This is seen especially in the attention given to Hegel's concept of being. The details of Marcuse's analysis are none too clear, but the main point stands out. The essential fact of being is its diversity:

> Every being is in a state of division, ambiguity and movement, while it is in existential relation with other beings, in order to build a new unity of being with some other being. It is only

simultaneously with its other side, its non-being, and with all that is different from it, through which it becomes determined and limited. Being is only in this movement, change and multiplicity and is only in them as unity, permanence and sameness.[12]

The idea behind this murky statement is in fact fairly simple, and can be illustrated by one of Hegel's own examples. Being is not static since it develops. The moments of being of a plant include the sprouting of the seed, flowering etc.; yet in each of these moments the plant remains a plant, and indeed it is only by going through each of these stages that a plant fulfils its full being.

Two consequences follow from this 'mobility of being'. Most obviously, as we have seen, life itself is presented as being two-dimensional. Great stress is placed on the necessity of a special type of dialectical logic for this to be understood. The origins of Marcuse's later attack on positivism are apparent in this passage in which he castigates taking 'facts' at their face value:

> To begin with, it appears that the existence of this factory is an entirely undisputed fact. It is 'the same' for everyone who sees it and sets foot on it, not only in its totality, but also in its machinery, workers, parts of buildings, and so forth. But when I really see the factory in its parts and the people in it, I should then know what they 'mean', what the factory, machine, worker, generally is and ought to be, what is their significance and purpose. If I do not know these things (this knowing is, of course, usually totally 'unconscious', an unnoticed, 'habitual knowledge'), I do not see a factory, machinery, workers, and so forth, but only an accumulation of stones, iron, people, etc. Of all this I do not really know what actually is, and what it is supposed to mean. When we realize that all this familiar and well-known meaning is simultaneously experienced and seen in our everyday process of vision, that without this we would not see, then suddenly the unequivocal givenness of such an object becomes doubtful. Is the factory really the same for those employed in it as workers, for its owners, for the idle traveler who happens upon it, and for the architect who built it? Or is it not each time the same and yet something quite different... To comprehend an historical object completely in its concrete reality, one has to grasp the totality of events. Such a comprehension is impossible if the historical object is considered rigid and isolated from its historical context, and treated as an identity free of contradictions 'throughout time', instead of seeing it as a many-faced coming into being, acting and passing away in time.[13]

Secondly, however, Marcuse draws a distinction between human and natural being. Only men can self-consciously realise their potential; the different moments of being of, say, a stone are not the result of consciousness but merely of blind collision with other objects. It is hard to see exactly what conclusion must be drawn from this. On the one hand, emphasis is placed on the uniqueness of man, and especially on the human capacity to become whole by recalling one's formative stages. It is not surprising that, in this vein, Marcuse suggests that nature is simply an object for men to work upon:

> Labour .... is precisely the doing of human beings as the mode of one's being-in-the-world: it is that through which one first becomes 'for itself' what one is, comes to one's self, acquires the form of one's being-there, winning one's 'permanence' and at the same time making the world 'one's own'.[14]

But, on the other hand, there are passages where Marcuse seems to be straining to very different conclusions. If all being has some sort of potentiality then man, as the conscious element in the world, should help it to be realised:

> In order for existence to simply continue to develop, all of these objectifications demand a specific kind of care, maintenance, securing, developing and overcoming based on them—a labouring that is in no way only based on the needs of the present, but must rather take into consideration the immanent want in these objectifications....[15]

This responsibility of man to nature is expressed even more clearly a few years later:

> Hegel does not mean that everything that exists does so in conformity with its potentialities, but that the mind has attained the self-consciousness of its freedom, and become capable of freeing nature and society. The realisation of reason is not a fact but a task.[16]

We shall hear more about this later.

What then are we to make of Marcuse's Heideggerian Marxism? The theory is terribly weak for three reasons. Firstly, it is open to a charge often justly brought against Sartre's advocacy of authenticity, namely that no judgement can be brought against someone who, as it were, authentically decides to live in bad faith or, in this case, chooses to endorse a one-dimensional world. I think Marcuse became aware of this and sought to make use of Freud to distinguish somewhat more rigorously between true and false needs. Secondly, and relatedly, Marcuse's glorification of labour as a permanent element of historicity is open to an obvious objection: if this is something permanent how could an alienated, one-dimensional world ever have arisen? What is to guarantee it not arising again? Marcuse does not even bother to systematically address this because at this period he is essentially a traditional Marxist optimist. He notes, for example, that:

> Since it is only in *labour* and in the objects *of his labour* that man can really come to understand himself, others and the objective world in their historical and social situation, the master, as a *non*-worker, cannot come to this insight.... the worker has an (as it were) irreducible advantage over him. He is the real factor of transformation; the destruction of reification can only be *his* work. The master can only come to this revolutionary insight if he becomes a worker, which, however, would mean transcending his own essence.[17]

The important implication of this passage is that the revolution is on the cards. But we are not told why this should be so, and this makes Marcuse's moral critique of capitalism rather empty. Finally, notice should be given to the first of several instances in which Marcuse produces assumptions that are breathtakingly optimistic. These assumptions are key and must be highlighted: I shall—pejoratively—call them his millenarian moments. In his essay, entitled 'Philosophical Foundation of the Concept of Labour', Marcuse withdrew his earlier insistence that socialism necessitates abolishing the division of labour, but without trying to specify sources of coercion that might be needed to make a complex industrial system work. No coercion would be necessary, we are assured, because once man has been freed from capitalist society his natural sociability will make non-coercive cooperation natural.[18]

The Frankfurt Years

Adorno reviewed *Hegel's Ontologie* and spoke approvingly of the tendency Marcuse exhibited in the work to move from abstract historicity to the analysis of actual historical situations.[19] As a review, this was probably misleading, but it does highlight the desire of Adorno and Horkheimer to produce 'negative' thought rather than to dream up new moral utopias. The essential rationale of what was a rather question-begging approach was that the radical aims of bourgeois society could be used to criticise its current practice—an approach which itself rested on the fundamental belief that the working class remained a revolutionary force. Marcuse accepted the argument that his society was not, as he had thought, totally reified and one-dimensional. But the acceptance was ultimately superficial for we can detect Marcuse beginning, in his analysis of materialism, to create a 'positive' argument that would later take him to Freud. His work in these years is best approached by considering four themes: the analysis of liberalism, the critique of positivism, the description of certain key two-dimensional concepts (especially hedonism and art) and the advocacy of a true materialism.

Marcuse's role in the Institute for Social Research, which he joined in 1932, was essentially that of a critic of philosophy, whilst other members were more or less responsible for more immediately political and social matters.[20] But this did not prevent Marcuse having a social theory underlying his essays, albeit one more or less borrowed from Pollock. This theory was essentially that fascism was to be seen as intimately connected with monopoly capitalism:

> .... the economic foundations .... are all essentially part of the transformation of capitalist society from mercantile and industrial capitalism, based on the free competition of independent individual entrepreneurs, to monopoly capitalism, in which the changed relation of production (and especially the large 'units' such as cartels and trusts) require a strong state mobilising all means of power.[21]

Marcuse argues that a particular fascist ideology is needed to justify this totalitarian world. In some brilliant and accurate pages he suggests that the core of the ideology depends upon a worship of heroism, vitalism, existentialism and naturalism. Naturalism is criticised since it suggests that there are laws beyond human control:

> The current crisis is 'nature's revenge' on the 'intellectual attempt to violate its laws....But nature always wins in the end...'. The transfiguration of economic and social relations to natural archetypes must inevitably and repeatedly come up against the so completely 'unnatural' facticity of the current forms of life.[22]

Such criticism is perhaps to be expected. But Marcuse's attacks on vitalism represents a rejection of the *Lebensphilosophie* of Dilthey which he had previously admired, whilst his powerful critique of political existentialism shows him distancing himself from Heidegger's self-identification with the Nazis.[23] On the basis of this analysis, one might expect Marcuse, given the title of his main essay on the subject, 'The Struggle Against Liberalism in the Totalitarian View of the State', to offer some sort of defence of liberalism itself. But the crux of Marcuse's argument is that liberalism contains the seeds from which totalitarianism springs. Just as capitalism breeds monopoly capitalism, so liberal philosophy is held to encourage fascist ideology. Both philosophies are but masks for various types of capitalist interest that remain unchanged:

> To be sure, we often encounter in heroic-folkish realism vehement invective against the monstrosity of capitalism .... But since the foundations of the economic order .... remain intact, such invec-

tives are always directed against only a specific type of bourgeois (that of the small and petty 'merchant' breed). They never attack the economic functions of the bourgeois in the capitalist production process.[24]

We will discuss the explanation of fascism in detail when considering Dahrendorf, but we can say here that Marcuse's 'agency theory' is deeply mistaken. It offers no explanation of why fascism did not occur in advanced capitalist societies like Britain and America, or indeed of the rise of fascist movements in agrarian countries such as Rumania.[25] As John Orr has brilliantly demonstrated, Marcuse's analysis of the ideology of 'total organisation' is more a criticism of an idiosyncratic thinker such as Junger than an accurate assessment of the policies proposed and adopted by the Nazi party.[26]

But given that fascism represented an attempt to create a one-dimensional world, it is important to ask from which position Marcuse himself was able to act as a social critic. The answer can be found in his championing of Hegel against the Nazis. In English-speaking intellectual life a connection has often been sought between Hegel's state-worship and Nazism itself: *Reason and Revolution* is best read as an attempt to refute such interpretations. Marcuse shows—quite easily—that the Nazis themselves were deeply suspicious of Hegel. For, when Hegel argued that 'the real is the rational', he did not mean that the presently existing social world was rational, but rather that the world, in order to be real, has to become rational. This is to say, that Hegel's dialectical logic is as much to the forefront of Marcuse's mind as it had been in *Hegel's Ontologie*. Consequently, Marcuse again stresses the role of men in realising the potential of the world:

> For there is, in the last analysis, no truth that does not *essentially concern* the living subject and that is not the subject's truth. The world is an estranged and untrue world so long as man does not destroy its dead objectivity and recognise himself and his own life 'behind' the fixed form of things and laws. When he finally wins this *self-consciousness*, he is on his way not only to the truth of himself but also of his world. And with the recognition goes the doing. He will try to put this truth into action and *make* the world what it *essentially* is, namely, the fulfilment of man's self-consciousness.[27]

There is, however, a slight difference in tone between Marcuse's two books on Hegel. The Hegel presented in *Reason and Revolution* is much more of a political thinker, and Marcuse offers both a defence and a criticism that are new. He defends Hegel against mere state-worship on the grounds that Hegel endorsed only the rational state; this state was progressive historically, in comparison with the conservative-populist student demands of the time whose wish to attack the state would have reaffirmed aristocratic control.[28] Nevertheless, Marcuse does feel that Hegel's advocacy of the state is unfortunate. He notes that Hegel's view of property followed from the insistence that will should control nature; and this in turn led to the Hobbesian need to create a strong state that would make all property holders obey the dictates of reason. The criticism of this position is simply that the law of the state only derives from a social problem:

> We have here a first example of Hegel's identifying a law of nature with the law of competitive society. The 'nature' of free will is conceived in such a way that it refers to a particular historical form of the will, that of the individual as private owner, with private property serving as the first realisation of freedom.[29]

This criticism of course introduces us to Marx. It is Marcuse's argument that Marx was able to take over the developmental view of history without falsely arresting it at the stage of competitive property holding. And even more important in Marcuse's interpretation, is the character of the Marxian dialectic. Hegel's recognition of coercion by the state in daily life led him to follow the tradition of German Protestantism in suggesting that the real sphere of freedom lay in thought, where reason was untrammelled by circumstances. Marx's dialectic is seen, in contrast, as definitely of *this* world:

> For Hegel, the totality was the totality of reason, a closed ontological system, finally identical with the rational system of history. Hegel's dialectical process was thus a universal ontological one in which history was patterned on the metaphysical process of being. Marx, on the other hand, detached dialectic from this ontological base. In his work, the negativity of reality becomes a *historical* condition which cannot be hypostatised as a metaphysical state of affairs. In other words, it becomes a social condition, associated with a particular historical form of society. The totality that the Marxian dialectic gets to is the totality of class society, and the negativity that underlies its contradictions and shapes its every content is the negativity of class relations.[30]

Marcuse contrasts the dialectical thought of Hegel, Marx and the Institute less with the particulars of fascist ideology than with the most sophisticated philosophical 'justification' for all non-dialectical thought, namely positivism. Marcuse suggests that the success of positivism originally sprang from philosophy falsely trying to emulate the physical sciences:

The human world was presented as governed by objective laws, analogous or even identical with the laws of nature, and society was set forth as an objective entity more or less unyielding to subjective desires and goals ... A strikingly conformist scepticism thus accompanied the development of modern rationalism. The more reason triumphed in technology and natural science, the more reluctantly did it call for freedom in man's social life.[31]

Marcuse is implying that we should reject positivism because the facts by which it wishes to judge are merely the facts of a false world; obedience to such facts can only result in conformist repression. This sort of sweeping assertion is very typical of Marcuse, and makes it even more important for him to be able plausibly to establish a second dimension lying below the facts. This style of condemnation eventually led to his attack on the western tradition of rationality as a whole. At this stage of his thought, however, his targets are smaller and more accessible.

Having admitted that thinkers such as Hume could adopt a critical attitude in matters such as religion, he turns his attention to the positivism of Saint-Simon and Comte. Saint-Simon is criticised for erecting laws of social life above the control of men, but Marcuse has much to say in favour of Saint-Simon's disciples.[32] In particular, they are held to have realised that Saint-Simon's pure industrialism was not possible in a world of social class. In contrast, Comte is attacked mercilessly. Marcuse detects a prefiguration of fascist thought in Comte's insistence on the need for resignation in the face of social contradictions so that industrialism may proceed:

Happiness in the shelter of a strong arm—the attitude, so characteristic today in Fascist societies—makes juncture with the positivist ideal of certainty. Submission to an all-powerful authority provides the highest degree of security. Perfect certainty of theory and practice, Comte claims, is one of the basic attainments of positivist method.[33]

And Marcuse goes further than this and anticipates one famous, later argument. He accuses Comte of fostering relativism so that no standard of judgement can be erected against his utopia. Such relativism is encouraged by a false tolerance:

The French Enlightenment who fought the absolute state gave no relativist framework to their demand for tolerance, but asserted that demand as part of their general effort to establish a better form of government.... Tolerance did not mean justice to all existing parties. It meant, in fact, the abolition of one of the most influential of parties, that of the clergy allied with the feudal nobility, which was using intolerance as an instrument for domination.[34]

Marcuse's attack on positivism is aimed at preventing the emergence of a fully integrated world. Another way of putting this is to say that Marcuse does not believe that the bourgeois world is *yet* totally conformist, and this can be seen particularly clearly in his analysis of hedonism, culture and the concept of essence. Marcuse's attitude towards each of these 'two-dimensional' realities is extremely ambivalent. As a Marxist he feels it necessary to point to the repressive functions of bourgeois culture, but his fear of fascism cannot prevent a tone of admiration for that culture, and we will see this tone turning into outright praise at the end of Marcuse's life. And one way in which this ambivalence can be seen is in Marcuse's urge to distinguish his analysis of philosophical doctrines from the 'undermining' practised by the sociology of knowledge:

> .... several fundamental concepts of philosophy have been discussed in this journal... These were not merely analysed sociologically, in order to correlate philosophical dogmas with social loci. Nor were specific philosophical contents 'resolved' into social facts. To the extent that philosophy is more than ideology, every such attempt must come to nought.[35]

'The concept of essence' is the most straightforward of the three topics examined. Marcuse argues that all great philosophies have drawn distinctions between the unimportant and the essential, the present and the hidden. This is held to be true even of Descartes:

> If the individual is to be salvaged and human freedom to be preserved, then the 'essence' of man must be located in thought. Here is where his authentic potentialities and the ontological certainty of his existence must be found: 'I conclude with assurance that my essence consists exclusively in my being a thing that thinks, or a substance whose entire essence or nature is only to think.'[36]

Marcuse's distrust of bourgeois society is seen in the fact that he regards limitation of the concept of essence to an internal, purely mental realm as a great loss. But, nevertheless, reality is still seen in two-dimensional terms, so that the possibility of criticising the given still remains. This possibility is being removed at the behest of phenomenology, dubbed here a characteristic thought style of late capitalist positivism:

> 'To the things themselves!' reveals its quietistic, indeed *positivistic* character as phenomenology progresses. The 'things' become so for phenomenology only after they have been stripped of their actual materially objective character and have entered the 'levelling' sphere of transcendental subjectivity for which everything is equi-valent.... A philosophy that considers 'all pre-given

beings with their exact evidence' equally 'prejudgements' no longer has any basis for distinguishing critically among those beings.[37]

The second topic treated is hedonism. Marcuse follows Hegel in arguing that hedonistic philosophies deserve criticism since they encourage enjoyment of an unjust order: this turns the idea of happiness into one of mere subjective enjoyment, when it should be, in Marcuse's eyes, much more. Marcuse is reasonably 'positive' when suggesting that this 'much more' must include a concern with the right ordering of the world and with satisfaction of personal relationships. Marcuse judges the last of these to be a demand incompatible with bourgeois society:

> .... the unpurified, unrationalised release of sexual relationships would be the strongest release of enjoyment as such and the total devaluation of labour for its own sake. No human being could tolerate the tension between labour as valuable in itself and the freedom of enjoyment. The dreariness and injustice of work conditions would penetrate explosively the consciousness of individuals and make impossible their peaceful subordination to the social system of the bourgeois world.[38]

And insofar as hedonistic philosophy keeps alive the demand for happiness, it is to be praised. So Marcuse praises the sociological realism inherent in the idea that pleasure is to be found only in consumption:

> Hedonism embodies a correct judgement about society. That the receptivity of sensuality and not the spontaneity of reason is the source of happiness results from antagonistic work relations. They are the real form of the attained level of human reason.... Happiness is restricted to the sphere of consumption. Radical hedonism was formulated in the ancient world and draws a moral conclusion from the slave economy. Labour and happiness are essentially separated. They belong to different modes of existence.[39]

In the most sophisticated piece of work of the Frankfurt period, 'The Affirmative Character of Culture', Marcuse argues that the bourgeois era tries to hide from the sociological realism of the ancient world in the matter of art. Marcuse praises Aristotle for insisting that the contemplation of beauty was only open to those who had leisure. Bourgeois culture is, on the contrary, criticised since it affirms the social order by arguing that beauty can be appreciated by anyone whatever his circumstances.[40] And Marcuse adds a further and much more interesting notion by deriving from

Kant a theory of the beautiful, albeit this is only fully developed later in Freudian terms. The beautiful is held to be the pleasurable; but pleasure can only be had when the actual sorrow and pain of the world are ignored and, insofar as art produces such a reconciliation, it effectively endorses oppressive reality.[41] Marcuse also looks on the other side. Despite, or perhaps because of, its affirmative role, art harbours a second dimension that allows sufficient room to portray— however briefly—an entirely different reality. As an example, Marcuse argues that:

> The idea of love absorbs the longing for the permanence of worldly happiness, for the blessing of the unconditional, for the conquest of termination. In bourgeois poetry, lovers love in opposition to everyday inconstancy, to the demands of reality, to the subjugation of the individual, and to death.[42]

Only art, Marcuse argues, is able to keep a sight of this second dimension at all times. Philosophy and religion, the other realms of culture, are in contrast becoming increasingly integrated. The essay ends with the curious argument that there is something, after all, to be learnt from fascism. The Nazis are described as attempting to use art in the service of their cause: in particular, the internalisation of a realm of freedom is used to justify the monstrosity of a social order in which the individual is completely sacrificed. The only way in which this can be contrasted is by making the vision of happiness and liberation contained in art serve in the political realm immediately.[43]

The last matter deserving consideration is Marcuse's conception of materialism. Here Marcuse clearly held fast to certain positive injunctions despite the influence of Horkheimer and Adorno. Thus, in 'Philosophy and Critical Theory' he argues that reason can be realised in the world:

> For when reason is accorded the status of substance, this means that at its highest level, as authentic reality, the world no longer stands opposed to the rational thought of men as mere material objectivity. Rather, it is now comprehended by thought and defined as a concept. That is, the external, antithetical character of material objectivity is overcome in a process through which the identity of subject and object is established as the rational, conceptual structure that is common to both.[44]

Such a rational comprehension should not be merely an intellectual matter, but something achieved by man as a material and sensuous being. Indeed, Marcuse argues that only a combination of hedonism and reason can draw forth human resources able to change the world:

> General happiness presupposes knowledge of the true interest: that the social life-process be administered in a manner which brings into harmony the freedom of individuals and the preservation of the whole.... The abstract reason of isolated individuals is certainly powerless over a happiness abandoned to contingency.[45]

This is, of course, another millenarian moment, assuring us that true happiness can only be found in the general condition of happiness. Marcuse argues that Marx's materialism is of this type:

> He contemplates a society that gives to each not according to his work but his needs. Mankind becomes free only when the material perpetuation of life is a function of the abilities and happiness of associated individuals.[46]

I am not at all sure that this is a correct interpretation of Marx, and it is certainly not the view famously adopted by Horkheimer and Adorno.[47] But once Marcuse has read this into Marx, he finds it very easy to accept without any sort of questioning the rest of the Marxist canon. Thus he adopts a vague if uplifting combination of *Capital* and the *Economic and Philosophic Manuscripts* which seems to suggest that 'the abolition of labour' will somehow transcend the division of labour; and he certainly believes that concentration in big business will lead to capitalism's collapse.[48] It is very surprising to find so much orthodoxy in a member of a school supposedly famous for originality and heresy. But this orthodoxy did not last.

Eros and Civilisation

All Marcuse's early work, whether 'negative' or otherwise, ultimately rests on the belief that the working class is a revolutionary force. This faith was, ironically, undermined for Marcuse as for other members of the Frankfurt School less by fascism than by the discovery that the working class was 'integrated' into American capitalism.[49] Marcuse reacted to this new climate by publishing only a single article, on Sartre,[50] in the years between 1942 and 1950. But after this pause his thought tried to deal with this new discovery in two ways. The first of these was essentially unlike the rest of the Frankfurt School, in being very optimistic. Onedimensionality could be avoided, Marcuse explained, for we could find alternative standards not in historicity but deep in the human psyche, and these would allow us to create a better world. The trouble with historical materialism had been that 'its concept of a free and rational society' promised 'not too much, but rather *too little*'.[51] These alternative standards could be discovered only with the benefit of Freud's late and speculative instinct theory. Marcuse became a very harsh critic of Fromm and other revisionists who sought to free psychology of these 'deep' instincts. This was crass positivism of the worst sort:

> Fromm revives all the time-honoured values of idealistic ethics as if nobody had ever demonstrated their conformist and repressive features. He speaks of the productive realisation of the personality, of care, responsibility, and respect for one's fellow men, of productive love and happiness—as if man could actually practise all this and still remain sane and full of 'well-being' in a society which Fromm himself describes as one of total alienation, dominated by the commodity relations of the 'market'. In such a society, the self-realisation of the 'personality' can proceed only on the basis of a double repression: first, the 'purification' of the pleasure principle and the internalisation of happiness and freedom; second, their reasonable restriction until they become compatible with the prevailing unfreedom and unhappiness.[52]

Marcuse's more radical use of Freud is taken up later. However, we can remark here that the second characteristic approach of his later years is that of extreme pessimism, consequent on a sociology stating that the liberal society would ignore alternative standards and become absolutely one-dimensional. There are hints of this in *Eros and Civilisation*, but they are only fully spelt out in *One-Dimensional Man* which is discussed in the next section.

Marcuse argues that modern industrial society is under the rule of the 'reality principle'. This principle insists that, in a world of scarcity, work and discipline must take the place of play and sensuousness. Order overcomes the urge for gratification. Marcuse argues that the manner in which this becomes possible is most fully explained only in the metapsychology of Freud's last years. In these years, Freud suggested that libido was divided into two instincts, one serving death, the other, life. Marcuse correctly points out that Freud was clearly fascinated by something that both these instincts shared, namely the conservative desire to return to a simpler form. Such a return amounts for Freud to an urge to abolish life altogether: this is obvious in the case of the death instinct, but is held to be just as true for the life instinct, which would apparently prefer peace to the difficulties encountered in trying to gain gratification in the world.[53] However, this common conservative search for Nirvana is usually avoided because the two instincts can work in different media. The life instinct (Eros) seeks to 'join together' things and experiences and it is held to triumph over the immediate aim of the death instinct (Thanatos) which is somehow linked to aggression.

Marcuse argues that both the history of the individual and the collectivity can be illuminated by understanding the process of conflict and fusion between these instincts. At the individual level, an understanding of these instincts underlies Freud's famous mental geography of id, ego and superego. The libidinal desire for gratification is located in the id, but is controlled by the ego and the social conventions inherent in the superego. In instinctual terms, aggression is held to provide some of the energy that the superego needs for its disciplinary measures, but the main impact of its force is now held to be directed against nature. This represents something of a taming of Thanatos, and it is paralleled by a taming of Eros. Most obviously, instant gratification is held back so that work can take place, but Eros is held to accept this because it can then gain secure gratification. However, Marcuse makes much of the loss involved in the genitalisation of sex. Certain sources of erotic delight are ruled out altogether:

> Smell and taste give, as it were, unsublimated pleasure *per se* (and unrepressed disgust). They relate (and separate) individuals immediately without the generalised and conventionalised forms of consciousness, morality, aesthetics. Such immediacy is incompatible with the effectiveness of organised *domination*, with a society which 'tends to isolate people, to put distance between them, and to prevent spontaneous relationships and the "natural" animal-like expressions of such relationships'. The pleasure of the proximity senses plays on the erotogenic zones of the body—and does so only for the sake of pleasure. Their unrepressed development would eroticise the organism to such an extent that it would counteract the desexualisation of the organism required by its social utilisation as an instrument of labour.[54]

This genitalisation of sex is, however, rejected by the perverted who continue to see sex in 'polymorphous-perverse' terms; and this unrestrained view of sex is held to have a hidden appeal for all of us.

At the collective level, Marcuse places great stress on Freud's anthropological-mythological account of the band of brothers who, having killed the authoritarian father, in their guilt reestablish repression. This sort of theory seems reasonably comprehensible as long as Marcuse simply argues that the primal crime is reenacted by every modern family.[55] But he wishes to stress that all of us have some sort of archaic memory of these events. The importance of these events for Marcuse has been neatly pointed out by Robinson:

> In Marcuse's hands the primal crime became a kind of capitalist allegory. Although he did not state so explicitly, he obviously transformed Freud's primal father into the capitalist entrepreneur and the band of brothers into the European proletariat.[56]

Marcuse suggests he has discovered here a psychic source for the non-appearance of socialist revolution. The guilt consequent upon the killing of the father led to harsher and internalised standards of authority, and this explains why most revolutionary movements are more than half defeated before they start. This might seem a decisive argument against the possibility of revolution, but Marcuse's argument seems to have the implicit assumption that understanding these deep mechanisms will allow us to escape them.

This very simple and rather vague description of instinctual theory might seem in philosophic terms to be pure ontology. But he argues, as he had with the concept of labour in his Heideggerian days, that the instincts are highly malleable and can appear in many different guises. More particularly, he joins these Freudian concerns with more traditional critical ones by introducing the concepts of surplus repression and performance principle. Roughly speaking, both of these refer to the fact that the level of repression in society is the result of more than the self-discipline needed so that scarcity can be conquered; repression is 'surplus' (presumably the resonance with 'surplus-value' is not accidental) insofar as a power structure exists which is held systematically to advantage some over others.[57] In the light of this argument, Marcuse attempts a 'depth' explanation of modern civilisation. As we have already seen, the development of civilisation is held to depend upon the taming of the death instinct. Increasingly, however, this balance between the instincts is tipped in favour of Thanatos. In Marcuse's words:

> Culture demands continuous sublimation; it thereby weakens Eros, the builder of culture. And desexualisation, by weakening Eros, unbinds the destructive impulses. Civilisation is thus threatened by an instinctual de-fusion, in which the death instinct strives to gain ascendancy over the life instincts. Originating in renunciation and developing under progressive renunciation, civilisation tends toward self-destruction.[58]

Marcuse's example of such self-destructive tendencies is fairly obvious: when he talks of regression to lower stages in which sado-masochism prevails, he clearly has fascism in mind.[59] And he insists that no substitutes can be found for the death instinct. In particular, work is usually so painful that little pleasure can be generated here.[60] And unleashing aggression onto nature does not somehow exhaust aggressiveness in its own right:

> .... extroverted destruction remains destruction: its objects are in most cases actually and violently assailed, deprived of their form, and reconstructed only after partial destruction; units are forcibly divided, and the component parts forcibly rearranged. Nature is

literally 'violated'. . . . . Destructiveness, in extent and intent, seems to be more directly satisfied in civilisation that the libido.[61]

Marcuse uses the instinctual model with great ingenuity, and it is tempting to question the whole terms of debate in which he engages. But I do not propose to follow that course since Marcuse's own account quickly becomes implausible in its own terms. The first way in which this is so concerns the sociology, mentioned above, which comes to the fore in *One-Dimensional Man*. This sociology is less scared by the terrible crisis created in civilisation by dark instinctual forces than it is petrified at the possibility that a repressive civilisation may be able to make itself psychically secure. On one occasion Marcuse suggests:

> Through the struggle with father and mother as personal targets of love and aggression, the younger generation entered societal life with impulses, ideas and needs which were largely *their own*. Consequently the formation of their superego, the repressive modification of their impulses, their renunciation and sublimation were very personal experiences. . . . Now, however, under the rule of economic, political, and cultural monopolies, the formation of the mature superego seems to skip the stage of individualisation: the generic atom becomes directly a social atom.[62]

This is to say that rebellion and criticism depend upon the struggles with a bourgeois and puritanical father; the absence of such a father may allow for the successful stabilisation of society. Secondly—and equally problematical—his optimistic account of the alternative reality under the rule of the pleasure principle is, in crucial ways, question-begging. Here, above all, are Marcuse's millenarian moments. In anticipation, we can say that these moments tend to take the following form: those instincts that are deep and dangerous when perverted are, in fact, beneficial and harmonious in their inner essence.

As noted, the instincts discovered by Freud are to be understood in terms familiar to us from the discussion of Marcuse's earlier Heideggerian Marxism, i.e. they are a permanent part of man's nature but are capable of taking on different forms. However, it is important to note that Marcuse's championing of the pleasure principle as an alternative to the reality principle enables him to advance his general position so as to escape the criticisms levelled at his Heideggerian Marxism. Firstly, Marcuse insists that the pleasure principle, understood either in terms of a hidden tradition of Western thought or in more conventional Freudian terms, represents 'real' needs. We shall see that these are not in fact spelled out very clearly, but Marcuse insists that they can be. Secondly, and most importantly, Marcuse is able to answer the criticism that an earlier and more primitive stage cannot have been so good since men deserted it. He does so, very simply, by saying that harsh reality has so far had to be obeyed because of the constraints of scarcity (and, of course, of domination as well). Now that affluence has been attained, true liberation is possible. Socialism, in a formulation Marcuse once accepted, can only flourish in rich countries.[63]

Marcuse follows Freud in arguing that what is repressed is remembered in phantasy. Art draws upon such phantasy, and thus contains the germ of an entirely alternative principle of social functioning:

> .... within the limits of the aesthetic form, art expressed, although in an ambivalent manner, the return of the repressed image of liberation; art was opposition.[64]

Marcuse effectively repeats the aesthetic theory first presented in 'The Affirmative Character of Culture', arguing that art's alternative view is achieved at the expense of being unreal and therefore ineffective, and here too Marcuse argues that the aesthetic should somehow become politically and socially active. But there is a slight addition to the argument: we are more or less told *how* art is able to reconcile us to evil reality in a way that makes it so pleasurable. It seems that this mysterious transformation can be explained in instinctual terms as the triumph of Eros and Thanatos: the bad reality is somehow reduced into an aesthetic form in which stillness and reconciliation are achieved.[65] This mysterious alchemy will prove important in a much larger sense in a moment. But before turning to this, a word should be said about the other source of Marcuse's alternative vision.

He finds in the myths of Orpheus and Narcissus a kind of poetic defence of the pleasure principle. His description of exactly how this sort of pleasure principle might be applied is exceedingly vague, but is worth noting. These myths summon up the vision of a world in which:

> .... the opposition between man and nature, subject and object, is overcome. Being is experienced as gratification, which unites man and nature so that the fulfilment of man is at the same time the fulfilment, without violence, of nature. In being spoken to, loved, and cared for, flowers and springs and animals appear as what they are—beautiful, not only for those who address and regard them, but for themselves, 'objectively'.[66]

This, of course, takes us back to his early dialectical insistence that man had some sort of duty to develop the full being of nature.

Insofar as this is a demand for ecology, it is comprehensible. But it must be stressed that there is no special reason to believe that scarcity has been so completely conquered that such a caring attitude towards nature is appropriate. Could not a *moral* case be made for the development of resources in many of the world to help solve perennial problems of poverty? Such matters bother Marcuse little. But of course Marcuse is here beginning to argue the Frankfurt School 'line', made famous by Adorno and Horkheimer's *Dialectic of Enlightenment*, that an entirely new attitude to nature is necessary as the domination of nature is held to lead to the domination of man. The mechanics of this link are by no means clear, and our discussion of the whole question can be delayed to the next section, where we consider Marcuse's criticism of modern science at its most ferocious.

Marcuse's alternative reality depends at many crucial points on those assumptions dubbed here as 'millenarian'. Firstly, at the end of the discussion of narcissism, Marcuse notes the accuracy of Freud's assessment of it as the archetypal 'oceanic feeling', and goes on to endorse this feeling openly:

> ....narcissism may contain the germ of a different reality principle: the libidinal cathexis of the ego (one's own body) may become the source and reservoir for a new libidinal cathexis of the objective world—transforming this world into a new mode of being.... The hypothesis all but revolutionises the idea of sublimation: it hints at a non-repressive mode of sublimation which results from an extension rather than from a constraining deflection of the libido.[67]

He concludes these observations as follows:

> Under such conditions, the impulse to 'obtain pleasure from the zones of the body' may extend to seek its objective in lasting and expanding libidinal relations because this expansion increases and intensifies the instinct's gratification.[68]

We can already see that Marcuse has argued that the perversions hold out the promise of unconstrained sexuality. This might seem as if Marcuse is somehow advocating or underwriting some of the lesser social virtues such as coprophilia or necrophilia. But, secondly, we are assured that this is not the case:

> ....the function of sadism is not the same in a free libidinal relation and in the activities of SS troops. The inhuman, compulsive, coercive, and destructive forms of these perversions seem to be linked with the general perversion of the human existence in a repressive culture, but the perversions have an instinctual substance distinct from these forms; and this substance

may well express itself in other forms compatible with normality in high civilisation.[69]

This is convenient and nice to know. And much the same is true, thirdly, of sexuality as a whole. Sexuality will cease to be genitalised, since all activity will give erotic reward. (*Eros and Civilisation*, like Wilhelm Reich's *The Function of the Orgasm* is not, as many had doubtless hoped, a dirty book after all: on the contrary, it is in the last analysis a document of prim German Romanticism.) And once all activity is eroticised, it seems that something Marcuse has hitherto resisted will become possible:

> .... if work were accompanied by a reactivation of pregenital polymorphous eroticism, it would tend to become gratifying in itself without losing its *work* content. Now it is precisely such a reactivation of polymorphous eroticism which appeared as the consequence of the conquest of scarcity and alienation. The altered societal conditions would therefore create an instinctual basis for the transformation of work and play.[70]

But this is not all. Fourthly, the instincts are apparently not resistant to order as such, for once reason becomes sensualised:

> It creates its own division of labour, its own priorities, its own hierarchy. The historical heritage of the performance principle is administration, not of men, but of things: mature civilisation depends for its functioning on a multitude of co-ordinated arrangements.... the liberty of the individual and that of the whole may perhaps be reconciled by a 'general will' taking shape in institutions which are directed towards the individual needs.[71]

We are not told exactly how such institutions will work and, in a sense, we do not need to be since there will be enough psychic goodwill to make anything possible. Finally—and crucially—we are told that the rush of civilisation to self-destruction can now be halted. When Eros is released, it will grow in strength and be able, as in art, to vanquish Thanatos:

> Pleasure principle and Nirvana principle then converge. At the same time, Eros, freed from surplus repression, would be strengthened, and the strengthened Eros would, as it were, absorb the objective of the death instinct. The instinctual value of death would have changed: if the instincts pursued and attained their fulfilment in a non-repressive order, the regression compulsion would lose much of its biological rationale. As suffering and want recede, the Nirvana principle may become reconciled with the reality principle. The unconscious attraction that draws the instincts back to an 'earlier state' would be effectively counteracted by the desirability of the attained state of life.[72]

Two criticisms of Marcuse's vision immediately follow from this. Firstly, Marcuse does not spend much time spelling out any specific political strategy; his concern is rather to find alternative standards by which a flawed world can be judged. But when he does briefly turn to the question of strategy, it is only to recommend dictatorship—perhaps not surprisingly since he knows our true inner needs. He boldly answers his own question as to how civilisation can create freedom from unfreedom:

> From Plato to Rousseau, the only honest answer is the idea of an educational dictatorship, exercised by those who are supposed to have acquired knowledge of the real Good.[73]

This seems to me to follow logically from his position, and a late attempt to say that it was merely thought-provoking[74] seems a terrible cop-out. But how long is such a dictatorship to continue? We have been told that instincts are historically mutable, and this, if it means anything, must surely suggest that the nasty instinctual character of repressive society will take a long time to remove. Secondly, and surely crucially, Marcuse's ingenious attempt to combine a picture of instincts as evil and nasty under capitalism and as nice and cooperative under socialism is far-fetched. This is an occasion in which it is simply impossible to have it both ways.

Marcuse has argued that absolute identity of subject and object is not strictly possible, although his theory comes close to this and he also wishes to argue that a minimum of repression will remain necessary.[75] But his own recommendations remain Freudian to a degree, and suggest that the elements of repression and unhappiness are likely to be very great. Thus he argues that the father is, in some sense, doing the work of Eros in preventing the son sleeping with his mother. This is to admit the Oedipus complex. Marcuse is well aware of this and tries to shuffle off its significance by arguing that the Oedipus complex is something that can easily be conquered without effect. His own arguments as to the benefit of having fathers who allow their children to find themselves by having something to fight against contradict this; he is hoisted on his own petard.

The Triumph of One-Dimensionality

One-Dimensional Man was Marcuse's most famous book, essentially because it served as the—largely unread—bible of the radical student movement of the late 1960s. It is by no means as lucid as *Eros and Civilisation*, and we are already familiar with some of its arguments. Hence, I shall concentrate here on its main theme, the argument that the progress of Western society directly undermines two basic values of Western civilisation, namely individualism and rationality.

Marcuse argues that individualism is becoming less and less of a reality in industrial society. Such individualism had been the result of the fight with the father, and it is highly valued by Marcuse who sees in it the space sufficient to lead to a criticism of the social order. Marcuse's move to pessimism thus depends upon him contradicting his earlier prediction that pleasure could not be released without destroying capitalism.[76] Equally, the move to pessimism results in a contradiction of his hope of a 'non-repressive desublimation' whereby the world could again become re-eroticised. Despair is endemic for Marcuse on the discovery, made as early as 1961,[77] that a measure of 'genital sexual liberation' could in fact serve to bolster the social order. Such 'repressive desublimation' conjures up Aldous Huxley's famous picture in *Brave New World* of a stooge-like population satisfied with heated contraceptives. Marcuse in such matters is extremely puritanical, and he speaks harshly of the 'sexualising' of work by means of attractive office girls.

His distaste depends in part upon his view of libido as somehow having a quantity; the implication here is that if it is frittered away in 'easy sex', no energy will be left for more important matters. The 'sexy business' of modern life is held to contrast with the room for contemplation and the imagination of more traditional societies:

> With its code of forms and manners, with the style and vocabulary of its literature and philosophy, this past culture expressed the rhythm and content of a universe in which valleys and forests, villages and inns, nobles and villains, salons and courts were a part of the experienced reality. In the verse and prose of this pre-technological culture is the rhythm of those who wander or ride in carriages, who have the time and the pleasure to think, contemplate, feel and narrate.[78]

Such romanticism, in my opinion, is at the centre of Marcuse's demand for a different attitude to nature. Here it is used to argue that the *promesse de bonheur* that the two-dimensionality of art had always succeeded in offering, is being lost by a process of integration. Madame Bovary's protest against the world would now be solved by the Yonville psychoanalyst, we are told, and Marcuse adds to this the observation that the popularisation of high art results in the loss of its message:

> .... the classics have left the mausoleum and come to life again.... True, but coming to life as classics, they come to life as other than themselves; they are deprived of their antagonistic force, of the estrangement which was the very dimension of their

truth. The intent and function of these works have thus fundamentally changed. If they once stood in contradiction to the status quo, this contradiction is now flattened out.[79]

No alternative language is held to be possible: the most outrageous of avant-garde styles is immediately robbed of its power by being ensconced in some museum.[80]

All this amounts, for Marcuse, to a sorry picture. The loss of critical range is held to amount to the confirmation of Orwell's view of 'doublethink', i.e., the control of our very conceptual apparatus is such as to disallow critical thought. Even worse, the 'happy consciousness' of integrated and seemingly liberated man in effect does away with conscience altogether, and this can only increase the ease with which atrocities can be committed.[81] And finally, Marcuse suggests that imagination itself becomes integrated since it is allowed to play some part in moulding high technology.[82]

Marcuse offers a very long and rather ill-sorted set of examples designed to prove that the individual is moulded directly by society through the 'introjection' of its values into his psyche. The details of this do not concern us. In summary, we may say that Marcuse is describing in concrete terms, and of course with disapproval, the sort of social consensus envisioned in the sociology of Talcott Parsons, a sociology, it must be remembered, that also placed emphasis on the Freudian 'introjection' of societal values into the individual. Marcuse's attack on Western standards of rationality takes off from this point. This rationality is seen as represented in technology:

> In this society, the productive apparatus tends to become totalitarian to the extent to which it determines not only the socially needed occupations, skills, and attitudes, but also individual needs and aspirations. It thus obliterates the opposition between the private and public existence, between individual and social needs.[83]

> A comfortable, smooth, reasonable, democratic unfreedom prevails in advanced industrial civilisation, a token of technical progress.[84]

Marcuse tells us that he is able to say this on the basis of two simple a priori values, namely, that life is worth living and that a society's achievement is to be measured against what it might otherwise manage with similar sources of wealth.[85] These values do not take us at all far, but the best approach to the argument is to analyse and criticise two separate strands within it: these are the social order produced by high technology and the 'project' involved in Western science.

Marcuse's sociology of advanced industrialism is avowedly based on no first hand empirical research; the examples Marcuse uses are all drawn from the United States, although this is justified on the ground that the American experience will soon become general. The analysis offered may be characterised as 'leftish end of ideology'. Society is held to be integrated by the welfare state (and the repressive desublimation that accompanies it) and by the agreement of all groups, business and labour in particular, to cooperate in a common national enterprise in the defence of freedom and against communism. Without this national purpose, capitalism might fall prey to the anarchy Marx expected; in particular automation might, in the absence of national purpose, cause 'system' problems.[86] This sociology interestingly places the advanced world, and developments within it, at the centre of attention; changes in the third world still depend on what happens at the centre.[87] Marcuse's own title for advanced industrial society is that of Welfare-Warfare society. This organisation is dubbed totalitarian, and Marcuse speaks directly of the Allied powers having been 'infected' by the war with Hitler.

Marcuse makes much of changes in the occupational structure in favour of white collar jobs since he believes that this is in part responsible for integrating the working class. Discussion of this point can conveniently be left till the chapter on Daniel Bell, on whom Marcuse here relies. But two criticisms of Marcuse can be offered now. Firstly, and most importantly, his general sociology is heavily Platonist in that it presumes that the working class is effectively socialised or indoctrinated into official ideologies. Empirical evidence does not lend support to this thesis.[88] This is not, however, to say that the working class is now or ever was the bearer of socialism. But I shall argue below that the Western working class nevertheless has 'bite' in ways that Marcuse completely ignored. Secondly, it is worth emphasising that he never seriously bothers to spell out how his society will work institutionally. It might, perhaps, be the case that a planned economy can coexist with a democratic government but, if so, this is far from obvious. This, however, is the mixture which, pressed, Marcuse falls back on.[89] There is no reason to follow a thinker who is so vague about something so crucial.

We have already noted several times that Marcuse has never unquestioningly accepted the true rationality of Western science. The origins of his discontent lie in his Hegelian insistence that all being needs to be fulfilled, rather than analysed on the basis of any single one of its moments; this doctrine implicitly underlay the neo-Freudian argument that reason should somehow be sensuous.

Marcuse's full case is that Western reason is not just misguided but is, in fact, a form of domination in its own right. This argument creates terrible difficulties for Marcuse for *Eros and Civilisation* had argued that a type of liberation was now possible *as the result of modern science*.

What becomes of these hopes once the 'project' of Western science is seen to create not just control over nature but a one-dimensional world as well? Marcuse never grasps this nettle clearly, although two lines of argument are hinted at, namely (in 1972) that a new science must be created and, alternatively, (in 1964) that Western science itself contains an inner dynamic that will mysteriously end domination. But before examining these and other matters, it is worth stressing the peculiarity of Marcuse's claim. John Orr has neatly characterised his position thus:

> The only sense that comes out of [Marcuse's critique] is that some teleological conception of nature is the only thing standing between man and wholesale destruction. For it alone offers the hope of pacifying man's destructive relationship with nature through reason. The desolate feature of modern science is that it holds out no promise whatever of such a Reason, hence Marcuse's extreme pessimism, and in its absence men cannot be trusted not to be totally destructive. In Marcuse's terms, the malaise of modern science lies in its, to his mind, ideological assertion that science yields no reason in nature, and no total ideology which can pacify technology. His only hope therefore seems to lie in an idea of secular reason manufactured where no evidence of it seems to exist, preferably by philosophers who are Hegelian in the cosmic sense.[90]

Marcuse's eventual discovery of a new science in 1972 that is sensuous and rational can, in other words, be interpreted as nothing less than an attack on naturalism itself. However sensible the demand for ecology, this—putting it bluntly—amounts to a type of mystical pantheism that is surely nonsense. Until convincing specifications are offered of a new science (and Marcuse never offers any specifications) there is no reason why we should believe it.

Marcuse's position is seen most clearly in his essays on Husserl and Max Weber. In the former, he follows Husserl in arguing that philosophy was once able to comprehend all of life, but that the unprecedented cognitive power of modern science has had the result of removing philosphy's self-confidence. This is of course a fairly commonly observed phenomenon, but Marcuse feels that Husserl is right in stressing that it is mistaken to admire the cognitive power of science so greatly:

Divorced from the validating 'ends' set by philosophy, the rationale set by science and the rationale of its development and progress became that of the *Lebenswelt* itself, in which and for which this science developed. Instead of rationally transcending the *Lebenswelt*, science comprehended, expressed and extended the specific rationale of the *Lebenswelt*, namely, the ever more effective mastery of the environment, including the ever more effective mastery of man. But that was not the inherent telos of science.... this entire development, this entire transformation of Reason, this essential, structural, internal commitment of pure Reason, pure theory and pure science to the empirical reality in which they originated, this entire transformation *remains hidden to science itself*, hidden and unquestioned. The new science does not elucidate the conditions and the limits of its evidence.... It remains unaware of its own foundation, and it is therefore unable to recognise its servitude....[91]

Marcuse redescribes his own position by arguing that Max Weber's concept of legal-rational authority did not represent the emergence of true rationality, merely the ability of a particular type of science to legitimate an ultimately irrational system:

The very concept of technical reason is perhaps ideological. Not only the application of technology, but technology itself is domination (of nature and men)—methodical, scientific, calculated, calculating control. Specific purposes and interests of domination are not foisted upon technology 'subsequently' and from the outside; they enter the very construction of the technical apparatus. Technology is always an historical-social *project*: in it is projected what a society and its ruling interests intends to do with men and things.[92]

The very last sentence here must be emphasized since it evidences yet another contradiction in Marcuse's thought. The fairly clear implication of the two quotations is that the very conceptual equipment of scientists is perverted by the particular project of Western science. But, as in *Eros and Civilisation*, Marcuse also from time to time suggests that it is the dominant capitalist interests which are responsible for the particular character of this project.[93]

In 1964 in *One-Dimensional Man*, Marcuse offers us a very peculiar escape from this view of technology, and this peculiarity is a measure of his pessimism. He suggests that:

.... the historical achievement of science and technology has rendered possible the *translation of values into technical tasks*—the materialisation of values. Consequently, what is at stake is the redefinition of values in *technical terms*, as elements in the technological process.[94]

This runs against everything that Marcuse has previously said about alternative sources of reason being available to control technology. Instead we are told that the extensions of technology's interests to moral values will in itself make it socially responsible. The hope that responsibility will follow power is surprising, as is Marcuse's sudden tacking on of the argument that:

> In the technology of pacification, aesthetic categories would enter to the degree to which the productive machinery is constructed with a view of the free play of faculties.[95]

But how is this possible since we have already been told that the very faculty of the aesthetic, the imagination, has been corrupted by one-dimensionality? No answer is offered.

Before finally turning to Marcuse's last work, it is necessary to look briefly at his analysis of Soviet industrial society. It has already been seen that he makes considerable use of the presence of communism to explain the cohesion of Western capitalism, and the argument is effectively reversed in his analysis of Soviet society—although certain apologetics are added to the picture.

It is slightly difficult to understand Marcuse's argument about Soviet society since he ostensibly limits himself to a discussion of the role of Marxism in Soviet society. This means that he refuses to countenance the view that Marxism is merely a veil which the leaders of Soviet society do not take seriously, although he is keen to distinguish core areas of belief from tactical elements that are considered inessential. This approach, however, does not in the end prove to be as great a disadvantage as it might seem since it is argued that certain social developments explain the direction in which Soviet Marxism has developed.

Soviet reality is held to be depressingly similar to that of one-dimensional capitalist America. This can be seen in four ways. Firstly, Marcuse argues that modern Soviet ethical theory, especially Stakhanovism, stresses labour discipline quite as much as the equivalent Protestant Ethic had done in the West. Secondly, Socialist Realism tries to abolish the 'second dimension' represented by art:

> Hegel saw in the obsolescence of art a token of progress. As the development of Reason conquers transcendence ('takes it back' into reality) art turns into its own negation. Soviet aesthetics rejects this idea and insists on art, while outlawing the transcendence of art. It wants art that is not art, and it gets what it asks for.[96]

Thirdly, Soviet philosophers turn dialectics into verbal dressage, whilst formal logic effectively comes to run the society. And finally, technological productivity produces a social world similar to the Western one. Marcuse's distaste for it is as great as was his hatred of modern America:

> The technological perfection of the productive apparatus domi-
> nates the rulers and the ruled while sustaining the distinction
> between them. Autonomy and spontaneity are confined to the
> level of efficiency and performance within the established pattern.
> Intellectual effort becomes the business of engineers, specialists,
> agents. Privacy and leisure are handled as relaxation from and
> preparation for labour in conformity with the apparatus. Dissent
> is not only a political crime but also technical stupidity,
> sabotage, mistreatment of the machine. Reason is nothing but
> the rationality of the whole. . . .[97]

This might seem as if it were a vicious condemnation of Soviet society *tout court*, but this is not so, for Marcuse offers several special pleas that excuse Soviet society and suggest that it is not so terrible after all. The central excuse for Soviet one-dimensionality is as simple as it is startling, namely that the Soviet Union only concerns itself with industrial production to such a degree because it fears for its own safety.[98] This type of omnibus argument has recently been adopted elsewhere,[99] and it of course implies that, but for the prior existence of Western industrialism, the Russian revolution might have taken a more humane form. Personally, I doubt this very much. For example, Lenin was clearly attracted to a massive industrialisation programme even before he arrived back in Russia in 1917, and certainly before he became aware of the dangers to the revolution posed by the West.

The possibility, for Marcuse, that Russia may not prove quite as unregenerate as the United States depends upon further sleights-of-hand. He first blandly argues that the Communist Party in Soviet society does not have special class-like interests that stand in the way of progress, offering no evidence to support this beyond the simple assertion that the party and the bureaucracy are the servants of the plan and have no autonomy beyond this role.[100] Secondly, he argues, Socialist Realism is at least honest. 'The most shocking notions of Soviet aesthetics', he notes, 'testify to a keen awareness of the social function of art'.[101] Marcuse, thirdly, suggests that the politicising of ethics, though at present repressive, holds out at least a potential of progress denied to the traditions of privacy associated with Western ethics:

> . . . . what holds true for the Soviet use of Marxism in general may
> also be applied to its ethical philosophy: once it has become an
> essential part of the physical and behavioural structure of the

individuals, once it has become a factor of social cohesion and integration, it assumes a momentum of its own and moves under its own weight.[102]

The Final Years

The story of Marcuse's final years is best told briefly. *One Dimensional Man* is deeply pessimistic since it argues that no alternative vision or means of transformation exists. This pessimistic conclusion means that any source of optimism discovered in his later years must contradict totally what had been hailed as irreversible; and such contradiction begins to occur with surprising regularity. From 1965 to the early 1970s Marcuse became extremely optimistic as the result of his belief that he had found in the student movement the troops necessary to realise his vision. In this period, we are offered nothing that is conceptually new; instead, Marcuse reverts to the vision of *Eros and Civilisation* and argues that the students have somehow managed to change their instinctual structure so as to be on the side of peace, sensuousness, liberation and so on. However, this period of renewed, and essentially unexplained, optimism did not last long. By the mid 1970s Marcuse had reverted to the pessimism of *One Dimensional Man*. Again, we are offered no really new analyses in this period, although some characterisations in *The Aesthetic Dimension* need to be noted since they neatly encapsulate much of the tenor of Marcuse's thought.

Marcuse saw students of the 1960s through the rosy spectacles of his Freudian period. He argues time and again that students have 'truer' needs in their demands for peace and togetherness.[103] This romantic view is, of course, only properly understood if contrasted to his continuing pessimism about the working class. *An Essay on Liberation* considers the working classes to have succumbed totally to the false needs that follow from the successful introjection of consumer standards. Hope rests with the students, and amongst those, especially blacks, who are not assured of a place in the Welfare-Warfare society. This argument is often dressed up in dubious conceptual language—thus the students, for example, are held to have a 'biological' urge for liberation. On occasion, Marcuse makes gestures towards other positions which contradict earlier arguments. Thus, he suggests that greater weight may after all be placed on the potential of third-world struggles,[104] and that automation might comprise a contradiction of capitalism.

What are we to make of the general argument that Marcuse offers us? Nothing can hide the paucity of the analysis, and three weaknesses stand out beyond all others. In the first place, the contrast with *One Dimensional Man* is total and cannot simply be left unexplained. How, for example, has it proved possible for middle-class students, of all people, to escape the processes of introjection upon which Marcuse's thesis so heavily relies? Even more important, perhaps, are his inconsistent statements on aesthetics. We have seen that in *One Dimensional Man* Marcuse argued that modern art had no chance of presenting a second dimension, especially as the imagination itself was beginning to be corrupted by technology. However, a mere three years later we are told that this is not in fact the case, and that art will *always* be able to picture a second dimension.[105]

Secondly, Marcuse grossly exaggerates the force of the opposition to affluent society. American blacks, as was perfectly obvious at the time, were concerned to gain a foothold in affluent society, and for that reason never easily allied themselves with white middle-class radicals. Moreover, the really fierce opposition of the latter depended less upon biological foundations than upon resistance to conscription for Vietnam; and this, as we now know, was a very temporary phenomenon. Bluntly, he has no realistic conception of social structure. Thirdly, Marcuse still offers us no guidelines as to the form any future society is likely to take. He rests content with condemnation of the present on the grounds that existing resources could, if used properly, create more happiness. As in *Eros and Civilisation*, he feels able to avoid any specification on account of the millenarian moments already noted, which assure us that all is possible once a new character structure has been established.

Marcuse, however, does spell out here his position on two matters more clearly than elsewhere. For one thing, he finally embraces the view that a 'new science' showing respect for nature is possible. As before, this endorsement is at times contradicted by the argument that only vested interests defile a natural technology,[106] but when the 'new science' is adopted it is done so in an uncompromisingly total way. Thus, Marcuse argues not just that man has a duty to respect nature and to develop its inherent potential, but that this in turn would lead to a biological need for freedom:

> Human freedom is thus rooted in the human *sensibility*: the senses do not only 'receive' what is given to them, in the form in which it appears, they do not 'delegate' the transformation of the given to another faculty (the understanding); rather, they discover or *can* discover by themselves, in their 'practice', 'new' (more gratifying) possibilities and capabilities, forms and qualities of things, and can urge and guide their realisation. The emancipation of these senses would make freedom what it is not yet: a sensuous need, an objective of the Life Instincts (Eros).[107]

Insofar as this is comprehensible it seems to me that it (and the allied argument that there is an instinctual need for the beautiful) is simply not true. No charge of incomprehensibility can, however, be brought against the second argument Marcuse developed in the spasm of optimism that gripped him in the late 1960s. This is stated with lucidity, and with every implication spelt out, in 'Repressive Tolerance'. Given that a few are already in possession of higher standards, and that their message is hindered by the false consciousness of affluence bred in the majority, what else should we expect than an argument in favour of intolerance? And this is what Marcuse does in fact recommend; he condemns the false, conformity-inducing tolerance of liberalism which treats good and evil alike, and suggests that a systematic bias in favour of the left be installed.

Marcuse was a brilliant polemicist and makes much of the obvious points, especially of the argument that intolerance towards the Nazis in the 1920s would have saved the world from disaster. But the essay is nonetheless pernicious. Forgetting for a moment moral arguments, the insistence on removing tolerance and politicising public life is, given (as Marcuse suggests) the predominance of the unenlightened, mere stupidity. And the rule of law is in any case valuable in its own right as other more sophisticated writers on the left have recently emphasised.[108] This makes some of Marcuse's assertions—such as the comparison between American police forces and the SS—worse than stupid.

By the early 1970s Marcuse had begun to distance himself from this naively optimistic radicalism. He claimed that the students had misunderstood him and were consequently throwing away the radical chances they had created. He insisted that students could only help raise consciousness, and would not be able to make a revolution in their own right. He was able to point to earlier passages in which he had, in fact, qualified stronger arguments with the insistence that the working class would have to be won over if a revolution was to be successful.[109] In addition, he came to criticise the anti-intellectualism and sectarianism of the student movement, and became deeply opposed to the relativism implicit in 'doing your own thing'. Whilst this was all perhaps realistic, two criticisms must be made.

First, Marcuse was in part responsible for some of the mistakes actually made. A classic instance of this is, unfortunately, terrorism. Marcuse condemned terrorism at the end of his life and argued that it had nothing to do with the left or with his theories.[110] This condemnation was disingenuous. For it was not at all surprising that Marcuse's own earlier disavowal of violence on *tactical grounds alone* was rejected by others who, convinced of the one-dimensionality of the world exactly in Marcusean terms, felt that terrorism *was* an appropriate tactic. Secondly, Marcuse's own political strategy in these very last years was in any case no thing of logical beauty. Thus, to give but one example, he argued in favour of a decentralised 'movement' but insisted that factionalism should be avoided and a central organisation created: doubtless some sort of true instinctual human being could manage to combine these, but most students found them contradictory. Finally, Marcuse came to review his aesthetic position, and here too he became a critic of the student call to abolish art.

His aesthetics as a whole can now be clarified by means of a diagram:

Table *1*. *Marcuse's Aesthetics as a Whole.*

	Eros		
	Arts 2nd Dimension	Aesthetic Reduction	
Politically Passive			Politically Active
	One Dimensional Art	Student Demand to end Art	
	Reality		

Marcuse had always admired art since its association with Eros allowed it to picture another reality, albeit the pleasure obtained in the enjoyment of art was capable of existing within an unjust society. As early as 'The Affirmative Character of Culture' (1937), therefore, Marcuse called for art to try to realise its vision in social life. However, in *The Aesthetic Dimension* he tells us that the way in which this had been done was disastrous.

The student demand to abolish art was apparently of the wrong type. Instead of realising the second dimension in reality, their anti-intellectual call to abolish art merely reinforced the one-dimensional world. With this sorry history in view, Marcuse came to argue that passive but two-dimensional art should be preserved at all costs. At times he continued to give the impression that this two-dimensionality might in the future be realised in practice. But increasingly he was drawn to absolute pessimism; however good a society, he argued, art would remain:

Art cannot sever itself from its origins. It bears witness to the inherent limits of freedom and fulfilment, to human embeddedness in nature. In all its ideality art bears witness to the truth of dialectical materialism—the permanent non-identity between subject and object, individual and individual.[111]

This seems remarkably like Samuel Johnson's view that the purpose of art is to console us for the tragedy of life, and it stands in complete contrast to everything he had hitherto championed.

Conclusion

Marcuse is an interesting thinker because he has, as it were, the courage of his convictions, and describes so completely a total moral vision that others subscribe to without any proper examination. As noted, I shall have more to say later as to why his view of complete class integration is mistaken. However, even without detailed sociological criticism, his vision can be dismissed. Firstly, his theory involves us deliberately in repression since there is no good reason to believe that the rule of the instinctually liberated would be an improvement on rule by any other set of self-elected saints. This is to repeat the charge that the millenarian moments that are supposed to convince us of the efficacy of repressive tolerance fail to convince.

Secondly, Marcuse's desire to oppose Western standards of rationality should be resisted. The extent of this critique—particularly the hope that nature can somehow again be seen in human rather than aseptic, natural terms—is quite remarkable, but this forms part of the problem. For the blanket nature of Marcuse's attack on Western science and reason simply deprives us of the very chance of creating a decent society. His Platonic view of man seems to me, in any case, to be false. This leads to a curious irony: if men are so gullible then how can we reasonably hope that they will become the spiritually independent members of his communal idea? Rousseau was at least more realistic; his utopia had to be 'totalitarian' *because* men were so weak. Marcuse was content to condemn and dream.

3 Jürgen Habermas

A Dream and a Nightmare

Jürgen Habermas made his name in Germany in 1962 with the appearance of *Strukturwandel der Öffentlichkeit* which quickly became recognised as a classic, particularly amongst the student Left. 'Öffentlichkeit' is rather hard to translate, but the general notion is that of the open society which allows for critical discussion as expounded by Popper. It is not, of course, surprising that a German of the post-war period—Habermas was a teenager at the end of the last war—should be drawn towards investigating the conditions and character of an open society; many of Habermas's generation turned to 'the German problem', although the consistency and bravery that Habermas has shown in attacking fanaticism on right and left is remarkable.[1] But Habermas's own voice is heard in his advocacy of the rigorous and striking version of 'positive' freedom.

Perhaps the key phrase we need to bear in mind in understanding Habermas's work comes from his inaugural lecture in 1965, when he spoke of 'the insight that the truth of statements is linked in the last analysis to the intention of the good and the true life....'[2] This is reminiscent of Marcuse and, as noted, Habermas is just as keen to produce constructive political philosophy, albeit the materials used are, as we shall see, very different from those employed by Marcuse. The best way in which to approach his thought is to try to establish its aims, in this section, before seeing how he tries to fulfil them; a consideration of *Strukturwandel der Öffentlichkeit* will reveal Habermas's conception of the 'good', i.e. his dream, and how this was destroyed by late capitalism in such a way as to produce his nightmare.

The account that Habermas offers us of the origins of the open society is perhaps closer in spirit to Marx himself than is that of other Marxists, for it rests on a very high valuation of bourgeois culture. The bourgeoisie, forced to oppose Enlightened Absolutism on account of its strict policies, mercantilist and otherwise, is held to become the champion of free discussion and reason. The very concept of Enlightenment is, for Habermas, enshrined in the dictum that *veritas non auctoritas facit legem*—a motto that could serve for all his own endeavours. The desire for public discussion created a newspaper press, although this initially served to advertise market conditions and new goods. The growth of museums and literary journals such as the *Tatler* are seen as showing the development of the right of the common man to 'sit in judgement'. This was indeed the case, and Habermas is quite right to stress that this period sees the enshrinement of the literate and well-informed man of taste as cultural arbiter.

Habermas notes one crucial difference between the public sphere of the Greeks and that of the bourgeois world. Whereas the Greeks had little conception of public and private, the European bourgeoisie made sharp divisions between these two spheres. Habermas particularly stresses that the family changes by developing ideologies of love that give the individual a certain interior privacy. Thus the core of his notion of a public sphere consists in the idea of a 'space' between civil privatism and the exercise of power in which a collective political will can be arrived at through the public use of reason. This is very much of an ideal type, but some attention is paid to the different European variants on the model. Habermas is particularly perceptive on the German and French cases, and makes much in the latter of the contribution played by the nobility in the formation of a public sphere.[3]

'Publicness' was an ideal embraced most fully by Kant but, in a discussion of intellectual history, Habermas shows that the ideal was illusory even at the peak of bourgeois society. More particularly, he accepts Marx's argument that only those with a measure of property were able to participate in public debate. And he again follows Marx when arguing that the creation of labour movements designed to secure social equality politicised social life and undermined the idea of free and disinterested discussion. But Habermas also points to a series of changes in society which Marx had not led us to expect. Marx failed to realise that the state could serve the interest of capital by introducing a measure of order into their chaotic relations. The economy, becomes in other words, 'repoliticised' so that Keynesian measures can avoid various capitalist crises. Habermas further argues that Marx's key notion of surplus value is outdated. For the state is held to promote organised science to such an extent that it becomes ridiculous to think of the surplus as coming from labour. Thus, the intervention of the state is seen as creating 'late' capitalism, and this mode of production is judged to work smoothly.[4] Hence Habermas feels that the Marxian motor of history, class conflict, has been irreparably co-opted in modern society; this is a point on which he has not had second thoughts.

If capitalism made 'publicness' only an ideal, late capitalism destroys it. The area of privacy created by bourgeois society is undermined. This, we are told, can be seen especially clearly in changing family functions. The family is held to lose its importance in any economic sense since private property loses its place in the world of corporatist monopolies. Moreover, he considers that:

> In losing its function in the process of capital formation, the family also increasingly loses other functions, such as upbringing and education, protection, care and guidance, in fact in transmitting basic traditions and orientations it completely loses its force as a determinant of behaviour in those areas which were regarded in the bourgeois family as the most intimate spheres of private life.[5]

In summary, we can say that the state replaces what had hitherto been private. But Habermas believes that exactly the opposite process is taking place at the same time, namely that the family, as a unit of consumption, is encouraged to retreat more and more into itself.[6] What is meant by this is fairly clear. Where the bourgeois family had been a sanctuary that bred independent individuals of active political views, the family of late capitalism is held to have lost its essential socialising function but, paradoxically, to have gained importance as an area of depoliticised consumption.

Habermas believes that the character of culture changes in such a way that it no longer serves to uphold rigorous and critical standards but provides 'entertainment' instead. His views in this matter are very close indeed to those of Horkheimer and Adorno's famous essay on the 'Culture Industry' of mass society, which they considered in large part responsible for integration into the status quo.[7] Habermas's picture of changes in the political functions associated with the notion of publicity also relies heavily on classic Frankfurt School analyses. Journalism no longer serves as a forum for political criticism but is reduced to lesser functions:

> There is a clear link between, on the one hand, the growth of large-scale capitalist enterprises and an oligopolistic restriction of the market, and, on the other hand, the proverbial soap operas, i.e. the kind of advertising permeating the whole culture of integration represented by the mass media.[8]

Newspapers also now have more directly political functions. Their role in public life changes from that of allowing rational discussion to that of publicising decisions made by an elite or, in other words, to 'engineering' consent for decisions beyond popular discussion. Associated with this decline, in Habermas's eyes, are new terms that show distrust of the people. The most important of these is held to be that of 'masses', and Habermas glumly notes that Le Bon's social psychology from the start sees the mass as irrational. Nevertheless, the nadir of modern social development is for Habermas seen in the character of modern elections. He has utter distaste for 'realistic' or revisionist theories of democracy such as that of Schumpeter, and it is not hard to guess why this is so. He tells us bluntly that public participation in power has been replaced by the mere 'engineering' of periodic acclamations.[9]

Habermas's account of the destruction of the public sphere shows he is not enamoured of late capitalism. But it is important to stress just how deep is his loathing. He tells us that late capitalism is beginning to produce a technological ideology that will dehumanise the world. His conception of this nightmare is neatly captured in these charges:

> Technocratic consciousness is, on the one hand, 'less ideological' than all previous ideologies. For it does not have the opaque force of a delusion that only transfigures the implementation of interests. On the other hand today's dominant, rather glassy background ideology, which makes a fetish of science, is more irresistible and farther reaching than ideologies of the old type. For with the veiling of practical problems it not only justifies a *particular class*'s interest in domination and represses *another class*'s partial need for emancipation but affects the emancipatory interest as such.[10]

> .... the self-objectivation of man would have fulfilled itself in planned alienation—men would make their history with will, but without consciousness.[11]

> .... the danger of an exclusively technical civilisation, which is devoid of the interconnection between theory and praxis, can be clearly grasped; it is threatened by the splitting of its consciousness, and by the splitting of human beings into two classes—the social engineers and the inmates of closed institutions.[12]

Underlying the charges quoted is Habermas's allegiance to the Greek view of politics so well spelled out by Hannah Arendt.[13]

A basic distinction was drawn by the Greeks between the type of knowledge to be gained over nature and the type of knowledge appropriate to human affairs. The former bred systematic, 'monologic' science, whilst the latter, given the ability of men to act and react, was capable only of creating prudential advice. Habermas follows the Greek ethic, especially as it was developed by Hegel in his Jena writings,[14] in arguing that two distinct spheres of human life have to be separated from each other. Knowledge produced in 'labour' is relatively unproblematic since it is designed to control an inert nature; in contrast, 'interaction' between human agents cannot produce the same sort of neutral scientific findings. In this distinction, of course, Habermas has firmly embraced the tradition of the *Geisteswissenschaften*. I shall have more to say in the next section about this basic division; here the reader must be warned that the philosophical problems that this division solves are counter-balanced—at least—by new ones it creates.

Habermas's charge against modern society is simply that the sphere of the practical, i.e. interaction, is being conceptualised in terms of, and is thus being swallowed up by, the technical, i.e. labour. Men are coming to be seen and treated as objects, not agents. The origins of this attitude are traced back to the seventeenth century scientific revolution. In a brilliant essay on Hobbes, Habermas describes how the Greek view of political knowledge was subverted by those who wished to create a 'science' of politics modelled after the sciences of nature. Whilst Habermas himself has great sympathy for rigour in the understanding of human action, he makes absolutely clear his own objection to the aping of natural science. Above all, such aping rests on a contradiction which he feels is well illustrated by the central failure of Hobbes's *Leviathan*. In that treatise the long description of an almost behaviorist vision of man accords ill with the demand for political obligation. In Habermas's words:

> Hobbes called *both* of these Natural Law: the *causal* connection of man's asocial instinctual nature *prior* to the contractual constitution of society and the state; and the *normative* regulation of their social cohabitation *after* this constitution. The difficulty here is evident: Hobbes has to derive from the causality of human instinctive nature the norms of an order whose function is precisely to compel the renunciation of primary satisfaction of these instincts.[15]

This can be put another way by saying that the view of man contained in the treatise does not fit in with the reasoning power expected of the reader. Habermas argues that the desire to create a science of politics influenced even Marx. The humanism of Marx's early writings falls, it is held, before an unfortunate late 'scientistic' attitude in which Marx argued that the 'self-generative' act of mankind occurred only in labour.[16] Habermas argues that this presumed methodology is insufficient to describe the explanations offered in Marx's own historical writings, and is especially poor in explaining why, at the subjective level, men would respond to certain social circumstances so as to create a revolution. The political consequences are held to derive from Marx's late, scientistic 'self-misunderstanding'. Most immediately, the belief that liberation lay in the realm of labour, rather than in developments in labour *and* in interaction, left us, we are told, unprepared for the modern world:

> .... Marx equates the practical insight of a political public with successful technical control. Meanwhile we have learned that even a well-functioning planning bureaucracy with scientific control of the production of goods and services is not a sufficient condition for realising the associated material and intellectual productive forces in the interest of the enjoyment and freedom of an emancipated society. For Marx did not reckon with the possible emergence at every level of a discrepancy between scientific control of the material conditions of life and a democratic decision-making process. This is the philosophical reason why socialists never anticipated the authoritarian welfare state, where social wealth is relatively guaranteed while political freedom is excluded.[17]

Moreover, and even worse, insofar as scientific Marxism could be reduced to the discredited formula of 'diamat' it proved capable of being used (and here Habermas could perhaps have Marcuse's *Soviet Marxism* in mind) in the interests of repression.

If this view of Marx is shared with Horkheimer and Adorno, it should be emphasised that Habermas's critique as a whole is novel. He is less haunted by the dangers of authoritarianism than by the Brave New World of Aldous Huxley in which men, he fears, adapt all too easily to enslavement:

> The manifest domination of the authoritarian state gives way to the manipulative compulsion of technical-operational administration. The moral realisation of a normative order is a function of communicative action orientated to shared cultural meaning and presupposing the internalisation of values. It is increasingly supplanted by conditioned behaviour.... Sociopsychologically, the era is typified less by the authoritarian personality than by the destructuring of the superego.[18]

Habermas argues, interestingly, that the consequence of conceiving of men in ontological terms, i.e. as fixed entities, is to release politics from ordered, rational constraint. Increasingly, reason comes to be seen in terms of technique. Reason is limited so as only to apply to instrumental action (by finding the best means to fit a given end) or to purposive rational action (by deciding between options on the basis of preference rules). Habermas attacks these limitations since they do not allow the content of values themselves to be discussed rationally:

> On the first two levels, the rationality of conduct enforces an isolation of values, which are removed from any and every cogent

discussion, and can only be related to given techniques and concrete goals in the form of hypothetically entertained imperatives; these relations are accessible to rational calculation, because they remain external to the values rendered irrational as such.... The subjective reduction of the interests which are decisive in the orientation for action to 'sentiments' or 'perceptions', which cannot be rationalised beyond that, is a precise expression for the fact that the value freedom central to the technological concept of rationality functions within the system of social labour, and that all the other interests of the praxis of life are subordinated for the benefit of the sole interest in efficiency and economy in the utilization of means. The competing perspectives of interest, hypostatised to values, are excluded from discussion. Revealingly enough, according to the criteria of technological rationality, agreement on a collective value system can never be achieved by means of enlightened discussion carried on in public politics, thus by way of a consensus rationally arrived at, but only by summation or compromise—values are in principle beyond discussion.[19]

This is a key passage in Habermas's work, and it can usefully be seen as directed against Max Weber.[20] As is well-known, Weber argued that science had nothing to say about ultimate values; men chose such values in existentialist style.

This probably delighted Weber since it left an area in which human life could not be disenchanted by science. Habermas is just as keen as Weber to escape 'disenchantment' but, though he accepts a division between science and social life, he does not accept Weber's characterisation of the latter.[21] Habermas refuses to accept that our 'gods' must divide us; such a view is held to be terribly dangerous since it leads to 'decisionism', i.e. the call for authority to decide between incommensurable values, and it is rejected by Habermas *tout court*.[22] Our task is not to specify the 'functions' of the political, but to complement the rationalisation of science with a rationalisation of our social life: we must examine our values in order to establish a valid social consensus, that is, we must systematically try and 'moralise' our political life.[23]

Although there is a clear affinity between Habermas's picture and Marcuse's one-dimensional world, there are two points at which Habermas distinctly rejects Marcuse. Firstly, his total rejection of all ontological and static, i.e. object-like, views of man, means that he does not follow Marcuse in seeking for human instincts that can be relied upon for liberation. What characterizes man for Habermas is the Hegelian ability to ceaselessly develop.[24] Secondly, Habermas wishes to distinguish two theses at work in Marcuse's views on science:

The first, and stronger version, is that there might be a possibility to develop a type of science which is generically different from what we have now; so that due to its very structure this new science could not be applied in the exploitation of nature. This idea is a very romantic idea. I don't want to be impolite to Marcuse, but I'm convinced that this idea has no real base. The other version is that there might be a change in the relationship between the scientific system and its environment, moreover, its political environment. A change, so that in the future developments in the science system might be stronger and stronger influenced and after all *guided* by political aims and by a discursively formed, politically reasonable will.[25]

Habermas sees the structure of science as invariant (although he has recently characterised its mode of operation anew), and objects only to this structure being applied in the very different field of interaction; and if rationalisation is possible inside social life, then there is no need to follow Marcuse in rejecting Western standards of reason and retreating to a non-specified pantheism. Saying this, however, leaves Habermas with a whole host of problems to sort out. What sort of non-technical knowledge about social interaction can be offered? How can such knowledge help create a rational society able, amongst other things, to control science itself? And, if it is possible to understand him when he rejects the so-called technical science of man as derived from repressive circumstances, what are we to make of the supposed link between truth and the 'intentions of the good and true life'?

Epistemology as Social Theory

Knowledge and Human Interests remains Habermas's most accomplished and exciting work. In it he does nothing less than offer a solution to *all* the problems, epistemological and social, that have been raised already. But the book is very much of a flawed diamond and it is important to realise why this is so; only when the character of the flaw has been seen can his later, slightly less systematic work be understood.[26] It should also be noted that the book is quite exceptionally difficult, since it is 'an immanent critique', i.e. it hides its own judgements behind a discussion of others' work.

The aim of the book is to attack positivism, defined here as a refusal to 'reflect' on the human subject. The notion of reflection is, as we shall see, a very troubling one, but his main point becomes clear when he attacks Mach's doctrine of elements on the grounds that it:

.... offers a far-reaching interpretation of reality, while contenting itself with a minimal definition of knowledge. Its own status is contradictory. By explicating the totality of facts as the object domain of the science and delimiting science from metaphysics through its replication of the facts, it cannot justify any reflection that goes beyond science, including itself.[27]

Habermas considers that the only way forward is to reopen the debate as to how human beings are capable of creating knowledge. He recognises Kant's critical philosophy as the greatest contribution in this area, but follows Hegel in judging the Kantian perspective flawed. Above all, Habermas is at one with Hegel in wishing to see the knowing subject as social and not just an isolated, static monad; and once this is granted, it becomes essential to investigate the ways in which the knowing subject develops, i.e. has its own history. Unlike Marcuse, Habermas can make no sense of Hegel's Absolute Idealism, but he finds much to praise in Marx's early writings. On the one hand, Marx recognises the developmental aspect of the knowing subject:

> . . . . the human species is not characterised by any invariant natural or transcendental structure, but only by a mechanism of humanisation. The evolutionary concept of 'the nature of man' unmasks philosophical anthropology as an illusion just as it does transcendental philosophy.[28]

Equally important, however, is Marx's insistence that this process occurs through 'social labour'. Epistemology is, in other words, to be seen as an aspect of social theory since it is as a social being that capacity for knowledge develops. But there is one obvious difficulty in Marx's approach: if we see nature only as the result of our own work upon it, how is it then possible to maintain, as both Marx and Habermas wish to, that the world exists in its own right, independently of our thought? This point is discussed later in this chapter.

Habermas maintains that the promise of Marx's early writings was not fulfilled. Labour came to be fetishised in Marx's later thought to such an extent that it excluded other realms of human significance. This was, as noted, very unfortunate in itself. But the epistemological consequence was that labour, and therefore Marxism, came to be seen in crassly positivist terms. The reflection on human capabilities was thus abandoned. Habermas's major claims in reopening this debate is that human beings attain three types of knowledge in accord with different social 'interests'. The position can be characterised thus:

Table 2. Habermas's Classification of Knowledge according to Social Interests

Knowledge	Interest	Medium	Example
Empirical Science	Technical Control	Labour	Physics
Historical-Hermeneutic	Understanding	Language	Textual Criticism
Critical Theory	Emancipation	Power	The Psychoanalytic Encounter; Reconstructed Marxism

The first two types of knowledge are familiar to us as labour and interaction, and they allow us to realise than an interest results from the necessity of solving certain problems, i.e. the control of the environment and the maintenance of social interaction, in order that social life will not die out. Such interests are considered to be 'quasi-transcendental', and one characteristic of them is described thus:

> The concept of 'interest' is not meant to imply a naturalistic reduction of transcendental-logical properties to empirical ones. Indeed, it is meant to prevent just such a reduction. Knowledge-constitutive interests mediate the natural history of the human species with the logic of its self-formative process.... But they cannot be employed to reduce this logic to any sort of natural basis.... On the human level, the reproduction of life is determined culturally by work and interaction. That is why the knowledge-constitutive interests rooted in the conditions of the existence of work and interaction cannot be comprehended in the biological frame of reference of reproduction and the preservation of the species. The reproduction of social life absolutely cannot be characterised adequately without recourse to the cultural conditions of reproduction, that is, to a self-formative process that *already implies* knowledge in both forms. Thus knowledge constitutive-interests would be completely misunderstood if viewed as mere functions of the reproduction of social life.[29]

This is an important point. Habermas is really saying that we need not fear any sort of Weberian disenchantment consequent on the explanation of our cognitive interests since these cannot be comprehended monologically or naturalistically, as development and learning mean that the object to be so understood is not static. We shall return to this point when the notion of a 'reconstructive science' is introduced. And the presence of a third interest—and an interest in nothing less than liberation—serves, of course, as an even greater rebuttal of Weberian fears of disenchantment. Such critical knowledge will not be technical in nature, since it will treat human beings as agents in their own right, but it will seek to enlighten people as to the restraints on their freedom. The truth of critical theory will be seen in the recognition by those it addresses of its view of a just social order. This notion of an interest in human freedom is, of course, a fantastic claim, and it is here that Habermas's scheme will come to grief. However, the types of knowledge need to be spelt out before such weaknesses are examined.

The positivist conception of natural science does away with the active role of the knowing subject, and sees truth resulting from the accurate but passive reflection of sense experience, or, technically, it presumes that truth depends upon a correspondence with the facts. Habermas considers Peirce's account of the origin of knowledge far more realistic. According to Peirce, scientific investigation occurs as a result of disturbances in our expectations about nature:

> Concepts and judgements can be explicated in syllogisms just as syllogisms can be condensed into judgements and concepts. But this 'movement of the concept' is neither absolute nor self-sufficient. It acquires its meaning only from the system of reference of possible *feedback controlled action*. Its goal is the elimination of behavioural uncertainty.[30]

This leads naturally to a second set of Peircean arguments that Habermas champions, namely those concerned with showing how it is that we obtain scientific theories. In this matter, Peirce wished to combine the arguments that we obtain knowledge about the world with the belief that an external and independent reality would serve to limit our theorising. This is essentially the dilemma of the young Marx, and Habermas's account is largely of how Peirce attempts to deal with the problem at various times through a theory of language, of ontology and of the logic of inquiry. Only in the last of these does Habermas see much hope. But he resists Peirce's own logic of inquiry on the grounds that it is insufficiently social:

> Deduction, induction, and abduction [i.e. Peirce's logic of inquiry] establish relations between statements that are in principle monologic. It is possible to think in syllogisms, but not to conduct a dialogue in them. I can use syllogistic reasoning to yield arguments for a discussion, but I cannot argue syllogistically with an other. In so far as the employment of symbols is constitutive for the behavioural system of instrumental action, the use of language involved is monologic. But the communication of

investigators requires the use of language that is not confined to the limits of technical control over objectified natural processes. It arises from symbolic interaction between societal subjects who reciprocally know and recognise each other as unmistakable individuals. This *communicative action* is a system of reference that cannot be reduced to the framework of *instrumental action*.[31]

Habermas, in criticising Peirce for surrendering in the last instance to positivism, suggests elusively that science must depend completely upon agreement reached in the community of scientists. And this agreement is somehow related to observation statements about the world. Habermas's discontent with the positivistic philosophy of science is obvious, but he is able to develop a clear alternative only when his theory of communicative competence has been elaborated.

The sociality seen here to be so important in natural science plays an equally important role in social life, hence Habermas has no liking for those approaches to the social world, especially phenomenology and existentialism, which try and build up a picture of the world starting from a single consciousness. Habermas is convinced that their attempt at a later moment to reintroduce a social dimension had no chance of success.[32] Habermas turns instead to the *Geisteswissenschaften* tradition, and to Dilthey in particular. This tradition suggests that each society has a set of social meanings that order its social life. The significance of this is that the understanding of another social world, i.e. the sociology of *Verstehen*, must be based on an attempt to understand the social meanings that allow an individual to act in a particular way. And this means that Habermas rejects those, such as the later Dilthey and Abel, who argue 'positivistically' that *Verstehen* only involves imputing fairly obvious and basic psychological meanings to actions that seem unusual to us. He thus criticises Abel's suggestion that a bad harvest leads 'naturally' to a fall in the marriage rate:

> There is no need for marriage to be judged primarily from the point of view of the economic burdens it occasions; in situations of insecurity [the establishing of] one's own family might just as well appear to be a security-enhancing formation of an intimacy group. How farmers will behave, in cases of crop failure, with respect to familial matters obviously depends on inherited values and institutionalised roles. Such cultural patterns and social norms, however . . . . . do not belong to the class of behaviour maxims that are seemingly introspected with certainty. Rather, they require a controlled appropriation through the hermeneutic understanding of their meaning . . . . Only if the symbolic content of the norms in force is disclosed through the understanding of meaning can motivational understanding comprehend observed

behaviour as subjectively meaningful action in relation to those norms.[33]

It is crucial to realise this if the interest of interaction is to be fulfilled. This is described by Habermas in these terms:

> Whereas empirical-analytic methods aim at disclosing and comprehending reality under the transcendental viewpoint of possible technical control, hermeneutic methods aim at maintaining the intersubjectivity of mutual understanding in ordinary language communication and in action according to common norms. In its very structure hermeneutic understanding is designed to guarantee, within cultural traditions, the possible action-orienting self-understanding of individuals and groups as well as reciprocal understanding between different individuals and groups. It makes possible the form of unconstrained consensus and the type of open intersubjectivity on which communicative action depends.... When these communication flows break off and the intersubjectivity of mutual understanding is either rigidified or falls apart, a condition of survival is disturbed, one that is as elementary as the complementary condition of the success of instrumental action....[34]

To insist that sociology bases itself entirely on the meanings of social actors represents a form of Platonism, and this raises all the problems traditionally associated with relativism. The supposed context-dependency of sociology seems, for example, far less liberal once it is realised that the values of some societies are harsh; in these circumstances the preservation of local standards can seem much more like complicity in repression. Habermas is, of course, a strong rationalist, and cannot rest content here, and the manner in which he tries to step beyond this leads us to his third interest in knowledge. He notes that the most celebrated contemporary Platonist account in this manner, that of Peter Winch, bases itself on a theory of language, that of Wittgenstein, which is exceptionally rigid. Language should be seen as flexible and changing, rather than as a closed system to be accepted wholesale.

Habermas's view, derived from Gadamer, suggests that it is very mistaken to presume that the sociologist wishing to understand another culture can simply learn its rules as he learnt its own. For one approaches another culture as one learns a second language, namely from the position of one who has a culture or language already; and this means that the interpreter must always be 'prejudiced'. This discovery that it is impossible to reach a 'neutral' understanding of the past or of another culture is used by Gadamer to support a conservative argument whereby respect should be paid to the traditions and values that have been given to us. Habermas insists that this is one-sided since the process of dialogue between two sets of values can lead to changes in either:

> Gadamer fails to appreciate the power of reflection that is developed in understanding. This type of reflection is no longer blinded by the illusion of an absolute, self-grounded autonomy and does not detach itself from the soil of contingency on which it finds itself. But in grasping the genesis of the tradition from which it proceeds and on which it turns back, reflection shakes the dogmatism of life-practices.[35]

Habermas's point here can be put more simply. Reflection on a particular set of social values can lead to the discovery that they have been formed in unfair and unequal conditions; a meaning system may serve as an ideology in the interest of some rather than all the actors.

This sort of critical knowledge is explicated in a discussion of Freud. Habermas is well aware that Freud's own ambitions were strictly mechanistic and positivist, but he thinks that the actual 'treatment' given in the psychoanalytic session is of a different character. Freud is seen as a 'depth-hermeneuticist'. By this is meant the investigation of areas of life that have become frozen or ideological:

> .....symptoms are signs of a specific self-alienation of the subject who has them. The breaks in the text are places where an interpretation has forcibly prevailed that is ego-alien even though it is produced by the self. Because the symbols that interpret suppressed needs are excluded from public communication, *the speaking and acting subject's communication with himself is interrupted.* The privatised language of unconscious motives is rendered inaccessible to the ego, even though internally it has considerable repercussions upon that use of language and those motivations of action that the ego controls. The result is that the ego necessarily deceives itself about its identity in the symbolic structures that it consciously produces.[36]

If this is the aim of the Freudian technique, however, its crucial characteristic is the nature of the cure that it offers. For psychoanalysis does not offer medicine for the organism, but creates the conditions in which the individual, by coming to reflect on his determinations, frees himself. Such 'critical' knowledge is not 'technical', and so can only be confirmed as the result of action on the part of the addressee in creating a just life. And Habermas contends that the psychoanalytic encounter serves as a model for all such active theory designed to enlighten. In his own words:

> The same configurations that drive the individual to neurosis

move society to establish institutions. What characterises institutions is at the same time what constitutes their similarity with pathological forms. Like the repetition compulsion from within, institutional compulsion from without brings about a relatively rigid reproduction of uniform behaviour that is removed from criticism..... [37]

This is reminiscent of his admiration for the unconstrained but rational judging of policy performed by the public debate of early bourgeois society. It suggests a world in which the abolition of hidden power relations will lead to an absolute purity of hermeneutic communication.

Knowledge and Human Interests has such a range that it raises numerous questions only some of which can be discussed here. Habermas has been much criticised for distorting the thought of those he discusses; however, a more pertinent criticism would be that he is often uncritical in what he seeks to appropriate. Thus he raises the important question as to whether the analyst suggests an interpretation to the patient that he then adopts; but he simply accepts Freud's insistence that easy acceptance will be as much distrusted by the analyst as outright rejection. [38] I do not share Habermas's faith here, and find it very disturbing that none of the considerable critical literature on Freud is even discussed. However, such details must be left to one side since it is more important to see why the scheme as a whole comes to grief.

Even Habermas's closest associates found it difficult to accept the linking of knowledge with liberation, or disinterested research with the actual organisation of political conflict. Given the relative weakness of thought, this objection has validity as Habermas himself now admits:

> ....the traditional use of the term 'reflection'...covers (and confuses) two things: on the one hand, it denotes the reflection upon the conditions of potential abilities of a knowing, speaking and acting subject as such; on the other hand, it denotes the reflection upon unconsciously produced constraints to which a determinate subject (or a determinate group of subjects, or a determinate species subject) succumbs in its process of self-formation. [39]

This is a very major admission since it undermines Habermas's attempt to, as it were, combine Kant and Marx in such a way that 'proper' knowledge would itself create the good society. This is not to say that the split between the transcendental and the more immediately political is all loss for Habermas. We shall see shortly that his renewed interest in extending Kant's philosophy by means of a theory of communicative competence will allow him to develop his much fuller account of natural scientific knowledge; in particular, this work will allow him to produce a concept of truth and thus escape the charge that his account of natural science in *Knowledge and Human Interests* amounts to mere pragmatism. But the turn towards such more formal, pure philosophy gravely weakens Habermas's notion of knowledge-constitutive interests. For how should we conceive of such transcendental knowledge? It is clearly not meant to be technical, but equally it is not part of normal social interaction. This question has not yet been answered by Habermas.

The really damaging consequence of the split, however, is felt in the more immediately political question as to how the good society is to be created. Even if it were the case that psychoanalysis works, as Habermas believes, a political theory cannot be based on the powers of self-reflection. Most obviously, the reason why psychoanalysis has a chance to work at all is that the patient enters analysis *seeking* enlightenment, and this is scarcely the case in politics. Or, to put it another way, liberation consequent on enlightenment cannot be applied to social life where interested parties resist and contest the views of one another. A firmer sense of social structure would have stopped him being so misled here; for, in fact, there is no general human interest in emancipation (Would that it were so easy!), and Habermas's recent rather murky remarks about the 'derivative' status of the emancipatory interest effectively admit that it is not in any way as basic as labour and interaction.[40]

This is a good moment to pause to comment briefly on the division between labour and interaction since this unlikely political strategy is a direct consequence of this radical separation. The more one thinks about the details of Habermas's division, and its relations to spheres of life, the more complex the matter becomes. The usual consequence of separating things into self-contained boxes in social theory is some substantive misunderstanding of the world. Habermas's division, firstly, tends to give the impression that knowledge of nature somehow runs separate from social communication; this clearly does not help us to understand those societies which anthropomorphically write their social world into their conception of nature. This division explains, secondly, why he ever countenanced such an unrealistic political strategy. Crucially, the sphere of social interaction is seen platonically as one in which men share a set of meanings (albeit these are sometimes unfair) and have their lives structured by them. The consequence of this is, of course, to presume that the undermining of distorted meaning (by showing it from the outside to be ideological) will itself result in liberation.

This is effectively to say that power, as Giddens has emphasised, is not really one of the permanent elements of social life with roots—as far as Marx was concerned—in the character of labour, but something that is essentially supernumerary.[41]

Habermas's initial conception of critical theory solved three 'problems' for him. Firstly, the fact that actors would recognise their oppression gave his criticism of society its status as truth. This meant that, secondly, the problems of theory and practice had been solved, for he confidently expected his ideals to be realised. Thirdly, Habermas had seemed to justify his claim that a special type of theory designed to enlighten human agents was a systematic possibility. His later work had to face each of these questions afresh once it became clear that transcendental self-reflection would not in itself lead to political freedom. His theory of communicative competence is designed to justify systematically his conception of unconstrained discussion. This theory seeks to show conclusively how we can 'ground' values; and the link with the good life emerges here once again. Habermas faces squarely the question of how social change in general, and of his own values in particular, may be realised by turning to history, and producing a whole theory of social evolution. The labour interaction division is here developed in terms of a logic of moral development, giving rise to an idealist view of ideology and historical change. Habermas is still attracted by the conception of a critical theory producing information that is not technical, and so the province of experts, but empirical/prudential and open to general discussion. Understandably, however, he is far more circumspect here than before.

Communicative Competence

The central idea justifying the theory of communicative competence is simple. In daily conversation, we assert, judge and express ourselves on various matters. These utterances, in Habermas's view make claims for validity that can be discussed and either accepted or rejected. Thus, communicative competence (or in his more recent formulation universal pragmatics) describes our ability to maintain communication with our fellows. We can see what Habermas has in mind in more detail by first remembering his critique of the linguistic philosophy of the later Wittgenstein. This philosophy centred upon the idea that language users 'followed the rule' of a particular language into which they had been socialised.

As we have already remarked Habermas criticised this view of language on the grounds that it artificially—indeed 'positivistically'—conceived of language as a static entity. He thus wants to propose a 'theory of language games' so as to be able to conceptualise that flexibility of language already mentioned. Habermas finds the most helpful guide towards characterising the sort of theory that he seeks to create in Chomsky's analysis of linguistic competence. He approves Chomsky's attempt to describe abstract rules, and also accepts that the only way in which the accuracy of such rules can be established is by consulting the normal speakers of a language.[42] Nevertheless, his programme differs in other ways from Chomsky's. Most obviously, Habermas wishes to create a theory for communicative, rather than merely of linguistic, competence:

> In order to utter a sentence, the speaker must fulfil general presuppositions of communication. Even if he fulfils these presuppositions in conformity to the structures that are already given with the sentence employed, he may very well form the sentence itself without also fulfilling the presuppositions specific to the telos of communication.... Whereas a grammatical sentence fulfils the claim to comprehensibility, a successful utterance must satisfy three additional validity claims: it must count as true for the participants insofar as it expresses something intended by the speaker; and it must count as right insofar as it conforms to socially recognised expectations.[43]

Further specification of the claims noted will be made in a moment.

It seems likely that Habermas is very suspicious of Chomsky's belief that innate abilities can explain language use, for such a view has an overtone of ontology that Habermas's developmental perspective seeks to avoid. For this reason he suggests that an explanation of competence should be in 'reconstructive' rather than 'empirical-analytic terms'. Habermas insists that reconstructive knowledge cannot somehow disenchant us about our own powers by applying science to human behaviour:

> An empirical-analytic theory in the narrow sense can (and as a rule will) refute the everyday knowledge of an object domain that we possess prior to science and replace it with a correct theoretical knowledge regarded provisionally as true. A proposal for reconstruction, by contrast, can represent pre-theoretical knowledge more or less explicitly and adequately but it can never falsify it.[44]

Moreover, 'reconstruction' is seen developmentally, as it is modelled on Piaget's tracing of the stages of development through which children pass. In itself, of course, this does not rule out some ontological view; it merely says that the human machine is a complex one that takes some time to mature. But Habermas is clearly attracted by a view which recognises development from the start, and his own use of the notion of reconstruction steers clear of any ontological view whatever.

Habermas draws upon the analysis of speech acts by the linguistic philosopher Searle to further his argument. An utterance is held to have both locutionary and illocutionary parts. In simple terms, the former of these carries information about the world whilst the latter contains information about the speaker's intentions; thus language is held to have a double structure such that communication at two levels is possible at the same time. The validity claims that Habermas thinks can be analysed result from paying proper attention to this division. More specifically, two claims are analysed which are normally ignored. Firstly, an utterance must be held to be made by someone who is sincere in his attitude, and not saying something merely to mislead. Such sincerity or truthfulness (*Wahrhaftigkeit*) can only eventually be borne out as the result of expectations fulfilled, and by the realisation that a speaker is not recommending something that he would not himself choose to do. Secondly, an utterance must be accepted as appropriate or right (*Richtigkeit*). This validity claim refers to the norms of the social world; if these are broken then assent will not be granted to the speaker. In addition to these two validity claims, Habermas recognises that two further claims of a more traditional nature can be made. A claim must be comprehensible (*Verständlichkeit*) if communication is to take place at all; but this is a claim that will be met by all except those ruled out by some incapacity from social life. Finally, Habermas recognises that the prepositional or locutionary part of a statement can be examined to see whether it is based on a true (*Wahrheit*) observation. These four claims can be diagramatically represented:[45]

Table 3. Habermas's Four Conditions for the Validity Claims of Language

Domains of Reality	Modes of Communication	Validity Claims	Speech Acts	Functions of Speech
'The' World of External Nature	Cognitive: Objectivating Attitude	Truth	Constatives	Representation of Facts
'Our' World of Society	Interactive: Conformative Attitude	Rightness	Regulatives	Establishment of Legitimate Interpersonal Relations
'My' World of Internal Nature	Expressive: Expressive Attitude	Truthfulness	Representatives	Disclosure of Speaker's Subjectivity
Language	———	Comprehensibility	Communications	———

On the basis of universal pragmatics Habermas now distinguishes between action and discourse. This distinction follows Peirce's separation of a logic of inquiry from a theory of the constitution of objects, and it is similarly designed to combine some sort of realism with an awareness of the part played by the knowing subject. Action, of course, is dominated by the two basic interests of technical control and social interaction; as long as no disturbance in technical or social worlds occurs, taken-for-granted pragmatic recipes will suffice. This stands in complete contrast to the objectivity that can be gained in discourse. Such discourse is resorted to whenever a breakdown occurs. The constraints of action are abandoned so that, in principle, validity claims can be freely discussed in order to achieve a rational consensus. In summary, Habermas has kept something of his notion of interests by relegating them to a lower level; at a higher level of discourse, we are offered a unitary conception of reason. This is a very important change, and can be seen at work in his analysis of truth and ethics.

Habermas has lost none of his distaste for naive positivism, and his theory of discourse is designed to serve as a theory of science. He argues that we all have experiences of the world; on this matter he feels that the transcendental inquiries of Kant are valid and have been confirmed by Piaget.[46] But a mere experience may be mistaken or misunderstood, and it is only intersubjective agreement, probably based upon experiment, that turns a state of affairs into a recognised fact. There is a difference between (in Habermas's adoption of Ramsay) 'Caesar's death' and 'the fact that Caesar died'.

> Facts .... are not happenings. That is why the truth of propositions is not corroborated by processes happening in the world but by a consensus achieved through argumentative reasoning.[47]

This view of science leads Habermas to criticise Popper's belief that a fact can judge between theories, as a vestige of naive positivism in an approach he otherwise endorses for doing so much better.[48] Observations and experiments are, in other words, held to make their impact because they can rely upon a shared set of cognitive norms. Habermas regards the crucial proof for this theory of truth to be the fact that progress in science has often been made without the discovery of new facts being involved in any way. He is arguing that the theoretical shifts in paradigms result simply from reasoning. Scientists can 'radicalise' their discourse and go beyond mere experimental 'puzzle solving' to criticise their presuppositions. It must be stressed, however, that Habermas is absolutely clear that progress has taken place in the technical sphere; any use of Kuhnian terminology should not detract from the fact that Habermas is a long way from the relativism that sometimes seems inherent in Kuhn's work.

One obvious objection can be raised against Habermas's arguments and it is important to see how he counters it. This is simply that consensus is different from truth, and that a consensus may be false. Habermas recognises the objection and seeks to deal with it by arguing that a true consensus can be reached only when 'ideal' speech conditions are discussed. In other words, truth is again held to depend in some measure on the good life. These conditions depend upon allowing, and indeed making sure, that a capacity exists for anyone to raise speech acts constantively, performatively, regulatively and, of course, communicatively, at any time. These conditions obviously rule out violence or any attempt to browbeat or manipulate: only the force of the better argument is meant to count. Habermas is well aware that such conditions have never been met and so he terms his assumption 'counter factual'. Nevertheless, he claims that such agreement as there is depends upon imagining, as in social contract theories, what would have been agreed upon in ideal conditions. And we shall see that the ideal serves him as the basis for his political programme of positive liberty.

Habermas's recent work on natural science has a slightly different tone to that of his earlier writing because it stresses that *we* are responsible for scientific progress; in contrast to empiricist epistemologies which tell us to manfully bare ourselves before a bombardment of sensation, everything here is held to depend upon our inventiveness. This is very important since it puts another nail in the Weberian theory of disenchantment: where, before, Habermas had seemed resigned to considering the technical as running on different principles from the *Lebenswelt*, it now seems as if we are responsible for this too. In one sense the positive tone is an accurate reflection of Habermas's position, which stresses that scientists have been free to 'discourse' as they wish from about the seventeenth century. But in the moral sphere Habermas is keen to argue that nothing like an equivalent 'institutionalisation of discourse' has as yet taken place, and this gives his remarks in this area a socially critical edge.

This is a good moment to pause in order to draw together and assess the three central arguments that Habermas offers against the 'disenchantment thesis'. Firstly, his anti-ontological, pro-Hegelian sense leads him to insist that there are very strict limits to the application of monologic, i.e. mechanical, models to human behaviour and this, of course, justifies separating labour from interaction. Men are subjects whose 'competences' allow them to interact; all that knowledge can do here is to describe the ways in which such competences mature. My objection to this argument is that it is by no means obvious that the insistence that man is complex, i.e. goes through various stages and so on, really takes the case very far: it might just demand that complex models of human behaviour are necessary. The second argument, the consensus theory of science that has just been examined, in a sense 'enchants' us with our powers. It is important to be specific here. Weber stressed that disenchantment would result simply from the destruction of magic, i.e. through making the world 'neutral' rather than homocentric, and we have noted Marcuse's peculiar attempt to escape this by creating an ineffable 'new science'. Habermas accepts that nature must be treated objectively, but balances any disenchantment so caused by the fact that it is *we* who create science in the first place. Habermas's argument here seems to get us into deep water very quickly. He first condemns positivists (most of whom are by no means as unsophisticated as Habermas claims) on account of his naive correspondence theory of truth. Then, when he realises that a consensus, even one reached under ideal conditions, can be incorrect, i.e. a free consensus of 'flat-earthers' would still be wrong, he introduces a measure of realism that prevents our theories going too far astray. This mixture of logic of inquiry *with* realism is a terrible mess. Insofar as realism is reintroduced it is a major matter that severely curtails Habermas's claim to have advanced far beyond positivism. And one final point is due in this regard: it is arguable that advances in science do not depend upon our ability to conceptualise the same facts anew, but on our ability to produce theories that enable us to gain new facts from investigating the world. The third argument against disenchantment can be noted here, but is considered in more detail below. It is simply that the rationalisation of our social world can complement rationalisation of our technical world. The character of the social identity that would result from such a social rationalisation is also discussed below.

It is not of course surprising to find that Habermas believes that argument at the level of discourse can rationally decide ethical or value questions. This position recalls his old insistence that reason should not be limited and decisions made in its place:

> If rightness as well as truth can qualify as a discursively redeemable validity claim, it follows that right norms must be capable of being grounded in a way similar to true statements. In the philosophical tradition two views (among others) stand opposed. One has developed in classical natural law theory and

says that normative statements admit of truth *in the same sense* as descriptive statements; the other has with nominalism and empiricism become the dominant view of today and says that normative statements do not admit of truth at all. In my view, the assumptions underlying both views are false. I suspect that the justification of the validity claims contained in the recommendation of norms of action and of evaluation can be just as discursively tested as the justification of the validity claims implied in assertions.[49]

On this basis Habermas puts forward two arguments about practical discourse. Philosophically, he argues that an equivalent to theoretical discourse's agreement to test statements by experiment can be found in the field of ethics, by insisting that only the most universalisable principle be accepted as valid. This principle is essentially Kantian, but Habermas thinks that he is able to propose a universalistic ethics that goes beyond Kantian ethics. The crux of the difference lies in Habermas's insistence that men decide what is important for themselves, and do not rely simply upon specifications laid down by Kant. This might seem a trivial point, but it is one of great moment for Habermas. In a word, Habermas is asserting that men can discuss and change their supposed needs in discourse; there is no need for any assumption of ontology in ethical matters:

> The limits of formalistic ethics can be seen in the fact that inclinations incompatible with duties must be excluded from the domain of the morally relevant, and they must be suppressed. The interpretations of needs that are current at any given contingent stage of socialisation must thereby be accepted as given. Only *communicative ethics* guarantees the generality of admissible norms and the autonomy of acting subjects solely through the discursive redeemability of the validity claims with which norms appear. That is, generality is guaranteed in that the only norms that may claim generality are those on which everyone affected agrees (or would agree) without constraint if they enter into (or were to enter into) a process of discursive will formation....communicative ethics guarantees autonomy (in that it carries on the process of the insertion of drive potentials into a communicative structure of action—that is, the socialisation process—'with will and consciousness').[50]

The second argument follows clearly from this and is more directly political in tone. Habermas's whole line of approach since *Strukturwandel der Öffentlichkeit* stresses the great potential that a newly institutionalised public sphere will offer for rational will formation. This public sphere can now only be formed on the basis of full participation, and it is for this reason that Habermas is such a harsh critic of various 'realistic' theories of democracy. His own political theory is based on a very different conception of democracy:

> [Rousseau] mixed the introduction of a new principle of legitimation with proposals for institutionalising a just rule.... If one calls democracies precisely those political orders that satisfy the procedural type of legitimacy, then questions of democratisation can be treated as what they are: as organisational questions. For it then depends on the concrete social and political conditions, on scopes of disposition, on information, and so forth, which types of organisation and which mechanisms are in each case better suited to bring about procedurally legitimate decisions and institutions. Naturally one must think here in process categories. I can imagine the attempt to arrange a society democratically only as a self-controlled learning process.... Democratisation cannot mean an a priori preference for a specific type of organisation, for example, so called direct democracy.[51]

One consequence of this is that Habermas does not think it appropriate to lay down strict guidelines telling us how people in a properly constituted public sphere will choose to live; this he believes is a matter for the participants alone.

The account offered so far of universal pragmatics can be summed up in a nutshell by saying that it amounts in philosophic terms to a socialisation of Kant. Habermas, as noted, accepts Kant's argument that individual human beings are capable of forming various judgements about the world. But he has chosen to go beyond the Kantian individual ego and he locates the subject of knowledge in social communication. Some assessment of the idea of consensus appears below, whilst the reader should note that Gellner (Chapter 7) offers an entirely opposed conception of both science and the disenchantment thesis. But here we must note that there is more to Habermas's universal pragmatics than this, as can be seen when we realise that a socialised knowing subject could still be seen in ontological terms. Habermas escapes from this by seeking to add a Hegelian and developmental moment to universal pragmatics that puts ontological considerations out of count. This depends on systematically reconstructing the human competences that make such developments possible.

Habermas believes that a research programme will be able to show that there is a logic of development to human competences:

> I would like to propose a systematically warranted division into cognitive, linguistic and interactive development; corresponding to these dimensions I shall distinguish cognitive, linguistic and interactive competences. This proposal signifies that for each of these dimensions . . . . . a specific developmental-logically ordered universal sequence of structures can be given. Following Piaget, I

suppose that these general structures of cognitive, linguistic and interactive ability are formed in a simultaneously constructive and adaptive confrontation of the subject with his environment, whereby the environment is differentiated into outer nature, language and society.[52]

As can be seen from the table on page 63, Habermas also considers that there is a fourth domain of reality, namely that concerned with inner nature. This fourth area is that of ego development and is more complex than the others since it integrates them, but Habermas nevertheless feels that it is possible to describe the necessary stages through which an individual must go in order to create his own ego. Habermas's programme is extremely complicated but the general line of his research can be seen by linking the principle stages of ego development with the development of one of the competences mentioned above, namely the ability to sustain social interaction. A general view of his approach is given in the following table.

Some explanation is needed for the table to be properly understood. The column on the left describes the three principal stages of identity formation. In the first the child is so much at one with his social and natural environment that he has no real identity at all. The first consciousness of separation occurs inside the family and is associated with the Oedipal crisis, but the identity that is achieved is 'conventional' since it is based on an uncritical acceptance of norms. Only in the third stage is a personal identity formed as a result of learning to communicatively criticise taken-for-granted norms. The next two columns describe, at the levels of action and motivation, what the development of ego identity means. But it is Habermas's argument that it is the development in the fourth column that is almost causally related to the development of different types of identity. The development of interaction capacity is seen as just the ability to resolve conflicts, and this is held to be linked to participation in a wider social framework.

This reconstruction of competences on Piagetian lines is really but a programme for research, so that it is rather easy to raise objections to it. As noted, it is very difficult to see how the pure knowledge obtained in this approach links with his earlier insistence that we must approach nature by means of particular knowledge interests. And whilst it is clear that interactive and cognitive competences bear a close resemblance to interaction and labour, what is to be said of the 'inner world' of the self? Is this too to be seen as an interest in knowledge? It is more likely, in fact, that there is no definite relation between competences and interests since Habermas

Table 4. Stages of 'Ego Development' according to Habermas.[53]

Ego Development	Actions	Motivations	Interactive Competence	Domain of Validity	Philosophical Reconstruction
Natural identity	Actions and consequences of action	Generalised pleasure/ pain	Maximisation of pleasure —avoidance of pain through obedience	Natural and social environment	Naive hedonism
			Maximisation of pleasure —avoidance of pain through exchange of equivalents		
Role identity	Roles	Culturally interpreted needs	Concrete morality of primary groups	Group of primary reference persons	
	Systems of norms	(Concrete duties)	Concrete morality of secondary groups	Members of the political community	Concrete thought in terms of a specific order
Ego identity	Principles	Universalised pleasure/ pain (utility)	Civil liberties public welfare	All legal associates	Rational natural law
		Universalized duties	Moral freedom	All humans as private persons	Formalistic ethics/
		Universalized need interpretations	Moral and political freedom	All as members of a fictive world society	Universal ethics of speech

has recently shown signs of introducing other human competences, notably the aesthetic, that need to be reconstructed. The reader should note that if there is something of a proliferation of competences then naturalistic explanation of human behaviour is made impossible, and the Weberian disenchantment thesis undermined still further.

It seems likely, however, that Habermas will direct his energies to this field, and two points are already clear. Firstly, reconstructive sciences offer a way in which the context-dependency, and thus the danger of relativism necessitated by the *Geisteswissenchaften*, can be avoided:

> Concept formation in sociology is obviously linked up with the everyday concepts in which members of social groups construct the normative reality of their social environment. This suggests developing sociological action theory as a theory that attempts to reconstruct the universal components of the relevant pre-theoretical knowledge of sociological laymen. Sociology would.... no longer choose its basic concepts conventionally, but develop them with the aim of characterising the general formal properties of the socialised subject's capability for action, as well as of those action systems. To be sure, the phenomenological research programme aims in a similar way to grasp general structures of possible social life-worlds; but the development of the programme was burdened from the start with the weaknesses of a method that is modelled after the introspective procedures of the philosophy of consciousness. Only the competence-theoretic approaches in linguistics and developmental psychology have created a paradigm that connects the formal analysis of known structures with the causal analysis of observable processes.[54]

This is not to say that Habermas has finished hoping for a theory that can enlighten active participants. Most obviously, the ideal-speech situation is designed to allow people to make up their own minds; in these circumstances theoretical knowledge and, indeed, experts as such will have no place. Nevertheless, this is an ideal for the future, and Habermas's hopes that the purer theoretical knowledge created by his communicative theory will have some sort of result in enlightened action are much vaguer than the original conception of critical theory. But, secondly, the knowledge gained here can be used in understanding historical change, and this is what we will see Habermas trying to do in the next two sections. It is worth highlighting how remarkable a claim is being made here. The keynote of Habermas's ethics is seen in the bottom line of Table 4 in which it is clear that the moment of greatest socialisation is also the moment at which a human being can finally develop his individuality. This might seem tenable as a claim in pure ethics, but Habermas is arguing that ethical development is a social and not just a philosophic fact. And it is a development that is held to have great importance.

Social Evolution as Reconstructed Marxism

If the theory of communicative competence 'grounds' or justifies Habermas's own critically rationalist views, it still remains to be asked how social change in general occurs so that some estimation can be made of the chances of these values being realised. This concern with social change amounts really to the construction of a proper sociological method to replace those of phenomenology, hermeneutics, systems theory and so on, all of which have been criticised *en passant*. This proper sociological method takes the form of an attempt to take apart, and reassemble in improved form, Marxism; it should be noted that this use of 'reconstruction' has nothing to do with the notion of reconstructive science. Not surprisingly, this theory centres itself on working out the distinction between labour and interaction; what is needed is:

> .... a level of analysis at which the *connection* between normative structures and steering problems becomes palpable. I find this level in a historically oriented analysis of social systems, which permits us to ascertain for a given case the range of tolerance within which the goal values of the system might vary without its continued existence being critically endangered .... Ranges of variation for structural change obviously can be introduced only within the framework of a theory of social evolution.[55]

Habermas is here following Godelier, the latest thinker to have influenced him, in arguing that a social system will have a certain economic and social range. If this could be spelt out for our society we would be in a position to decide whether it was most meaningful to speak of 'late-capitalist', 'industrial', 'post-capitalist' and so on, and thus able to make some estimate of our historical chances. In this section Habermas's very ambitious general scheme is outlined, whilst its application to our own society is examined in the next section.

Habermas begins his reconstruction by analysing four of the crucial points of Marxism; in each case it is worth noting that the boldness of his thought is such that many Marxists would feel that he is throwing out far too much of their canon.

(1) It is not surprising to find that Habermas begins by considering the concept of social labour to which he retreated extensively in *Knowledge and Human Interests*. He considers that the idea of social labour and of that labour organised into an economy *is*

useful and helpful in distinguishing between the life of hominids and primates. But he insists that humans can themselves be distinguished from hominids only by emphasising the importance of socialisation in families:

> We can speak of the reproduction of *human* life, with homo sapiens, only when the economy of the hunt is supplemented by a familial social structure. This process lasts several million years; it represented an important replacement of the animal status system.... The rank order of the primates was one-dimensional; every individual could occupy one and only one.... status. Only when the same individual could unify various status positions and different individuals could occupy the same status was a socially regulated exchange between functionally specified subsystems possible. The animal status system was based on the occupant's capacity to threaten, that is, on power as an attribute of personality. By contrast social role systems are based on the intersubjective recognition of normed expectations of behaviour and not on respect for the possibilities of sanction situationally available to a role occupant because of peculiarities of his personality structure. This change means a *moralisation of motives for action*.[56]

The implication of this argument is simple; learning takes place in our social life as much as in our technical ability, and it is the ability to pass on such learning through socialisation that can explain the extraordinary diversity of human culture.

(2) Habermas does not wish to draw any conclusion from the diversity of cultures that would in any way undermine the notion of evolution and development. He is thus much kinder to the second Marxist canon, that of the history of the species (*Gattungsgeschichte*), than he was to the first—indeed he wishes to strengthen rather than weaken it. Habermas recognises that there are weak points in the notion of evolution via the canonical five modes of production. In particular he finds it hard to accept the implication of a 'unilinear, necessary, uninterrupted, and progressive development of a macrosubject.'[57] But he feels that these are excrescences on the basic theory which can survive without them. This can be seen in his rejection of the idea of a macrosubject:

> Historical materialism does not need to assume a *species-subject* that undergoes evolution. The bearers of evolution are rather societies and the acting subjects integrated into them; social evolution can be discerned in those structures that are replaced by more comprehensive structures in accord with a pattern that is to be rationally reconstructed.[58]

Habermas insists, however, that evolution be seen to retain a directional sense, and he is most unwilling to accept the watering down of this world story by objections, noting the complexities and 'mixtures' achieved by particular modes of production. He argues that instead of allowing case studies to dilute the directional component, a preferable strategy is to reconceptualise the notion of modes of production in a more abstract and inclusive fashion. His own suggestion is that this can be done by reference to a very few 'organisational principles':

> By principles of organisation I understand innovations that become possible through developmental-logically reconstructible stages of learning... The organisational principle of a society circumscribes ranges of possibility. It determines in particular: within which structures changes in the system of institutions are possible; to what extent the available capacities of productive forces are socially utilised and the development of new productive forces can be stimulated; to what extent system complexity and adaptive achievements can be heightened. A principle of organisation consists of regulations so abstract that in the social formation which it determines a number of functionally equivalent modes of production are possible. Accordingly, the economic structure of a given society would have to be examined at two analytic levels: firstly in terms of the modes of production that have been concretely combined in it; and then in terms of that social formation to which the dominant mode of production belongs.[59]

Habermas has suggested on one occasion that perhaps the three most basic organisational principles are those of kinship, power and the economy.[60] This suggests that his view of history is, essentially, trinitarian: kinship societies seem in Habermas's account to be preagrarian, whilst the state emerges with organised agriculture and the economy as a means of social integration with industrialism.

(3) The third canon of Marxism that Habermas comments upon is that of the metaphor of base and superstructure. Habermas is clear that this is of little use if understood in a naively economist fashion. Such was not apparently the actual usage of Marx himself:

> The context in which Marx put forth his theorem makes it clear, however, that the dependency of the superstructure on the base was intended in the first instance only for the critical phase in which a society passes into a new developmental level. It is not some ontological interpretation of society that is intended but the leading role that the economic structure assumes in social evolution.[61]

Habermas adds that the base should not, anyway, be seen in economic terms. As the organisational principles mentioned above indicate, society can be structured in entirely different ways. It is on this point that Habermas is perhaps most divorced from traditional Marxism. Some revisionist Marxists might allow that kinship or the state were necessary for the conduct of economic life; but Habermas seems to suggest that kinship and power are modes of organisation in their own right.

(4) The final canon that Habermas discusses is that of the relation between forces and relations of production. Traditional Marxism has often seen this in what Habermas considers to be a crassly determinist and technologist fashion whereby changes in the forces of production dictate what changes take place in the relations of production or form of social life. More subtle but often questioning-begging forms of Western Marxism have tried to escape this crudity by suggesting that there is, for example, a certain autonomy of social and political life but that such autonomy cannot step beyond certain limits laid down by a mode of production. Habermas recognises the worth of this enterprise, but does not believe that it has proved very successful. Godelier's argument, for example, is dismissed since it fails to describe the mechanism of social change adequately and remains far too unaware of the character of independent social change.[62] In fact, Habermas wishes to reject the idea of base and superstructure completely since he does not think that the historical evidence supports any such 'technological' theory:

> .... the great endogenous, evolutionary advances that led to the first civilisations or to the rise of European capitalism were not conditioned but followed by significant development of productive forces. In these cases the development of productive forces could not have led to an evolutionary challenge.[63]

This argument leads to Habermas introducing the argument which is behind all his critical comments on the Marxist canon:

> It remains an open question, *how* [an evolutionary] step is taken ..... only an analytic answer can explain *why* a society takes an evolutionary step and how we are to understand that social struggles under certain conditions lead to a new level of social development. I would like to propose the following answer: the species learns not only in the dimension of the technically useful knowledge decisive for the development of productive forces but also in the dimension of moral-practical consciousness decisive for structures of interaction. The rules of communicative action do develop in reaction to changes in the domain of instrumental and strategic action; but in doing so they follow *their own logic*.[64]

Habermas is suggesting that there is a logic of stages of social development that has the same character as the stages of development for individuals described by Piaget. This is a very difficult notion to grasp, and Habermas is certainly not happy about the word 'logic' itself. He is careful to deal with some of the more obvious objections immediately:

> Of course, we ought not draw from ontogenesis over-hasty conclusions about the developmental levels of societies. It is the personality system that is the bearer of the ontogenetic learning process; and in a certain way, only social subjects can learn. But social systems, by drawing on the learning capacities of social subjects, can form new structures in order to solve steering problems that threaten their continued existence. To this extent the evolutionary learning process of societies is dependent on the competences of the individuals that belong to them. The latter in turn acquire their competences not as isolated monads but by growing into the symbolic structures of their life-worlds.[65]

This refusal to allow that there is a difference between individual and society means that, of course, Table 4 illustrates not just the development of ego identity but also the logic of development in social morality. This development is, Habermas stresses, a social resource and the result of adaptive abilities since it allows for the regulation of conflict with greater and greater success. And Habermas offers further examples of the development of legal norms, providing some illustrations of the homologies between the development in societies and the development in modes of social integration.[66]

Simply to state that there are two dynamics does not in itself provide a theory of social evolution: this requires saying how the two are related to each other. Habermas has offered the most general theory which does relate the two, and in the abstract it stresses three crucial stages. In the first of these, Habermas still considers that his account is materialist since he suggests that a social system will come to be faced by problems that emanate from its base (although the base is not in every society an economic one). Secondly—and crucially—the successful taking of an evolutionary step depends upon the logic of moral development.

> I would even defend the thesis that the development of these normative structures is the pacemaker of social evolution, for new principles of social organisation mean new forms of social integration; and the latter, in turn, make it possible to implement available productive forces or to generate new ones, as well as making possible a heightening of social complexity.[67]

Finally, Habermas suggests that a theory of social movements is probably necessary to discover how the conditions under which the learning achieved under the old system can be mobilised in order to take the evolutionary step:

> Functionalism explains evolutionary advances by correlating functionally equivalent solutions to systems problems. It thus steers away from the evolutionary learning processes that could alone have explanatory force. This explanatory gap.... can be filled with a theory of social movements.... Naturally, the action orientations that achieve dominance in social movements are, for their part, structured by cultural traditions. If one conceives of social movements as learning processes through which latently available structures of rationality are transposed into social practice—so that in the end they find an institutional embodiment—there is the further task of identifying the rationalisation potential of traditions.[68]

We shall hear more on this question from Gellner. But Habermas's final stage sees, on the basis of a newly established social order, the development of the unleashed productive forces.

Habermas surrounds his theory with many reservations, some of which have already been noted: the most important of these emphasise that there is no automatic correlation between evolution and increase of happiness and that regression below an available moral logic, as with fascism, is always possible. Nevertheless, the theory is exceptionally bold and I have quoted from it at length in order that my own lack of sympathy should not prevent comprehension. The theory is an advance on Habermas's earlier conception of emancipatory interests, both in recognising that a moral change needs a social movement to realise it and in seeing men less as the prisoners of an ideology than as actively trying to change a particular moral tradition. Moreover, the questions that Habermas asks are certainly important, especially since it is plainly the case that ideology plays a significant role in the evolution between modes of production.

But to admit this is not to agree that higher levels of moral consciousness provide the key to social evolution. In the transition from agrarian to industrial societies, for example, it is extremely doubtful whether any such development in morality occurred. Wallerstein has argued that this transition did indeed depend upon learning as a means to create a new form of social life, but he insists that the learning that took place was limited and in the interests of the few.[69] Similarly, Mann has argued quite rightly that the development of industrialism is associated with the growth of nation-states; and this means that the European ideology of medieval Christianity was replaced by the more particularistic ideology of discrete national units.[70] And it is almost certainly the case that to develop a country quickly requires centralised power that is thereafter unlikely to be given up: technical growth, in other words, depends upon creating very unfortunate moral arrangements. These general doubts can be summed up by saying that Habermas's presumption that morality develops according to its own logic, seems here to pay insufficient attention to the ways in which ideologies can be the result, rather than the cause, of material circumstances. But the general theory can be more accurately evaluated by referring to its use in his concrete analysis of the crises of late capitalism.

Motivation Crisis

Habermas's *Legitimation Crisis* begins by analysing the notion of crisis itself. The key distinction between labour and interaction is used to separate a system crisis from an identity crisis. As we might expect from the discussion of social evolution, the difficulty in steering a social system only becomes critical when the *Lebenswelt* of social actors is undermined to the extent that they no longer feel sure of their identity. Thus there is a movement in Habermas's discussion from the first to the last of four crises that he classifies thus[71]:

Table 5. Habermas's Classification of Crisis.

Point of Origin	System Crisis	Identity Crisis
Economic System	Economic Crisis	—
Political System	Rationality Crisis	Legitimation Crisis
Socio-Cultural System	—	Motivation Crisis

Each of these crises, as well as the movement between them, needs to be spelled out; this is not an easy task given the denseness and suggestiveness of Habermas's account.

Marx was a theorist of economic crisis. *Capital* is not, however, completely clear on how this crisis will arise, whether from overproduction or underconsumption, but its origins in the anarchic conditions of capitalism forcing too great an investment in machinery with a consequent fall in profit are clear. Habermas considers late capitalism nothing less than a social form designed to prevent precisely this economic crisis. Crisis is avoided by Keynesian demand management, and by the use of science to create value from machinery—a possibility that Marx did not systematically countenance. And, of course, the success of the economic machine in combination with cultural consumption is held to integrate the working class. Habermas, however, argues that the politicisation of the market (for this is what late capitalism amounts to) raises other problems elsewhere. He now considers the market to have served not just as an economic mechanism, but as a source of legitimation as well: each just exchange in the market place is held to underwrite *laissez-faire*. The politicising of the market consequently raises the question as to the source of legitimation in a more highly politicised world. Roughly speaking, this analysis is—ironically—that proposed by economists such as Hayek and Friedman who, however, insist that the economy be uncoupled from politics since *no* legitimation can be found there. This is not Habermas's position, and he is in any case sensible enough to realise that it is unlikely that any Western government is able, in the face of democratic pressures, to give up all tools of economic management and to allow depressions to take their course.[72]

Two sets of crises may develop inside the political system. Most obviously, a rationality crisis develops whenever the state is not allowed to carry out its task of ironing out the problems of capitalism. This can occur when the state is overburdened in the provision of the necessary social infrastructure for economic growth, when, in other words, its finances are broken by having to provide schools, welfare, research and development and so on. Alternatively, the capitalists might refuse to allow the state to serve their best interests, especially perhaps by trying to make it responsible for capitalist failures. Habermas does not think, however, that this need necessarily happen:

> .....there exists no *logically necessary* incompatibility between interests in global capitalist planning and freedom of investment, need for planning and renunciation of intervention, and independence of the state apparatus and dependency on individual interests. The possibility that the administrative system might open a compromise path between competing claims that would allow a sufficient amount of organisational rationality, cannot be excluded from the start on logical grounds.[73]

Indeed, Habermas does not think that a rationality crisis need develop in any way as long as one condition is fulfilled. This condition is that people trust the state and accept its priority of seeking to make capitalism work. In other words, problems in rationality could ensue where there is a deficit in the amount of legitimation that the state can draw upon. It is at this point that real dangers for late capitalism begin to become apparent. The administrative system needs a certain amount of room and independence if it is to be able to act, and this means that democracy, the formal source of legitimation, must not take on active participatory forms. However, the very activity of the state in planning hitherto untouched private areas of life tends to breed activity amongst its citizens:

> Thus, traditions withheld from the public problematic, and all the more from practical discourses, are thematised. An example of such direct administrative processing of cultural tradition is educational planning, especially curriculum planning. Whereas school administrations formerly merely had to codify a canon that had taken shape in an unplanned, nature-like manner, present curriculum *planning* is based on the premise that traditional patterns could as well be otherwise. Administrative planning produces a universal pressure for legitimation in a sphere that was once distinguished precisely for its power of self-legitimation.[74]

Doubtless the state would like to create new ideologies to justify its activities but Habermas considers that the attempt to produce social meanings 'administratively' will soon be seen through. Perhaps more importantly, the public attempt to create shared meanings would lead to recognition of the latent class structure: thus 'in the final analysis, *this class structure* is the source of the legitimation deficit'.[75] Nevertheless, Habermas believes that it may prove possible for the state to replace meanings with value, i.e. to secure cohesion through economic growth. This would be possible just as long as the cultural realm does not systematically produce demands that cannot be satisfied in these instrumental terms. But Habermas considers that this is precisely what is beginning to happen, and it is this that makes the motivational crisis the key to his whole discussion.

The account of motivational crisis has two essential parts.[76] Firstly, the core components of received bourgeois ideology are apparently being irreparably dismantled. A whole series of analyses are referred to in support of this point. Most importantly, Habermas suggests that 'possessive individualism' is being eroded both by the discovery that money cannot buy 'social goods' and by the fact that fewer people are dependent on the market place since, for example, technological developments place a high premium on long periods of university study. In a nutshell, Habermas is subscribing to the spirit, albeit not to the specifications, of Schumpeter's famous argument that capitalism has no ideology of its own and slowly depletes the ideology on which it once smoothly ran. Secondly, and crucially, Habermas wishes to argue that the new ideas that are being produced by the cultural realm are directly opposed to the needs of late capitalism. The most crucial oppositional ideas have two sources. Modernist art is held, following Daniel Bell, to pose a cultural contradiction to the system:

> In the artistically beautiful, the bourgeoisie once could experience primarily its own ideals and the redemption, however fictive, of a promise of happiness that was merely suspended in everyday life. But in radicalised art, it soon had to recognise the negation rather than the complement of its social practice. In the aura of the bourgeois work of art—that is, in the cultist enjoyment of the already secularised, museum-like shrine—was mirrored a belief in the reality of the beautiful illusion. This belief crumbled.... The truth thereby comes to light that in bourgeois society art expresses not the promise but the irretrievable sacrifice of bourgeois rationalisation, the plainly incompatible experiences and not the esoteric fulfilment of withheld, but merely deferred, gratifications.[77]

Habermas draws on his communications theory to argue that the only viable ethical system now available must be that of communicative ethics. He criticises Kantian formalistic ethics on the grounds that it is too limited. This can be seen, he argues:

> ....in the fact that inclinations incompatible with duties must be excluded from the domain of the morally relevant, and they must be suppressed. The interpretation of needs that are current at any given contingent stage of socialisation must thereby be accepted as given. They cannot be made in turn the object of a discursive will formation.[78]

Communicative ethics, in contrast, allows participants in a dialogue to question everything. Most importantly, Habermas believes, socialisation patterns have already changed so much that this new morality is 'determining typical socialisation among several strata, that is, they have achieved motive-forming power'.[79] Habermas refers in this context to studies of personality structure among students. He is aware that there is no guarantee that political activism will result from these new patterns, but nevertheless insists that a fundamental change in social values that will cause a motivational crisis is occurring.[80] This could only finally be prevented, he tells us, if a way of socialising people were found such that questions of justice and truth were deemed to be irrelevant. This is naturally rejected on moral grounds, but, more importantly, it is also made to seem somewhat unlikely.[81]

Two rather separate points are being made about the cultural sphere. On the one hand, Habermas is arguing that these new demands are such as to cause a crisis for the state. This is presumably because he feels that there will be enough people, amongst them students, who will refuse the bidding of the status quo and thereby cause problems for society. Secondly, however, Habermas argues that these developments represent normative learning that could be used so as to allow Western society to move from late capitalism to a socialism based on free communication. This part of his argument is most clearly outlined in a lecture dealing with the question of whether complex society can achieve a rational social identity. Habermas's answer to this is clearly affirmative. If the distortions of class on communication are removed, then a genuine hermeneutic consensus on the good life will emerge: we are told that it would be presumptuous to prejudge those discussions by specifying the good life now.

What are we to make of Habermas's argument? Thomas McCarthy has criticised its form as being rather 'technical'—in other words, it allows little room (except at the moment when free communication amongst equals is established) for enlightenment of participants by means of a critical theory.[82] Insofar as this is true, it seems to me to be something of an advance on Habermas's earlier, implausible political strategy. Nevertheless, the weaknesses of that approach unfortunately resurface here. To be frank, Habermas still displays an insufficient grasp of social structure in believing that art and new forms of socialisation are strong enough forces to bring down our social order. Even more pertinently, it is at least questionable whether modernist art and some of the newer student demands deserve to be taken so seriously. Is it really the case that the more outrageous tricks of modern art are opposed to the social order? Might not Marcuse be right in saying that some 'outrageous' modern artists provide desired entertainment, and are highly paid for so doing? (This will be discussed further when we examine Daniel Bell's extended versions of this theory.) But much the same point could be made about the student movement. Whatever its achievements, it is hard to ignore the fact that it was often based on low-quality ideology. And the climate of the 1980s in universities is one in which the traditional bourgeois virtues seem to be doing rather well.

This criticism of Habermas—that the optimism of his 'logic' of moral development leads him to miscalculate available social forces—does not mean that his analysis is of no use. On the contrary, it will be argued below that class remains a sufficiently powerful factor to cause a rationality crisis. But other, related criticisms of Habermas's insistence that communicative ethics represents the highest level of moral development are much more damaging. A part of the great appeal that Habermas exercises derives from the hope that we can escape the disenchanting effect of science by rationalising social life in order to realise a new collective social identity. This is a very complex matter, but the way in which he describes the situation of open communication makes it doubtful that it will produce identity. For the continual questioning of anything whatever is surely enough to undermine the taken-for-granted assumptions that make up the very definition of identity. Habermas's argument is, moreover, of a *carte blanche* variety presuming that consensus and truth will emerge once repression is taken away. In the first place, this is very unlikely to lead to any sort of political action.

Insofar as social movements are based on ideas, they gain their success from aiming at some sort of alternative ordering of society; nothing more than generalised resentment will form around the idea that the future should somehow be open. Secondly, the commonsensical view that Habermas's conception of consensus is too utopian must be upheld: Habermas should, for example, pay attention to the failure of G.D.H. Cole's very strenuous labours to explain how a completely participatory democracy would be possible.[83] Such a naive view can only be held because Habermas has continued to treat power as something external to social life, rather than as a permanent characteristic of the relations between men.

In a sense, Marcuse is more realistic than Habermas in insisting, as he did in an interview with Habermas shortly before his death,[84] that a new character structure is needed if a 'rational' society is to work. But granted that we cannot expect this, there is much more to be said in favour of the dull workings of the only sort of democracy we know. Habermas might be more aware of this were his social organisational principles—kinship, power and the economy—rather different. Eastern Europe surely shows us that the industrialism can be run on a power basis, and this should make us realise how peculiar is Western social evolution. None of this means that liberal democracies are havens of social justice, as will become clear. There is, however, much to be said for judging a social order against what is possible rather than condemning it facilely by invoking—and here the word is used pejoratively—'utopian' dreams.

Conclusion

It is scarcely necessary to say that Habermas is an exceptionally striking thinker of very great range. Many of the issues he raises surface in later chapters: in particular, it has been noted that Gellner offers a very different view of both science and ideology. In conclusion, however, it is worth emphasising the basic charge I have made against Habermas. This is that his very idiosyncratic version of idealism is implausible both in the early Platonic conception of the emancipatory interest, and in his more recent work, abstract and concrete, on the place of moral development in social evolution. We can see the idiosyncracy of his idealism at work when he notes:

> The idea of an identity become reflective, to be collectively established in the future, would now be the last illusory husk before collective identities as such could be given up and replaced by the permanent variation of all reference systems. Such a state of affairs also bears utopian features; for in it all wars—as organised efforts of collectives that demand from their members a willingness to die—would be thinkable only as regressive states of emergency but no longer as something institutionally expected to happen.[85]

We shall see later Raymond Aron, a thinker as much influenced by the *Geisteswissenchaften* as Habermas, contesting this.

Habermas's conception of a logic of moral development thus runs the danger of writing his own hopes into history. Other thinkers have done this before: there is, for example, a quite uncanny resemblance between some of Habermas's formulations about science, moral development and social evolution and those offered by L.T. Hobhouse in his *Morals in Evolution* and *Social Development*.[86] Furthermore, it seems to me that Habermas has already fallen into the trap of placing his hopes above analysis in his description of our own society. It was stated earlier that in 1973 he considered that a motivational crisis was a distinct possibility. However, his most recent pronouncements give the impression that late capitalism is surviving this problem rather well. He notes, for example, that:

> .... the work ethic is incredibly reinforced: there is a rehabilitation of competitive behaviour, pursuit of gain, and exaltation of virtues conducive to a high mobility of labour. For it is necessary to induce people to accept work that they would not otherwise perform of their own free will, or for which they have not had the necessary preparation. The accent is thus placed on an acquisitive ethic and instrumental values. This orientation penetrates deeply into the first years of schooling, to the point of dominating the whole educational system.[87]

This passage gives the impression that, contrary to the predictions of *Legitimation Crisis*, social values and, above all, possessive individualism are still capable of supporting late capitalism. The possibility of a motivational crisis perhaps never represented more than Habermas's dreams.

4 Daniel Bell

Homo Duplex

At first sight it might seem as if Daniel Bell inhabits a completely different universe than that of Habermas. But this is not really so for as a graduate student at Columbia University in 1943–44 Bell worked with Leo Löwenthal and Paul Massing on the Institute's 'Study of Anti-Semitism in American Labour'.[1] More importantly, his belief that we are coming to live in a 'post-industrial' society does not, as is often held, blind him, to use Habermas's concept, to the very different necessities of social interaction. Indeed, his definition of culture reflects the fact that he too is deeply grounded in the *Geisteswissenschaften*:

> I would define culture as the modalities of response by sentient men to the core questions that confront all human groups in the consciousness of existence: how one meets death, the meaning of tragedy, the nature of obligation, the character of love—these *recurrent* questions which are, I believe, cultural universals, to be found in all societies where men have become conscious of the finiteness of existence.
>
> Culture, thus, is always a *ricorso*. Men may expand their technical powers. Nature may be mastered by scientific knowledge. There may be progress in the instrumental realms. But the existential questions remain.[2]

This concern with meaning led Bell, for reasons to be examined, to argue that capitalism is coming to face a cultural contradiction; this argument is very favourably cited by Habermas in his *Legitimation Crisis*, and there is a distinct overlap in analysis.

But if the concerns are not so dissimilar, the values which Habermas and Bell bring to them differ dramatically. Habermas's views are, as it were, all cut from the cloth of rationalism: rationalisation in society is needed so that technical knowledge and its effects may be controlled. Bell's position, in contrast, is more complex. The work he did with the Institute apparently discovered an appalling reservoir of anti-semitism and nativism in America; the fear of what might happen to the Institute were this made known prevented publication of the report. But the lesson for Bell of this and, crucially, of contemporary events in Europe was that human bestiality could not simply be blamed on irrational social structures and the like: the truth that Bell felt he had discovered was the old one that *homo homini lupus est.* This is implied in the definition of culture just given: where Habermas would speak of rationalising and developing culture, Bell suggests that cultural wisdom is static and somehow concerned to teach the 'finiteness' of human life. We shall be taking up Bell's interesting and—curiously—neglected views below. But a second more obvious difference from Habermas should be stressed. Bell does indeed speak of technological developments with warmth and enthusiasm. The central reason for these lyrical tones can be highlighted immediately: if the industrial system changes so as to demand more and more highly skilled labour, then that class war which terrifies Bell may no longer be on the cards.

There are two very different personae housed inside the soul of Daniel Bell. One of them is akin to a latter day Saint-Simon or, better, H.G. Wells, keen to tell us about the Promethean possibilities offered by modern science and industry. But the other is aware of the evil that men can do, and seeks to place some limit on human vanity. This other is best dubbed 'Rabbi—not just because of the calling of Bell's own father, but because he so frequently refers to the wisdom enshrined in old rabbinical writings. It is exciting to try to combine these two personae but—obviously—they are more contradictory than complementary; and the reader may anticipate that the attempt to run them together will cause problems.

One preliminary is in order. Much of Bell's most striking work is contained in essays, and it is in fact only recently that he has sought to develop a 'general theory' of modern society. These essays cannot be ignored since they introduce us to his main themes, and I have chosen to consider those on America and the 'end of ideology' thesis before approaching his more ambitious 'general sociology'. At times the implications of some of the early essays are best brought out by later arguments, and I have not hesitated to refer to them. This tactic is justified given the stability of Bell's view of man, and it need not obscure the occasions on which Bell has changed his views.

Moralism and the Complexities of America

It is appropriate to note that biographical circumstances give Bell a slightly ambivalent view on America. On the one hand, as a New York Jewish intellectual appalled at the potential for evil amongst, importantly, those supposed according to the Marxist scheme to usher in liberation, Bell is afraid of America. This fear can be seen in two of his earliest articles. In 'The Grass Roots of America Jew-Hatred' he suggests that 'the country where anti-semitism can emerge in the most violent shape and unabated fury is the United

States'.[3] And in 'Notes on Authoritarian and Democratic Leadership' he complained that it was difficult to ensure democratic leadership given that all 'basic social patterns are authoritarian and tend to instil feelings of helplessness and dependence'.[4] However, it is worth remembering that Bell's fears have not been fulfilled. On the contrary, he has done well out of America, being labour editor of *Fortune* before pursuing an acclaimed academic career at Columbia and Harvard. I believe that Bell's personal fears and hopes are projected onto the interpretation we are offered of American history and society. This interpretation is not Bell's alone but is also endorsed, with slight differences of emphasis, by Shils, Lipset, and, most strikingly, Hofstader. It is impossible now to decide who originated this interpretation, although Bell clearly played some creative part; and we can leave the question of attribution to others and turn, albeit with some knowledge of the work of the other writers,· to the interpretation itself.

American society is held to be especially prone to a simplifying political style—well nicknamed by Hofstader the 'paranoid style in American politics'.[5] Bell dubs this style 'moralism', and suggests that it has two sources:

> [Firstly] This has been a middle-class culture, and there may be considerable truth to the generalisation of Svend Ranulf that moral indignation is a peculiar fact of middle-class psychology and represents a disguised form of repressed envy. One does not find moral indignation a feature of the temper of aristocratic culture.... This moralism, itself not unique to America, is linked to an evangelicalism that was largely unique.... While puritanism, and the 'New England Mind', have indeed played a large intellectual role in American life, in the habits and mores of the masses of the people, the peculiar evangelicalism of Methodism and Baptism, with its high emotionalism, its fervour, enthusiasm and excitement, its revivalism, its excesses of sinning and of high-voltage confessing, has played a much more important role in colouring the moral temper of America.[6]

It is important to realise that 'enthusiasm' is here used pejoratively, for mass enthusiasm is held to have characterised Nazism. But the full dangers that are implicit in moralism are illustrated for Bell in Populism and McCarthyism, two movements capable of appealing to the American psyche. The first of these flourished in the years after the Civil War, and came to a peak in 1896 with the bid of Bryan for the Presidency. It appealed to the poor farmers of the West and South whose fate was increasingly determined by the railroads. Essentially, according to the interpretation offered, populism, aided by simplifying moralism, turned paranoid; this paranoia is held to be epitomised by the anti-industrial, anti-semitic and even neo-fascist demagoguery of Tom Watson in his later years. The unpleasantness of McCarthyism is more generally known. Bell feels that its crusading fervour can only be understood if it is realised that communism became equated with sin in the fundamentalist mind.[7] Bell is thus arguing that the seeming differences between the movements—one being of the left and consequently attacking Eastern financiers, the other of the right opposed to effete intellectuals—are superficial. Both were radical movements appealing to the same fundamentalist mind, and both movements are held by Bell to be nativist and anti-semitic.

If one novelty of this interpretation was a marked distrust in the beneficence of the untutored mind, another lay in the concept used to explain radicalism, namely that of 'status politics' or, to be precise, of 'status anxieties'. Bell insists that it is a mistake to see all politics in class terms, and a blunder to use this European tool uncritically in the American scene. More particularly, it is claimed that American politics need to be analysed in not one but two dimensions; class *and* status are capable of producing political action. Where class politics are bred by economic hardship, status politics are held to emerge from prosperity:

> Contrary to the somewhat simple notion that prosperity dissolves all social problems, we see that prosperity brings in its wake new social groups, new social strains and new social anxieties. Conventional political analysis..... cannot fathom these new social anxieties nor explain their political consequences.[8]

In other words, those suffering from social dislocation will cling desperately to, and act upon, their customary moral certainties. Bell has not written in detail about Populism, but his analysis of McCarthyism illustrates the general argument. Three groups with status anxieties are held to have contributed to McCarthyism. Firstly, the independent small town businessman is held to feel threatened by New Deal politics although these do not affect his economic interest adversely. In Bell's words:

> ... the social group most threatened by the structural changes in society is the 'old' middle class—the independent physician, farm owner, small-town lawyer, real estate promoter, home-builder, automobile dealer, gasoline-station owner, small businessmen, and the like—and that, regionally, its greatest political concentration is in the South and the Southwest, and in California. But a much more telltale indicator of the group that feels most anxious—since life-styles and values provide the emotional fuel of beliefs and actions—is the strain of Protestant fundamentalism, of

nativist nationalism, of good and evil moralism which is the organising basis for the 'world view' of such people. For this is the group whose values predominated in the nineteenth century, and which for the past forty years has been fighting a rearguard action.[9]

Secondly, the new managerial elite is held to suffer from grave insecurities despite the considerable economic rewards that it can command. It is made to feel particularly powerless when government interferes in labour relations, and this leads to support for the radical right. Finally, Bell suggests that the increasing sophistication of weapons technology has led to an undermining of the authority of the traditional military elite by a new group of intellectual strategists able, for example, to understand the games theory at the basis of nuclear strategy. All three groups are held to be 'dispossessed'; they suffer less from the envy that came to dominate Populism than from 'the sour impotence of those who find themselves unable to understand, let alone command, the complex mass society that is the polity today'.[10] Such people are ripe for conspiracy theories liberally populated with Jewish or communist villains—or possibly both.

In his early 'Notes on Authoritarian and Democratic Leadership', Bell suggested that democratic leadership can only be achieved by creating a democratic electorate. The implied activism of this remark rapidly waned, as can be seen from the manner in which he speaks of the character of British politics as revealed by Edward Shils's *Torment of Secrecy*:

> In the elite structure of British politics, control is not in the constituencies...but in the small parliamentary caucuses, which have a legal as well as historic independence from mass party control. The British elite wedded to a 'politics of civility', tends to dampen any extremism within the top political structure, while the control system keeps the masses outside and makes it difficult for them to be mobilised for direct pressure on the government.[11]

Established leaders, in other words, are admired since their levels of education will make them loyal to 'the democratic system'. Bell bitterly regrets the fact that the American political system allows populist incursions that disrupt the elite, and so prevent it from systematically restraining the inclinations of the masses.

But despite all these criticisms of America, Bell remains convinced of American virtue. The fact that Great Britain had an established elite perhaps prevented the excesses of the 1930s but it is the prevalence of these excesses throughout Europe that really occupies his attention. One central reason, Bell argues, for the intensity of conflict in Europe was the cultural division imposed on top of class divisions, a famous example of this being France, where resistance to economic injustice led of necessity—given the symbiosis of church and state—to anti-clericalism.[12] In America, by contrast, culture and politics run on separate axes, and this is a source of delight to Bell since it means that radical status politics are unlikely to completely polarise the society. This point is just the first of several designed to show that America's exceptional circumstances have allowed it to avoid the internecine conflicts of Europe in the twentieth century. This exceptionalism explains why Bell, despite his fears of radical politics, remains an optimist about America. The burden of these points, succinctly summarized by Bell recently,[13] is that even if the elite is not always sufficiently established to restrain the masses, the circumstances of America are such that the same result is achieved. These beneficent and idiosyncratic circumstances deserve to be listed.

(1)   America appeared as the promised land to those who, from the Puritans onwards, were expelled from their own country. Bell notes that 'all of Marx's co-workers in the German Workers Club who came to the United States after 1848...abandoned socialism....',[14] and he is able to demonstrate how American socialism itself faltered before the ideal and (during the expansion of America) the reality of individual achievement.

(2)   Bell endorses to some extent the 'Turner thesis' in arguing that the development of the country could take precedence over internal social conflicts.

(3)   As a result of the first two factors, America became culturally diverse. Despite the great attempts to Americanise immigrants, 'the melting pot' failed to work.

(4)   The fact of diversity played its part in defusing conflict. More important still in escaping from the total conflicts of Europe, was the fact of the sheer physical size of America. This was very significant since there had been more actual violence in American labour history than in that of most European countries. But, Bell says:

> ...the remarkable fact about labour violence was that, while it was more explosive and intense (involving dynamiting, gun battles, and the use of troops and police) than in the ideology-riven countries of Europe, this violence (in the coal mines, the timber camps, the textile mills) took place largely at the 'perimeters' of the county. It took a long while for those shock waves to reach the political centre, and by that time their force had been dissipated.[15]

(5)   The tremendous success and resilience of the American

economy allowed social improvement to take place in an unplanned, i.e. non-political manner. One clear example of this has been the way in which crime has served as a peculiar avenue of social mobility for different ethnic groups in American life. Each ethnic group that has been associated with organised crime—the Irish, Italians and, perhaps currently, blacks—has taken enough out of it to allow the group as a whole to move upward in American society.[16] The essay in which Bell demonstrates this point is a very clear example of the sort of reverse muck-raking that characterises his approach: what had seemed scandalous is held in fact to have 'functional' side-effects.

(6) The twentieth century in America has seen 'the breakup of family capitalism'. In Bell's words:

> Two 'silent' revolutions in the relations between power and class position in modern society seem to be in process. One is a change in the *mode of access* to power insofar as inheritance is no longer all-determining; the other is a change in the *nature of power holding itself* insofar as technical skill rather than property, and political position rather than wealth, have become the basis on which power is wielded.[17]

In short, Bell is arguing that capitalism was objectionable and likely to lead to social protest as long as the rich had direct access to power. But America no longer has a ruling class of any sort; power is, on the contrary, very hard to 'locate' as it results from negotiations between all the groups of a pluralist society.

(7) One final factor must be mentioned: the very lack of ideology of the exceptionally flexible American two-party system is held to be of great advantage. American parties are quick to take over the demands of protest movements, and to make them their own; this makes it exceptionally hard for ideological politics to emerge. Bell of course recognizes that even in America the 1930s saw something approaching ideological politics, as American labour began to participate in a social movement with political aims. But what impresses him in retrospect is that labour, once recognised as a legitimate interest, quickly reverted to bread and butter 'market unionism'—a position he does not expect to change given one development yet to be discussed, namely that of the declining importance of unions resulting from changes in the occupational structure. He sums up his whole case thus:

> We have learned...to include the 'excluded interests', the populist farmers and the organised workers. These economic interest groups take a legitimate place in the society and the ideological conflicts that once threatened to disrupt the society,

particularly in the New Deal period, have been mitigated. The new divisions created by the status anxieties of the new middle-class groups pose a new threat. The rancour of McCarthyism was one of its ugly excesses. Yet the United States, so huge and complex that no single political boss or any single political grouping has ever been able to dominate it, may in time diminish these divisions. This is an open society, and these status anxieties are part of the price we pay for that openness.[18]

This listing of 'factors' that make America exceptional should not give the impression that Bell's view of America is wholly deterministic. That this is not the case can be seen from his fine essay 'Marxian Socialism in the United States'. Here Bell demonstrates quite convincingly that American socialists failed in the art of politics; more specifically, they were unable to turn a generalised critique of capitalist society into practical policies either for running capitalism or for transcending it.[19] This essay is also full of asides that say much about Bell's own political attitudes. He remarks, for example, that many leftist intellectuals of the 1930s were 'left with burnt fingers when, for reasons of expediency, the party line was changed'.[20] I do not know whether, or to what extent, Bell suffered political disillusion in his early years. One thing is certain, however, that he came to 'cast his lot with America' since it was sufficiently large and complex to frustrate dangerous radicalism, and open enough to allow social groups to achieve social reform without the benefit of any centralised political plan.

Let us now assess Bell's view of America. We can begin by drawing upon the very severe criticisms made of his accounts of populism and McCarthyism. Bell's picture of a half-crazed and dangerous popular mind is considerably overplayed, it is argued. C. Vann Woodward, the distinguished historian of Southern Populism, insists that the paranoid turn of Populism only came very late; until then Southern Populists were closely associated with very progressive movements:

> ...in the efforts they made for racial justice and political rights they went further toward extending the Negro political fellowship, recognition, and equality than any native white political movement has ever done before or since in the South. This record is of greater historical significance and deserves more emphasis and attention than any anti-Semitic tendencies the movement manifested...[21]

Michael Paul Rogin, the author of *The Intellectuals and McCarthy*, a much praised monograph on the 'status politics' theory, makes very similar points. He suggests general reasons for believing that mass political action need not invariably lead to dangerous and simple-minded intolerance:

> ...political issues determine which segment of an individual's total bundle of attitudes will become relevent. White workers may be prejudiced against Negroes in the abstract and if mobilised on the issue of neighbourhood housing may take anti-Negro positions. But if they are mobilised on the basis of common economic grievances, as happened in the organisation of the CIO in the 1930s, the activity of white workers may be pro-Negro.... There is no reason to assume that the anti-democratic attitude of masses mobilised by depression or discrimination will affect their actual political activity. Indeed, their activity may change their attitudes. Members of elite groups, with 'better' attitudes in the abstract, may engage in anti-democratic activity out of fear of mass movements. Behaviour cannot be predicted from attitudes alone.[22]

And Rogin goes somewhat further in arguing that such activity is often necessary for reaching a conclusion, given that elite groups can be *less* liberal then their followers. There is one famous example of this: the central European aristocracy at the turn of the century fostered the agrarian roots of fascism and anti-semitism.[23] In the American context, Rogin argues:

> At least since World War II, leaders of the Republican Party have been far more conservative than their own party supporters—who are on many issues closer to Democratic leaders than to Republican ones. Here, then, is a pressure to the Right in American politics from a powerful elite group. Deference to those leaders would increase conservatism in particular, not democratic stability in general.[24]

This brings us to a second point, namely, that the concept of status politics does not, as it is claimed, represent a conceptual breakthrough in the understanding of American history. This is not to say that the idea of protest movements born from prosperity is altogether mistaken and I shall, in fact, try and add to Bell's formulation later in this chapter, but status politics confuse more than it helps us when it comes to interpreting Populism and McCarthyism. Most obviously, Populism was not the result of anxieties caused by prosperity:

> ...the conditions under which Populism rose were exactly the opposite: severe depression, critical unemployment, and crippling currency contraction, when few were able to improve their economic position—and certainly not farmers in a cash-crop staple agriculture.[25]

Woodward prefers to call Populism 'agrarian interest politics', but a loose use of the concept of class that stresses economic complaint need not distort, and certainly allows for, a more accurate understanding of the aims and social roots of Populism than that offered by Bell. The basic programme of Populism might have been simple-minded, but it was perfectly rational; there is no reason to conjure up demons in order to understand it. The case of McCarthyism is somewhat different. Here the crucial point to realise is that, pace Bell, the movement received as much support amongst the elite as amongst the moralising mass of the people.[26] Perhaps Bell's portrayal of the dislocation suffered by managers, the military and the small-town middle class does add to our picture of the movement. But if the movement gained the support of only a conservative fraction of the elite and, unlike populism, attacked its enemies, one wonders if the perspective of class should be abandoned altogether.

These historical arguments lead to general conclusions about Bell's thought. Two points need to be made about his habitual tendency to reduce the analysis of mass movements to an understanding of human psychology. Firstly, this tendency prevents Bell grasping very basic social structural facts explaining the appeal of Populism. The trouble is not in his insistence that rational men's interests include their values to the same extent as more immediately instrumental goals, but rather that his portrait of man as irrational prevents a proper analysis of the circumstances that lead to, or help to support, a particular belief. This accounts, in turn, for his failure to distinguish between two very different programmes. Given that Bell considers himself a pluralist theorist, this failure is surprising although comprehensible in the light of the long debate in sociology as to whether society is best seen in conflictual or consensus terms. As noted, virtually all those who attempted eclectically to distil the best of both these positions have argued that only certain sorts of conflict can be permitted if a society is to survive, i.e. that conflict must be bound by a measure of consensus. This rather unexciting conclusion is correct, and it has been taken a little further above by noting that bounds may be placed on conflict for 'material'—as compared to 'ideal'—reasons, i.e. because the society delivers the goods rather than because people, or at least their leaders, 'believe' in the system. As will be seen, Bell really endorses the latter position. But the important thing to note is that the boundaries on conflict are drawn very tightly; or, alternatively, it is necessary to 'believe' *in the virtues of the American system as a whole.* Anybody who chooses to question these virtues is dubbed irrational or moralist. I do not wish to be understood as attacking the ideal of pluralism per se since as an ideal it is admirable; but nevertheless there is much to object to in the narrowness of the limits drawn by Bell.

Frankly, Bell's picture of America as a just and open society is overdone. Two general aims here are of especial importance, namely the question of differential rewards and that of power holding. Bell intimates in his early essays (and formally spells out in *The Coming of Post Industrial Society*) that the distribution of rewards is just, as it is based on a meritocratic principle. This picture is presumably supported by Bell's argument that inheritance is losing its salience as capitalism becomes managerial rather than familial. It is certainly not the case that the American class system is a perfectly oiled caste machine, and perhaps there has even been as much recent social mobility in America due to changes in the occupational structure as there has been in England and Wales.[27] Nevertheless, such evidence as there is goes clearly against Bell. Firstly, wealth continues to be concentrated and handed down.[28] Secondly, there is continuing evidence that the propertied classes can influence, sometimes through family connections directly and other times by coalitions of major shareholders, managerial capitalism.[29] Thirdly, meritocracy is not, as it were, pure and virtuous, but is rather much sullied by class connections: the privileged are well aware that the life chances of their children may depend increasingly on their having a good education.[30] In a nutshell, some people systematically do better out of America than others, and the warm aura of achieved justice that surrounds Bell's account of America is unwarranted.

The second area, that of power holding, is more complicated. A standard charge made against Bell's pluralism is that it fails to realise that some social groups have more say and impact than others, and prima facie evidence of this proposition is held to be the continuing inequality of rewards in Western society as a whole. This is, however, a very complicated matter, and I shall later argue that in Western Europe unions possess at least obstructive or negative power. One wonders if the access to power of labour is nearly as assured in America. The revelations consequent on Nixon's downfall evidence the attempts, at the least, by large corporate groups—a power in the land that Bell's account of the breakup of family capitalism curiously ignores—to control decisions. But as with pluralism, I do not wish to be misunderstood here: imperfections of Western society do not mean that the constitutional freedoms they offer are somehow worthless.

These points could be summed up by saying that to attack social movements as ideological and dangerous per se is to cast a slur upon reforming politics that may be free from chiliasm, morally just and in general perfectly rational. The English conception of working people trying to bring about a just social democracy, created by, for example, Tawney, is of this type. This is not to say that Bell is wrong in his belief that unions are increasingly playing the market rather than acting as troops for such a social movement; frankly, Bell's sociological description—however, regrettable this may be—seems justified. But the characterisation offered here in place of that of Bell is nonetheless important in directing our attention to a crucial and very weak assumption of Bell's analysis. He assumed that meritocratic pluralist society would be both stable and successful because people, or their leaders, would believe such a society to be just. Bell no longer holds this view, as we shall see, since he has come to recognise that social stability has depended more on the Keynesian ability to increase the size of the cake than on any belief in the system as such.[31] For it is becoming clear, in part because of the failure to expand the cake in recent years, that the combination of social inequality and democracy by no means leads to smooth running of society, as inflation demonstrates. The situation in which groups try and catch up with those above them causes, to use Habermasian terms, a rationality crisis. But more will be said on this later, especially on the vexed question as to whether this rationality crisis is the result of greedy group activity per se, or of some sort of disillusion with capitalism.

Finally, I think that Bell's endorsement of America represents a poor strategy for intellectuals of a progressive turn of mind. One historian of the American intelligentsia has noted in an acute essay on the American intellectuals' part in the Congresses for Cultural Freedom that:

> In associating themselves with the war-making and propaganda machinery of the state in the hope of influencing it, intellectuals deprive themselves of the real influence they could have as men who refuse to judge the validity of ideas by the requirements of national power or any other entrenched interest. Time after time in this century it has been shown that the dream of influencing the war machine is a delusion. Instead the war machine corrupts the intellectuals.[32]

Tawney was far more realistic in believing that a measure of support from a social movement was necessary if those at the centre were ever to do more than pay obeisance to progressive ideas.[33] And this is as true of America as elsewhere. The social reforms of the 1930s were achieved by something approaching a social movement, and they have been long-lasting. In contrast, some of the reforming plans implemented in the 1960s have been transitory in the extreme.[34]

Religion and Ideology in Europe

Where America has been fortunate, Bell wishes to argue that Europe has suffered. One reason for these different fates has already been mentioned: European conflicts are held to have been intensified by the superimposition of cultural divisions upon economic ones. There is great justice to Bell's charge here, as there is to his observations on the ability of the sheer size of America to dissipate the force of conflict. But there is a second factor about European politics in the twentieth century that is of even more importance for Bell: its passionate ideologies. Bell's thought here is complex and allusive, and it is as well to bear in mind perhaps the key passage from all his work:

> ...religion...was a way for people to cope with the problem of death. The fear of death—forceful and inevitable—and more, the fear of violent death, shatters the glittering, imposing, momentary dream of man's power. The fear of death, as Hobbes pointed out, is the source of conscience; the effort to avoid violent death is the source of law. When it was possible to believe, really believe, in heaven and hell, then some of the fear of death could be tempered or controlled; without such belief, there is only the total annihilation of the self.
>
> It may well be that with the decline in religious *faith* in the last century and more, this fear of death as total annihilation, unconsciously expressed, has probably increased. One may hypothesise, in fact, that here is a cause of the breakthrough of the irrational, which is such a marked feature of the changed moral temper of our time. Fanaticism, violence, and cruelty are not, of course, unique in human history. But there was a time when such frenzies and mass emotions could be displaced, symbolised, drained away, and dispersed through religious devotion and practice. Now there is only this life, and the assertion of self becomes possible—for some even necessary—in the domination over others.[35]

Here all Bell's fears about human nature are implied. As is well known, the nineteenth century saw the development of a counter-enlightenment philosophy associated above all with the names of Dostoyevsky and Nietzsche.[36]

Nietzsche conceived of man in naturalistic Darwinian terms, and argued that he was driven by deep and dark forces, the most important of which were aggressive and sexual in nature. Although Bell does not accept Nietzsche's recommendation that we should follow our instincts, he endorses the picture of the 'demonic' in man. Religion has been vital for civilisation since it has systematically restrained human instinct. Ideology does not even try to restrain the restless strivings of the human heart. On the contrary, the great appeal of ideology lies in the messianism which makes the eschatological promise of the leap to the kingdom of freedom, the release from all necessity.[37] This promise, so prevalent for Bell in Marxism, is exceptionally dangerous since it leads to the sacrificing of people to the vision of a new order. 'Is it an accident', he asks, 'that the modern world, having delimited the authority of religion in the public sphere, has been the first to create "total power" in the political realm—the fusion of beliefs and institutions into a monolithic entity that claims the power of a new faith?'[38] This is to say, that ideology can draw upon the unbridled passion of human nature. There are hints in Bell's writings that ideology draws upon precisely those demons inside man described by Nietzsche: in particular, he would describe the concentration camps, I believe, in terms of some sort of mass sadism.[39]

Bell considers ideologies the products of intellectuals. The loss of religious faith is held to have affected them deeply, and Bell points to five typical responses to this predicament by modern intellectuals— rationalism, civil religion, existentialism, aestheticism, and political religion.[40] This is an interesting list, and we can look forward to Bell himself analysing each fully,[41] but some comments can be made here. The first two would probably be regarded by Bell as too effete to have much general social appeal. Perhaps the most interesting thing about the last three is their interrelationships. For example, Bell notes how Lukács moved from aesthetics to politics, and a strong case could be made for Sartre's politics being an attempt to deal with essentially moral problems.[42] Further analysis of aestheticism follows below. But it is political ideology which is finally the most important for Bell. In his interesting discussion of Lukács he tries to argue that the bedrock of the intellectual's relationship to political ideology is only struck when the party member is prepared to lie in the service of his cause; his argument is, as it were, a gloss on the mentality immortalised in Arthur Koestler's *Darkness at Noon*.[43]

Bell considers the age of ideology to have ended. The expression 'the end of ideology' had been coined by Edward Shils to describe the central idea circulating at the Congresses for Cultural Freedom in the 1950s. Bell justified his adoption of the expression thus:

Today, these ideologies are exhausted. The events behind this important sociological change are complex and varied. Such calamities as the Moscow Trials, the Nazi-Soviet pact, the concentration camps, the suppression of the Hungarian workers, form one chain; such social changes as the modification of capitalism, the rise of the Welfare State, another.... Few serious minds believe any longer that one can set down 'blueprints' and through 'social engineering' bring about a new utopia of social harmony. At the same time, the older 'counter beliefs' have lost their intellectual force as well. Few 'classic' liberals insist that the State should play no role in the economy, and few serious conservatives, at least in England and on the Continent, believe that the Welfare State is the 'road to serfdom'. In the Western world, therefore, there is today a rough consensus among intellectuals on political issues: the acceptance of a Welfare State; the desirability of decentralised power, a system of mixed economy and of political pluralism.[44]

The Third World is specifically exempted from this general analysis since, there, ideologies of nationalism and modernisation are likely to continue to have very great appeal. But Bell's careful analysis of changes in Marxism-Leninism—which makes very similar points to Marcuse's *Soviet Marxism* whilst choosing to point to a different moral—argues that advanced state socialist societies, aware of new complexities inside their own societies and of the limitations of Marxism, may in their turn suffer an end to ideology as well.[45]

His thesis is considered, however—with some justification—to be complacent. It is no accident that this thesis is appended to a collection of the essays on America discussed earlier. For Bell is effectively saying that Europe too can look forward to achieving the success of a modern society somewhat along American lines. I have already argued that the American—and indeed Western—reality is not quite as beautiful, or, more importantly, as stable as Bell suggested. This makes his position rather unattractive, as was pointed out by Denis Worng:

> ... the celebrated virtues of moderation and compromise cannot become manifest unless, to begin with, there are conflicting political demands to be moderated and compromised.... But the total absence of any influential body of radical opinion in the country has the effect of narrowing the spectrum to the point where 'moderation' becomes simple 'stand-pattism'. When intellectuals begin to look at politics through the eyes of the professional politicians, they are failing to perform their role as unattached critics and visionaries.[46]

A distinction must be made here. Some of those who have charged Bell of complacency have done so in the belief that old ideological politics retain their importance, or that they are being replaced by new ideologies—of students, nuclear protestors or whoever. I believe that certainty on both these counts is misplaced, and therefore my charge of complacency is weaker. My view, briefly, is that Bell misdescribes our society (and in so doing slanders non-millenarian movements for social reform) and facilely assumes that a pluralist society relatively free from ideology will function easily. There is an air of resignation about Bell's phrasing of the position of the modern intellectual that is most unfortunate given how hard it is proving to make modern Western societies work:

> The young intellectual is unhappy because the 'middle way' is for the middle-aged, not for him; it is without passion and is deadening... Politics offers little excitement... The trajectory of enthusiasm has curved.[47]

But the considerable discussion engendered by the end of ideology thesis has failed to notice another, more substantial weakness. This can be approached by noting how curious is Bell's argument for the end of ideology namely that the modern intellectual will no longer seek to embrace ideology. In itself this is exceptionally naive since intellectuals are surely capable of producing all sorts of rubbish at any time. Certainly Bell's mode of expression would not have occurred to a European familiar with the resilience of Marxism in academic circles.[48] But what Bell is implying here is that the great passions of the 1930s were merely the product of a radical intelligentsia. One can understand why he should make this claim—he is naturally worried that a section of the elite should encourage the ever-present passions of the mass mind—but it is surely misleading.

Bell fails to ask *why* such ideologies appealed to men at that particular time, and why they are less attracted by the ideologies on offer in the last twenty years or so—that of Sartre, for example. The reason for their appeal is surely not so hard to find and, in a sense, is hinted at in his comments on ideology in the Third World. Men need to interpret their position as a whole at moments when their lives are being uprooted by large-scale social change, such as archetypically characterises the move from agrarian to industrial societies. In such rare circumstances when belief is of exceptional importance, intellectuals are an important social factor. Once more Bell's picture of the human psyche—as a lake ready to do damage the moment the dam of restraint is removed—leads to a regrettably weak grasp of social structure. Perhaps visions of man as either harmonious or evil, beneath an alienating social veneer, both necessitate poor sociology. Certainly Bell's view entails too great a pessimism about our condition since, for example, Nazism is less a product of the modern situation, than, as we shall see in the next chapter, the curious pathology resulting from an interrupted transition to industrialism. In calmer circumstances, men may calculate (calculation being a factor scarcely taken into account in

Bell's view) that it is not necessary, for example, to exterminate a rival group.

This brings us to Bell's characterisation of religion as, contrary to ideology, somehow a restraining force on human instincts. I doubt this very muct. Some Third World countries are able to make use of puritanical Islam rather than Marxism as a modernising ideology, but the mass enthusiasms thereby engendered do not seem more restrained or morally superior to secular ideologies. After all, millenarianism is itself a *religious* expectation of the establishment of a reign of justice and peace. And this is an important point since it does much to discredit Bell's recent arguments in favour of a revival of religious belief—a revival that might not in any case be necessary if man is more than the bundle of pent up passions that Bell imagines.

An Anti-Holistic General Theory

In recent years Bell has produced the outlines of a general theory of modern society. There seem to be two reasons for this move away from his earlier, striking but less systematic essays. Most immediately, and probably as a result of the fame brought him by the *End of Ideology*, Bell spent some time in the 1960s serving as Chairman to the American Academy's investigations into the shape of our future in the year 2000.[49] These investigations did not themselves suggest new ideas to Bell—he had, for example, first clearly formulated the concept of a 'post-industrial society' as early as 1964[50]—but they do seem to have encouraged more systematic thought. Secondly, Bell has come to argue, perhaps too pessimistically, that many of the factors that made America 'exceptional' have now disappeared.[51] The 'melting pot' has finally succeeded although, ironically, this has not prevented the ever greater use of ethnicity in political life, albeit essentially for instrumental ends. Most important of all, America is now held to have become a 'national society' for the first time. The communications revolution means that Washington is now as much a 'cockpit' as was Paris in 1789 or 1870. This is no source of comfort to Bell. The decentralisation of America did away, as it were, with politics as it is usually understood, i.e. a fight for power at the level of the central state. If society is to remain stable it will become more and more necessary to produce, for the first time, some form of social accounting, especially given that economic planning is now necessitated by an ever greater concentration of industry.

The general theory that we are offered is of a very unusual kind. Society is held to comprise economy, polity and culture, each of which is run on completely different axial principles:

The techno-economic order is concerned with the organisation of production and the allocation of goods and services. It frames the occupation and stratification system of the society and involves the use of technology for instrumental ends. In modern society, the axial principle is *functional rationality*, and the regulative mode is *economising*... The polity is the arena of social justice and power: the control of the legitimate use of force and the regulation of conflict... in order to achieve the particular conceptions of justice embodied in a society's traditions or in its constitution, written or unwritten. The axial principle of the polity is legitimacy... The implicit condition is the idea of equality, that all men are to have an equal voice... I mean by culture... the realm of symbolic forms... Modern culture is defined by this extraordinary freedom to ransack the world storehouse and to engorge every style it comes upon. Such freedom comes from the fact that the axial principle of modern culture is the expression and remaking of the 'self' in order to achieve self-realisation and self-fulfilment. And in its search, there is a denial of any limits or boundaries to experience.[52]

Bell tells us that his own political values are similarly split. In economics, he regards himself as a socialist, not because he believes in the abolition of private property or the like but because he believes the economic sphere should be seen as a means of fulfilling social needs. But in cultural matters, as we would expect, he regards himself as a conservative, whilst his concern for the rule of law makes him a liberal in politics.[53]

It is important to realise that Bell regards this 'distinction of realms' as a recent phenomenon, since classical capitalist society is held to have been cemented by religious belief. In the case of the economy:

...the unrestrained economic impulse was held in check by Puritan restraint and the Protestant ethic. One worked because of one's obligation to one's calling, or to fulfil the covenant of the community. But the Protestant ethic was undermined not by modernism but by capitalism itself. The greatest single engine in the destruction of the Protestant ethic was the invention of the instalment plan, or instant credit. Previously one had to save in order to buy. But with credit cards one could indulge in instant gratification.... When the Protestant ethic was sundered from bourgeois society, only the hedonism remained....[54]

This lack of a transcendental ethic has deleterious effects on the remaining two realms. The lack of restraint in cultural matters encourages, as we shall see, the release of the demonic that Bell fears, albeit this release has not as yet been canalised onto any great and threatening ideology. And the removal of religious restraint has turned the polity into a battleground of competing and incompatible claims on the state budget.

Before examining the ways in which developments in one realm affect others, it is as well to pause once again to offer some comments. The reader may have already noticed that Bell's view of social cohesion in America by benefit of shared Puritancial belief does not entirely accord with his earlier interpretation of American society. In the early essays on America the fundamentalist mind of Protestantism seemed to pose some sort of threat, whereas here he sings the praises of religious belief. Perhaps Bell would reconcile these positions by saying that 'radical' politics in America were never very much of a threat. But what is interesting here is the way in which the consensual nature of Bell's social theory expands. He begins to sound more and more like Durkheim in his description of the religious sources of cohesion of the past; and he goes beyond Durkheim in arguing that religion, and not just the 'cult of the individual', is necessary if social cohesion is to be reestablished in Western society. This heavily Platonic position is highly implausible. In 1851, for example, the Victorians discovered, to their horror, that the English working classes did not even have the chance to be socialised into the central value system since there were insufficient church seats to accommodate them; in other words, religion was perhaps *never* the social cement that Bell claims it once was. And such religious belief as there was amongst the English working class, i.e. nonconformity, encouraged them at the end of the nineteenth century to oppose the status quo. In general, it is unlikely that a complex society *can* consensually socialise members of different social groups into a *single* belief-system.[55]

A Post-Industrial Society?

Bell's claim that industrial societies are about to enter a new 'post-industrial' stage has received an enormous amount of attention[56] and it is well to approach the matter carefully. The first question to be answered is whether this concept really goes beyond the post-capitalism of his early essays on America. If it is no advance on this position, then 'post-industrialism' is sailing under false colours. Alternatively, if post-industrialism is indeed novel, then Bell is describing something of the utmost importance. The change from agrarian to industrial societies caused a spectacular revolution in human destinies, and the transition between the two ages was characterised by the play of the ideologies that Bell so hates. If the 'mode of production' is going to change once again, is it the case that similar upheavals will result? These are the sorts of questions and expectations that Bell's thesis arouses.

Unfortunately, *The Coming of Post-Industrial Society* has justly driven reviewers and critics to distraction since Bell hedges his bets time and time again. This is clearly true of the principle of post-industrialism, theoretical knowledge, which is described thus:

> ...a technocratic mind-view, one can say with some sense of paradox, is more than just a matter of technique. In its emphasis on the logical, practical, problem-solving, instrumental, orderly, and disciplined approach to objectives, in its reliance on a calculus, on precision and measurement and a concept of a system, it is a world-view quite opposed to the traditional and customary religious, aesthetic and intuitive modes.[57]

Bell nevertheless insists that he is no naive technocrat, that, in other words, his 'post-industrialism' depends upon politicians if it is to be realised. In his own words:

> Technical knowledge—the administration of things—is a necessary and growing component of many kinds of decisions, including political and strategic ones. But power—the relations between men—involves political choices that are a compound of values and interests and cannot always be 'ordered' in a technical way. The technocrat in power is simply one kind of politician, not a *technicien*, no matter how much he employs his technical knowledge.[58]

This obscures more than it clarifies. The account offered by Marx and Weber of the transition from feudalism to capitalism gained its plausibility from the picture of a class strong enough (largely because of its position in European towns) to destroy the old order that was restricting its activities. Even if theoretical knowledge is a new principle in the same sense that bourgeois rationality was, is it the case that the men of knowledge will be able to dominate politics sufficiently so as to institutionalise their world view? Indeed, do these new men feel that such drastic steps are called for? Are they inevitably forced to oppose the status quo?

The Coming of Post-Industrial Society does not just hedge its bets; it is also exceptionally unclear, and at crucial points self-contradictory. But the main characteristics of a knowledge society can be distinguished below the welter of rather uncritically presented statistics, and can be spelled out in turn. First, the economy is held to be moving from the production of goods to the production of services. The guiding notion behind this assertion seems to be that the more advanced society becomes the less do goods provide satisfaction; as we get richer, in other words, our new and more sophisticated needs must be met by services rather than by things.

The main proof offered on behalf of this proposition is the speed at which the service sector is expanding. And there are two riders to the service sector argument.

On the one hand, Bell suggests that the nature of work itself may change. Where industrial workers fought against nature, the post-industrial professional—for it is the professional who apparently characterises the new order—must participate in 'a game between persons'. This is an interesting idea, but unfortunately one that is not much developed.[59] On the other hand, Bell notes that the increase in service jobs can cause problems for the polity since service work cannot be made much more productive:

> As a larger portion of the labour force shifts into services, there is inevitably a greater drag on productivity and growth, and the costs of services, private and governmental, increase sharply... one then faces a painful contradiction, for if the wages in the service sectors, especially government, rise without compensating gains in productivity, they become additional claimants on social resources,... while some gains are possible [in service sector productivity], intrinsically these will always lag behind the 'progressive' industrial sectors.[60]

The second characteristic, that more and more jobs will be in the services, follows closely from this, and is little more than a restatement of the early argument that the occupational structure was changing so as to diminish the strength of organised labour. This argument is of obvious import for political life:

> The crucial fact is that the 'labour issue' *qua* labour is no longer central, nor does it have the sociological and cultural weight to polarise all other issues along that axis.[61]

What is new in Bell's argument, however, is the emphasis he now feels due not to service work as a whole, but to the faster growing sections of it, namely those trained professionals who make use of the vastly expanding number of doctorates in research and development. This is the real home of theoretical knowledge and these are the new men who are at the centre of Bell's argument. But Bell's scheme of the social structure of post-industrial society makes clear that he is not at all sure that the new men have—as yet—sufficient *esprit de corps* to form a significant bloc in society.

More specifically—and thirdly—he suggests that it is quite likely that a major source of conflict in post-industrial society will be that between situses rather than statuses (or, more crudely, classes). By this he means that the skilled may associate themselves with one of these locations of occupational activity: the enterprise, government, universities, social complexes (e.g. hospitals, social service centres), and the military. This introduces the fourth point. The economic enterprise is seen here as one occupational activity amongst others, rather than, as is more usual, the pacesetter by virtue of the effect of the profit motive on society as a whole. Bell defends this position:

> The private enterprise system has been the primary institution of Western society not because of its coercive power but because its values—economising and increasing output of material goods—were congruent with the major consumer values of society. With all its obvious imperfections the system 'worked'. Today, however, those values are themselves being questioned, not in the way socialists and radicals questioned them a gene-ration ago—that they were achieved at the cost of exploiting the worker—but at the very core, the creation of more private goods at the expense of other social values.[62]

The discovery of social costs, and of the necessity for social ac-counts, is leading to change in the mode of operation of the corpor-ation: instead of being an 'economising' venture it is becoming concerned with 'sociologising' its activities.[63] Bell remains firmly convinced that shareowners have no control over managers, espe-cially given the increasing self-financing of corporations. Therefore, a complete 'sociologising' of the corporation may depend upon the creation of a 'second chamber' at directorial level of elected repre-sentatives of the community, which will insist on the corporation fulfilling its social responsibility.[64]

And this takes us to a fifth and final point. Such a second chamber can only work if it has an adequate conception of social needs. Bell waxes eloquent on the difficulties of creating any workable social indicators, let alone a fully fledged system of social accounting. Nevertheless, his own involvement as an adviser to government has led him to believe that a good deal of progress can be made in this direction by, presumably, academics of his own ilk. Such a responsi-bility can only fulfil this task if America at last learns to accept the need for an established and progressive elite. Much progress was made in changing popular attitudes on this matter in the early 1960s, but the 'anti-intellectual' attitude of those who resisted the Vietnam war is held probably to have undone this.[65] One thing is certain for Bell: the relative failure of many of the 'great society' type programmes of the 1960s reflected less a lack of political will than a basic lack of information as to how to improve society.

This set of arguments does not establish the increase in theoretical knowledge as sufficient to take us to a new stage of social development. This is most obvious from the fact that, as Bell himself stresses, the vision he is describing has been variously intimated by Saint-Simon, Veblen, Bruno R., Marx (in the third volume of *Capital*), Galbraith, Richta and others.[66] In Giddens's words:

> ...Daniel Bell is acutely conscious that most aspects of the notion can be traced back to the early years of the nineteenth century. This may be construed as indicating that the theory has a reputable ancestry; but it is also something of an embarrassment, for the point of the idea of post-industrial society is to attempt to encompass some of the most 'modern' features of the advanced societies.[67]

Even more importantly, most of the concrete changes that Bell describes began occurring a considerable while ago. In the words of Peter Stearns:

> ...Bell's view of industrial society is that of early industrial England. He does not understand that by 1850 or even later the working class consisted of many service workers (or more properly partial service workers, as with many artisans) and certainly only a minority of actual factory labour. Hence his comparisons with what has occurred since then are at best oversimplified. Above all he does not know what to do with the century of industrial history after 1850 or 1870. Being an honest observer he often admits that trends he terms post-industrial are quite visible by 1870; the rise of white-collar workers, the speeding up of transportation processes, and so on. But he offers no overall assessment of the society in which these developments took place. Should we call it pre-post-industrial?[68]

Krishan Kumar has made the same point by demonstrating how the retention of a large agricultural sector until very recently in such countries as France prevented the emergence of a fully-fledged industrial society.[69] And such a logical fulfilment of industrialism is, in fact, what Bell describes: this is especially clear once we realise that theoretical knowledge is only the fulfilment of the basic rationalising attitudes enshrined in the scientific revolution of the seventeenth century. This is not, of course, to say that many of Bell's observations are not acute and that changes do not occur inside industrial society. But changes inside a society used to change should not be equated with the move from relatively static agrarian societies to much more mobile industrial societies.

Bell's more detailed arguments are equally dubious. In his authoritative analysis of the service sector argument, Gershuny notes:

> The thesis has, in essence, three stages: first, as we get richer, we develop new categories of needs or demands; second, that these

needs have to be met by services rather than by goods: third, an increase in the demand for services leads to increased numbers in service employment. Bell provides us only with data to substantiate the final prediction... But... to take this generalisation as evidence for the whole 'goods to services' thesis involves an invalidly reversed implication; for while increased service consumption necessarily requires more service workers, more service workers do not necessarily imply more consumption of services, for *service workers are also concerned in the manufacture of goods.*[70]

Gershuny goes on to demonstrate that the increase in, as it were, non-productive service work in the United Kingdom is not really very striking. This increase is to be counterbalanced by the virtual extinction of certain traditional services (laundries, domestic servants, and, increasingly, railways) as people begin to buy labour-saving goods that can replace them—a process that Gershuny reckons by no means yet to have peaked. A consequence of realising that much service-sector work is productive is, of course, to undermine Bell's argument that the service sector is a drain on productivity. So long as a fair measure of service-sector work is for industry, as in Germany and Japan, then Bell's suggestion is almost the opposite of the truth.[71] And one point can be added to this critical view of the service sector thesis. The largest production of research and development in the United States goes on the war machine; this seems less like a post-industrial society than science applied in the traditional interest of state-power.

The analysis of class and the corporation is, if anything, even weaker. What chance is there really that business managers—in any case, pace Bell, still very much the tool of blocs of shareholders—will choose to be dictated to by some board of responsible community leaders? Here Bell's hopes wildly outrun what one may reasonably expect.[72] And the distinction between property and skill as modes of access to power is misleading. On the one hand, as we have seen, it is false to ignore the continuing concentration of property and the significant link between privilege and education. On the other hand, this notion may set up a polar opposition that is exceptionally crude. For, as Weber stressed, the market place established by classical capitalism did not rule out those with special skills being able to gain privileges for themselves; the market mechanism, in other words, certainly allowed those with property to be rewarded for it, but it also established a labour market in which some did better than others. And one final point in this area is in order. Bell's picture of the post-industrial professional is exaggerated, and no better comment on the matter is available than one he himself made in an early essay:

The effort to 'professionalise' work has become the major means for giving one's job a badge of honorific quality which the nature of the work itself denies. We have schools of hotel management, as well as of social work. The garage becomes the 'lubritorium'; individuals do not say 'I sell pots and pans' but 'I am in selling'; the janitor becomes the 'superintendent'; the hospital superintendent turns into the 'administrator'; the secretary becomes the 'executive assistant'; and the minister, if he is unable to rise to bishop, measures his success in terms of the social class of his parishioners.[73]

The implication of this is that low quality white-collar jobs may be as open to unionisation in the long run as were blue-collar jobs. This seems to be happening in Europe and Japan already, although the picture is, as Bell stresses, different in the United States.

Finally, it must be noted that Bell contradicts himself endlessly on the important question as to whether the men of knowledge will in some way come to power. Formally, he insists that he is no technocrat, and that politics must be separated from the 'analytic construct' of the post-industrialism he is offering. Yet in more optimistic vein he notes:

> ... those in possession of knowledge ... are not yet in a position to form a unified social group, a new clergy, and they are not even considering the possibilities of doing so, although one may wonder whether circumstances will not impose upon them a vertical hierarchy along ecclesiastical feudal lines, perhaps without their ever realising it ... For me science, being a quasi-autonomous force, transgresses capitalism. The scientific corps, when it finds its ethic and cohesion will become the monad containing the image of the society of the future.[74]

Such hints are dropped time and again, and it is therefore worth emphasising on two counts the weakness of technocratic theories. Firstly, possibly the most brilliant pages in *The Coming of Post Industrial Society* demonstrate the power of established authority to quell the moral demands of scientists. The case study of this process that Bell offers shows the military discrediting, by fair means and foul, scientists who had been radicalised by the realisation that their knowledge had led to the possibility of nuclear war.[75] Secondly, for most of the time, scientists and professionals of all sorts do not seem to have the kind of ethos that Bell demands of them. Again his own work demonstrates this cogently. In a fine essay on Veblen's *The Engineers and the Price System*, he shows that the engineers on whom Veblen placed some hopes were interested not in establishing Soviets, but in gaining professional autonomy in American life.[76] So

Bell's hopes, hidden and even denied as they are, must be considered mere illusions.

A Cultural Contradiction of Capitalism?

The fact that 'post-industrialism' is a pseudo-concept does not by itself say anything against the notion that Western societies, understood in a more realistic manner, may be suffering from a cultural contradiction; indeed, we have seen Habermas arguing precisely this case. Moreover, the problem of this realm is judged by Bell to be the crucial one that faces our society:

> But the deeper and more difficult questions are the legitimations of the society as expressed in the motivations of individuals and the moral purposes of the nation. And it is here that the cultural contradictions—the discordances of character structure and the disjunctions of realms—become central.[77]

The reasons for this estimation are not hard to seek: unless men can find some answers to the existential question that haunts them, the demonic side of man might again be unleashed upon the world.

The baseline for Bell's views on modern culture is the celebrated analysis of modernist art proposed by the late Lionel Trilling, the famous American cultural critic with whom Bell taught a 'Literature and Society' course at Columbia University. Trilling argued that modern art had an 'adversary intent' such that is was opposed not just to particular social forms but to the 'social' as such. Trilling recognised the brilliance with which modernism captured what are, at times, our inmost feelings, but he nevertheless regarded the blanket character of the attack as disturbing, even dangerous. Almost thinking against himself, he argued that:

> ... art does not always tell the truth or the best kind of truth and does not always point out the right way ... it can even generate falsehood and habituate us to it ...[78]

In particular, Trilling came to believe that the emphasis of modernist art on the authentic—and thus often amoral—feelings of the individual failed to acknowledge how necessary it was for some order if civilisation were to continue at all.

Bell endorses Trilling's view of modernism, but adds to it his concept of the demonic. As we have seen, he considers that the historic function of religions has been to control the demonic. Furthermore, when religious belief faded the investigation and examination of the demonic became the prerogative of art; and in particular of modernism. Bell leaves us in no doubt that aestheticism was dealing with dangerous realities:

In this proclamation of the autonomy of the aesthetic—indeed, in the argument that only as an aesthetic product can life be justified—Nietzsche declared war on the most profound tradition of Western culture. The writers of the Old Testament, as any religious Jew knows, had a horror of the aesthetic because of the implications of its claims. For if the aesthetic was autonomous, it was not bound by moral law, and anything was possible in its search for experience lived to the highest peak as art.[79]

Bell seems to have in mind here the attitude of Raskolnikov at the start of Dostoyevsky's *Crime and Punishment*, and in this vein he quotes a note of Baudelaire on the sinister seducer Valmont: 'Je fus toujours vertueux sans plaisir; j'eusse été criminel sans remords'.[80] And this search for heightened experience is paralleled in the form of modernist art by an 'eclipse of distance' designed to affect the viewer or reader in a total way so that he is no longer in control of the aesthetic experience. Both these points can be encapsulated in Bell's dictum that modernism is essentially anti-rational.[81]

It is only beyond this analysis of modern art, i.e. culture in a narrow sense, that Bell offers us his thesis about the cultural—in the broader anthropoligical sense—contradiction of capitalism. In fact, Bell offers us something like a worst and a best case of the way in which this contradiction may be worked out: like Marcuse, he likes at once to terrify and to cheer. The worst eventuality results from the evil that unrestrained instinct may do in society. We have already seen that he has intimated, in the case of men like Lukács, some sort of link between modernism and the creation of total ideologies. He surely has in mind here the way in which thinkers who are aware of the anguished condition described by the modernist art make 'a leap of faith' or 'retreat to commitment': this is the route signposted by Kierkegaard, and which Bell claims Lukács to have taken.[82] But Bell is not accusing recent modernist intellectuals of producing similar 'total ideologies'; he has not, in other words, changed his mind about the end of ideology thesis. Moreover, he cannot bring himself to reject the modernist classics, and rather softly excuses them when arguing that:

> Traditional modernism, no matter how daring, played out its impulses in the imagination, within the constraints of art. Whether demonic or murderous, the fantasies were expressed through the ordering principle of form. Art, therefore, even though subversive of society, still ranged itself on the side of order and, implicitly, of a rationality of form. Post-modernism overflows the vessels of art. It tears down the boundaries and insists that acting out, rather than making distinctions, is the way to gain knowledge. The happening and the environment, the street and

the scene, not the object or the stage, are the proper arena for life.[83]

This reference to post-modernism is directed at the popularisation of modernism so that the culture as a whole is affected by its standards. This 'modernism in the streets' is exemplified by the new 'pornotopia' so prevalent in New York and *Amsterdam*; Bell finds this revolting, and is a harsh critic of some of the fads and fashions characteristic of the 1960s. One wonders if Bell would recognise the Jonestown massacres as the result of lack of restraint consequent on the democratisation of modernist values. It seems more than likely that he would, since he warns us that the release of the demonic has by no means yet done its worst:

> ...the postmodern mood, touching deeper springs of human consciousness, and deeper, more restless longings than the overt political search for community, is only the first act of a drama that is still to be played out.[84]

We are not told exactly the form that this drama will take; but it is clearly to be a tragedy.

After such sentiments, it is very surprising indeed to encounter Bell's optimistic case. He argues in the first place that modernism is so exhausted in the arts that it is virtually becoming self-parodying. More importantly, however, he believes that the democratisation of its message is about to be countered:

> Despite the shambles of modern culture, some religious answer will surely be forthcoming, for religion is not (or no longer) a 'property' of society in the Durkheimian sense. It is a constitutive part of man's consciousness: the cognitive search for the pattern of the 'general order' of existence; the affective need to establish rituals and to make such conceptions sacred; the primordial need for relatedness to some others, or to a set of meanings which will establish a transcendent response to the self; and the existential need to confront the finalities of suffering and death.[85]

The revival of religious belief is led, ironically, by American Fundamentalism. The bearers of this particular ethic are now held to be representative of the common man's need for 'simple pieties, direct homilies, reassurances against their own secret impulses'.[86] And the fact that the Fundamentalist Church is expanding so fast in America suggests to Bell that others are fed up with the modernist ethic and have come home to the reassuring certainties of religion.

The presence of two incompatible scenarios does much to damage the notion of a cultural contradiction to capitalism. In particular, it is very hard to see why, if the instincts represent what we really, most deeply want, unrestrained man should suddenly decide to accept humdrum and restrained hymn singing. And Bell's discussion of art is also open to criticism. Firstly, Bell far too easily accepts Trilling's view that the classics of modernism have an adversary intent. Some do indeed consider social alienation—Sartre's *No Exit* and *Nausea* spring to mind immediately. However, this is certainly not the case with all modernistic classics, and it is not true of perhaps the best of them. Thus, Proust ends *A la recherche du temps perdu* on a note of affirmation as Marcel discovers a true vocation, having for so long been misled by false 'trails'; and Molly Bloom, as is well-known, ends *Ulysses* by affirming nothing less than 'life itself'. Significantly, neither of these works could be dubbed anti-rational, although they are interested in trying rationally to investigate areas of life which had hitherto been left untouched. And, frankly, I do not believe that the insights into character and the technical sophistications of modernism are likely to be left behind.

The best modern novelists—including Bell's own contemporary, Saul Bellow—reject the anti-enlightenment views of some modernists. They write realistically, but are obviously and profoundly influenced by the achievements of the great modernist writers. Bell also exaggerates the extent to which modernism has been democratised in popular art. Romantic novels and popular drama tend, in the United Kingdom at least, to be morally conservative, as a glance at any Barbara Cartland novel shows.[87] All this is to say that there is not the contradiction between culture and society that Bell claims. However, I do not wish to be misunderstood: Bell is perfectly correct to say that the history of art must often be understood in its own terms, i.e. as something which has its own history and development.

Bell is open to a much more solid criticism insofar as he argues that art will prove capable of undermining society. This really exhibits very little sense of social structure; I can think of no society brought down by the antics of its artists. Of course, Bell must be understood as arguing something slightly more general, namely that the *popularisation* of a self-centred hedonistic style of life may somehow disrupt the social fabric. This seems to me equally unlikely, and here again Bell is something of his own worst enemy. He notes that:

> Today one finds asceticism primarily in revolutionary movements and revolutionary regimes. Puritanism, in the psychological and sociological sense, is to be found in Communist China and in the regimes which fuse revolutionary sentiment with Koranic purposes, as in Algeria and Libya.[88]

This is entirely correct, but gives rise to the reflection that the feckless hedonists that Bell portrays are unlikely to have the self-discipline to be able to change anything. For good or ill, revolutions tend to be made by, or at least led by, Puritans in the mould of Lenin or the Ayatollah Khomeini. And this suggests that there is a strong argument for seeing modern culture as completely *functional* for the society. In a nutshell, pornotopia sounds very much like Huxley's (or Marcuse's) brave new world: unpleasant but not in the least dangerous.[89]

Bell's hopes seem to me, if anything, more implausible. They are Platonist in presuming that culture can give cohesion to the social order, but their greatest weakness is surely in the argument for the revival or religion. A standard criticism made against Durkheim's *Elementary Forms of Religious Life* is that it mistook an analysis of the functions of religion for religion itself.[90] Exactly the same problem arises here. I am certainly not going to join any religious movement because its side effect is held to be that of social cohesion. Religious belief depends upon a theology, and this Bell does not offer us. This is immensely important since it seems more than likely, pace Bell, that the cognitive style that characterises the scientific world view is such as to slowly undermine religious belief. If we presume that the physical world runs in a law-like manner, can we then really believe in miracles? This is, of course, an immense issue; suffice it to say that very many arguments could be directed against Bell's hopes. And perhaps, in any case, these hopes are somewhat disingenuous. Raymond Aron has recalled how Léon Brunschvicg told him at the end of the 1930s that 'Nuremberg is religion according to Durkheim, society adoring itself'.[91] May not social cohesion be bought at too great a price?

Liberalism Revived?

Bell's view of the modern polity is of much greater interest than his question-begging views on post-industrialism and modernist culture. He offers us two sets of arguments, each of which needs to be examined: the first seeks to locate the sources of our present political ills, whilst the second attempts, via the notion of a 'public household', to revive liberalism in such a way as to cure them. Roughly speaking, Bell is very valuable when diagnosing problems, but unconvincing when trying to solve them.

We have seen Bell argue that creation of a national society leads to the politicising of all social life with the result that the state is seen to be responsible not just for economic management, but for social welfare as well. Bell's analysis on these points is rather close to that offered by Habermas. The polity can best be analysed, Bell claims, by deriving from Schumpeter a notion of 'fiscal sociology', the basic tenet of which is that politics consists of groups competing at state level for the largest possible share of the state budget. There are many groups which seek to play their part in this competitive fight:

> They comprise functional economic groups (business, labour, farmers); symbolic status groups (religious, national, racial); socially disadvantaged groups (poor, aged, handicapped); cultur- ally expressive groups (women, youth, homosexuals); civic- purpose groups (civil rights organisations, consumer and environ- mentalist groups); economic special-purpose groups (taxpayer's associations, veteran's lobbies); cultural special-purpose groups (universities, scientific and professional associations, art associa- tions); functional political associations (conferences of states, or city or municipal organisations) and 57 other varieties.[92]

Two points about Bell's argument are worth highlighting. Firstly, he considers that the claims are made for what are considered entitlements; presumably the practice of inter-group comparison encourages one group to say that what another group has should be its own as of right. Secondly, Bell claims that the recent resurgence of ethnic group identity (and we may add regional, or 'national' identity) should be understood in fairly instrumental terms. It may suit immediate economic interests to 'play the ethnic card', rather than to emphasise, say, class divisions—in particular, Bell believes that class loyalties are likely to depend upon recession.[93] This argument is strikingly put and, in general, convincing. One could, however, perhaps add a rider to it. Ethnic politics in the United States grew in the wake of the special treatment handed out to Blacks in the 1960s. This new-found identity does indeed deserve to be considered instrumental, but its relationship to prosperity is slightly more complex than Bell allows. Such identity is not simply the result of greedy competitive groups fighting in a period of prosperity for the state budget: rather it is the politics of the prosperous—or potentially prosperous[94]—keen to resist the central state's desire to redistribute.

The result of, as it were, politicised pluralism is disastrous in Bell's eyes. The state is overloaded with problems some of which it can never be expected to solve, others which it does not yet have the capacity to deal with. Above all, however, the modern state seeks to buy off competing groups by means of inflation. And the result of this in the long run is likely to be a permanent blow to the growth potential of Western societies. Bell takes this very seriously since he is more aware than formerly that Western society has depended for much of its stability on the phenomenal growth rates achieved in the post-war years.[95]

Bell's analysis is much more detailed and subtle than this cursory examination shows. But two critical points may nevertheless be made. Firstly, Bell blames the 'rationality crisis' of the state upon the greed enshrined in 'bourgeois hedonism'. This is to say that modern culture contradicts capitalism not just in the strong sense of releasing the demonic, but also in the weaker one of trying to run a society purely upon calculations of self-interest. There is an amusing contrast here with Habermas who speaks—surely unrealistically— of the decline of 'possessive individualism'. Bell's hope is that the revival of religion will somehow both restrain the demonic and place some limits on bourgeois hedonism; the implausibility of such a general revival tells heavily against Bell's political theory. But I baulk at describing group egoism as 'bourgeois hedonism' since this gives the impression that Hobbesian-type greed is somehow socially transient, and thus lends automatic plausibility to Bell's avowed intention of disconnecting liberalism's respect for the rule of law from the acquisitiveness of economic man. Against this, I would argue that it is very difficult indeed to see how a dynamic economic society could ever reduce the drive of economic man.

More to the point, corporate egoism surely characterises most human societies, albeit it is only in certain circumstances that the state has insufficient coercive power to force its way out of a situation in which contending groups 'stalemate' the society. This brings us to the second point. It is not really the case that all claims on the polity have as much impact as each other. On one occasion Bell notes that labour is the most powerful group making such claims, although he qualifies this by saying that the strength of its resistance is somehow related to its desperation at the discovery that post-industrialism is undermining its power base.[96] Bell's arguments on this point, as we have seen, are less than convincing since there is no reason to believe that union power is diminishing generally. Both these points are important in assessing Bell's attempt to revive liberalism by means of the public household.

The key to solving our political problems, apparently, is to see the state in different terms. Instead of a 'nightwatchman' for the general interest, we should recognise that the state has a positive task in looking after the good of the public. In particular, the state should take formal responsibility for social policy and, more generally, for the servicing of those needs that individual wants cannot provide for unaided. Bell's position here is not entirely clear: in particular, it is not at all certain whether he has some philosophical theory that allows us to say what is a need rather than a want, or whether he is simply arguing that the state should administer matters whenever wants conflict. But whatever is the case, one presupposition of Bell's position is quite clear: the state must be given sufficient breathing space free of political pressure to plan for the general interest in a rational manner. This presupposition leads Bell to be very critical of what he considers to be recent political fashions. He has no time for the demand for greater participation in government since he feels that this is likely merely to institutionalise political stalements.[97] Similarly, he insists that the rational state can only do its work if the principle of meritocracy is firmly accepted. This leads him to attack the Populists who wish either to change the egalitarian debate so as to achieve not equality of opportunity but of result,[98] or to institutionalise quotas for underprivileged ethnic groups. Writing of the latter, he notes:

> The historic irony in the demand for representation on the basis of an ascriptive principle is the complete reversal of radical and humanist values. The liberal and radical attack on discrimination was *based on its denial of a justly earned place to a person on the basis of an unjust group attribute.*[99]

In summary, it may be said that Bell favours representative democracy in politics so that the benefits of a liberal elite keen to institutionalise a system of public accounting, may accrue to Western society. The problem that he feels needs countering is not in any way that of capitalism, but that of an excess of democracy.

How plausible is Bell's claim that liberalism can be revived by replacing bourgeois hedonism with a Public Household? Will Bell be able, in other words, to solve the problem of theory and practice by taking his place in a liberal establishment that is allowed to plan for social welfare? There is everything to be said for his desire to make the constitutionalism of liberal society work more efficiently, for this constitutionalism, as he rightly stresses, is currently under considerable strain. Moreover, he is surely right to stress the 're-politication' of society, as well as to emphasise that group egoism is not equivalent to the Marxist expectation of capitalism crumbling under the assault of a united proletariat armed with a vision of a new social order. This lack of stability has been referred to earlier as resulting from the combination of social inequality and democratic rights, and we must now ask whether, pace Bell, this lack of stability is to be blamed in any way on capitalism.

Bell rightly observes, following W.G. Runciman's *Relative Deprivation and Social Justice*, that those at the bottom of society do not harbour in their day-to-day lives many thoughts about the injustice of 'the system'. It is a long way from this negative point to the more positive one that Bell is trying to argue here, namely that people—if not 'envious' Populists or Social Democrats[100]—will come positively to endorse the 'rules of the game' of Western society and that, in particular, the able risk-takers will be judged to deserve high rewards. The trouble with this is that the more publicity is thrown onto the system of social rewards the more generally apparent it will become that there is a structure of privileges in Western societies—a structure, it should be noted, sufficiently strong to curtail many of the more ambitious reforming plans of the liberal establishment Bell so values. The more publicity there is, the less likely is general consensus. However, although general resentment is growing on account of the growing publicity, there is still reason to doubt, given the lack of a clearly delineated and realistic alternative, that mass social democracy is about to enter into its own.

There is, admittedly, still much in Bell's argument that remains valid. If we make the thought-experiment of imagining a truly meritocratic society in operation, it is still likely that the combination of democracy and inequality, albeit not 'unfair' or inherited inequality, would be unstable. Furthermore, it is hard to imagine a democratic socialist society, i.e. a pluralist, market socialist society, that does not suffer from exactly the same problems. Yugoslavia is a case in point. In this circumstances there is perhaps much to recommend Bell's proposal that we learn how to make political use of the market. His argument here, in fact, is limited to the insistence that welfare is best achieved by the state giving citizens money so that welfare can be bought on the market rather than provided by the state. I am not at all sure how progressive a notion this is—it is, after all, so much easier to cut money than actual services—but there is something to be said for the extension of the political market as a whole. Is it utterly inconceivable that the tradition of rewarding the best jobs with the best pay might not best be broken? Something along these lines has been argued by Fred Hirsch, and the general proposal is discussed below. It is full of difficulties, and may in fact be inoperable. Nevertheless, something as imaginative as this may be necessary for the stability of Western societies. Daniel Bell's very traditional proposals will not revive liberalism.

Conclusion

The tensions in Bell's thought make it consistently intriguing but hard to untangle. I have, however, been forced to interrupt my presentation of his ideas at several points to dispute the correctness of certain key assumptions—particularly his view of man filled with demons ready to cause chaos the moment religious restraint is removed. As a sociologist, Bell is curiously lacking in a sense of social structure. If he is unattractive as a political thinker, this is not because no defence can be made for the capitalist—but liberal—democracies of the West. I shall argue later that Raymond Aron provides a brilliant defence of these societies in the full knowledge of their imperfections. Bell brushes away the imperfections, which is irritating, as is his habit of name-calling—those who disagree with him are 'Populist' or 'envious'. This is not, however, to say that he is wrong to argue that labour has lost its crusading ideological vigour, and is only one of the most powerful interests in Western societies. But the lack of understanding exhibited has something to do with his having produced a political theory that is unlikely to be able to solve the current problems of Western society—problems, however, that his thought has done much to help us understand.

5 Ralf Dahrendorf

Sex Appeal

It would be impossible to understand Dahrendorf's thought without taking cognisance of two biographical facts. Firstly, Dahrendorf was placed in a concentration camp by the Nazis for his precocious schoolboy anti-Nazi activities.

> The concentration camp afterwards was a very different experience really; dark mornings queuing in the icy east wind for a bowl of watery soup, the brutal hanging of a Russian prisoner who had stolen half a pound of margarine, slices of bread surreptitiously passed to a sick or an old man; a lesson in solidarity perhaps, and above all one in the sacredness of human lives. But it was during the ten days of solitary confinement that an almost claustrophobic yearning for freedom was bred, a visceral desire not to be hemmed in, neither by the personal power of men nor by the anonymous power of organisations.[1]

Dahrendorf is thus a sociologist of liberty, and it was not surprising that his first book *Marx in Perspektive* argued that the wildly utopian dream of a classless society was very dangerous in encouraging politics of total social engineering.[2] This sort of argument led him to study at the London School of Economics, and it was here—secondly—that Dahrendorf became a follower of Popper.[3] The Popperian insistence in openness combined with Dahrendorf's own 'visceral desire' for freedom, and his resulting sociology is best seen as a type of social transposition of the Popperian ethic.

Most of this chapter is devoted to the passionate, rigorous and striking sociology contained in *Class and Class Conflict in Industrial Society*[4] and *Society and Democracy in Germany*[5]. The 'conflict sociology' of these works caught the spirit of the time both in attacking functionalism, and in insisting that the fate of Eastern Europe be placed at the centre of analysis; and Dahrendorf's concern to realise his views himself, by going into FDP (Liberal Democrats) politics, made him all the more striking a figure. But I shall argue that a deeper reason for the appeal of Dahrendorf lay in his possessing—and the expression is used without prejudice—a type of academic sex-appeal. This was his ability to delight two audiences simultaneously. On the one hand, the Popperian-inspired love of conflict made him seem a very radical figure but, on the other, the argument, derived from T. H. Marshall (a second LSE influence on Dahrendorf), to the effect that Western society was becoming 'post-capitalist' made him acceptable to moderates. I shall describe how a single vision—for such it was—could encapsulate both camps, albeit not, in the final analysis, in a way that was to carry complete conviction.

Dahrendorf's period in German politics (1965–1970) was followed by a term at the European Commission (1970–1974).[6] But in 1974 he became Director of the LSE and has, remarkably, found time in that position to offer us, with his experience of political complexities much in mind, a rather different political theory. To be frank, his 'vision' has now faded and, ironically, his thought has now come to rest upon some of the very views he once attacked so strongly. This is a fascinating development, and deserves analysis even though the later political theory that results is implausible.

The Warrior Code

The cornerstone of Dahrendorf's social theory is commendably simple and realistic: in every society some people rule over others. This argument underlies Dahrendorf's two-fold attitude to Marx which needs to be spelled out here. On the one hand, Dahrendorf is a critic of Marx. He opens *Class and Class Conflict* with a brilliant version of Marx's uncompleted 52nd chapter of the third volume of *Capital*. He stresses that Marx sees classes as originating in modes of production, and that classes conflict because a new class bears the seed of a new mode of production; conflict, in other words, occurs between two main blocs and results in the transition to a new stage of history. Dahrendorf pours scorn on this:

> For if private property disappears (empirical hypothesis), then there are no longer classes (trick of definition)! If there are no longer any classes, there is no longer alienation (speculative postulate). The realm of liberty is realised on earth (philosophical idea).[7]

The rationale for this criticism is simple: Marx is held to have believed that power is derived only from the economy or, more accurately, from the position of classes within a particular mode of production.

The other side of the picture is much more positive. Although Dahrendorf wishes to remove the millenarian, utopian element in Marx, he does not wish to argue with the general Marxist view that some gain and some lose in every society. Indeed, his desire to extend this sort of picture to all societies, and beyond the mere fact of reward, can be seen in the contrast he draws between two types of social theory. He suggests in *Class and Class Conflict* that the dominant view of social theory is that which sees social cohesion as being gained through the sharing of social norms. Such consensus, or Platonic-theories, are held to depend upon these factors:

(1) Every society is a relatively persistent, stable structure of elements.
(2) Every society is a well-integrated structure of elements.
(3) Every element in a society has a function, i.e. renders a contribution to its maintenance as a system.
(4) Every functioning social structure is based on a consensus of values among its members.[8]

Dahrendorf does not dispute in his earlier work the value of this approach, but he does insist that it is limited. Certain types of change can usefully be seen as the internal workings of a complex system, but others cannot. Those shot down on the streets of East Berlin in 1953 or, we may add, of Tehran in 1978, wanted a new system altogether. The conflict model of society needed to understand such events also rests on four presuppositions:

(1) Every society is at every point subject to processes of change; social change is ubiquitous.
(2) Every society displays at every point dissensus and conflict; social conflict is ubiquitous.
(3) Every element in a society renders a contribution to its disintegration and change.
(4) Every society is based on the coercion of some of its members by others.[9]

It is worthwhile pausing briefly to endorse the value of Dahrendorf's starting point. That there are some very considerable defects in his analysis of post-capitalism will be argued later, but far too often when these are noted the false implication is drawn that Dahrendorf's whole scheme is wrong (and usually, therefore, that Marx is right after all). Personally, I find Dahrendorf's scepticism about the very possibility of a consensual society refreshing after, say, the inverted Parsonianism of Marcuse. But, more important, is the use to which Dahrendorf's approach can be put. It is unfortunately the case that *Class and Class Conflict* is essentially a formal book without benefit of historical examples that would strengthen his case. But such examples are not hard to find. Michael Mann's work-in-progress on 'sources of social power' is effectively an attempt to prove Dahrendorf's basic contention that all societies have power relations, and that only some of these are best judged to be economic; thus Mann convincingly argues that the Roman Empire and China between the Han and Ming dynasties were based upon military power.[10] And it should by now be well known that there are many other cases, perhaps most clearly African feudalism (well described by Jack Goody[11]), in which authority has roots which are not economic.

Many people before and after Dahrendorf have, of course, argued that domination is universal. His originality lies in the argument that the cause of conflict is the differential access to power. It is here that Dahrendorf may be seen as transcribing the Popperian ethic. Ernest Gellner has wittily remarked that this ethic is really much akin to old German warrior codes since it insists that glory lies in baring oneself to refutation just as warriors were supposed to face up to the enemy rather than to defeat him by various underhand subterfuges.[12] Dahrendorf's social actors are Popper's: contentious, anarchic and brave. This is a source of enormous satisfaction to Dahrendorf, and it is responsible for imparting to his advocacy for liberty an air of optimism and certainty. Conflict cannot be suppressed, he tells us, since men will always attack the powers that be: '1984 could not last', he believes, since 'authoritarianism was bound to produce a liberal revolt against it, a 1989 so to speak'.[13] It is important to stress that this warrior ethic is designed to explain the origins of social conflict. And once this is understood, a standard criticism of Dahrendorf, namely that he, unlike Marx, does not explain how these interests are generated that lead to conflict, can for the moment be dismissed:[14] no such explanation is called for as men *are* warriors (with the exception of a few cowards over whom we shall see Dahrendorf agonising later), and warriors fight. But more will to be said about this.

We can see the warrior ethic clearly at work in his comments on two terminological matters. The first of these is related to the consensus-conflict dichotomy. Dahrendorf reconsidered this dichotomy in 'On the Origins of Inequality among Men'. He argues, on the face of it surprisingly, that inequality results from the fact that each society is a moral community which positively or negatively sanctions behaviour in the light of its leading values. This seems in general less than exciting, but Dahrendorf makes an interesting argument from it nonetheless. Just as he wishes to argue that property was not the source of power, but merely an instance of it, so he seeks here to argue that the division of labour does not explain inequality since that division itself depends upon a prior moral evaluation. This is, in other words, to say that status hierarchies are not necessarily in line with market forces. And, we are told:

> Because there are norms and because sanctions are necessary to enforce conformity of human conduct, there has to be inequality of rank among men.[15]

But this explanation of the origins of inequality will not apparently serve to explain the origin of the distribution of power:

> Thus the theory advanced here does not explain the origin of power and of inequalities in the distribution of power. That the origin of power also requires explanation ... is evident from the discussion of the universality of historicity of power ... What an explanation of inequalities of power might look like is hard to say....[16]

The rather surprising use Dahrendorf has made of the concept of moral community has understandably misled one critic, who points out that the necessity of applying sanctions *implies* power.[17] This is of course correct, but Dahrendorf is wishing to argue something further, namely that moral standards are those *imposed by the powerful*. It is this that explains the first of two amendments to the initial characterisation of the conflict concensus debate:

> ... I was convinced that there was a strict logical equivalence between the analysis of social classes and constraint theory, and between the analysis of social stratification and integration theory. The considerations developed in the present essay changed my mind. I have now come to believe that stratification is merely a consequence of the structure of power, integration a special case of constraint, and thus the structural-functional approach a subset of a broader approach. The assumption that constraint theory and integration theory are two approaches of equal rank, i.e. two different perspectives on the same material, is not so much false as superfluous; we get the same result by assuming that stratification follows from power, integration from constraint, stability from change. Since the latter assumption is the simpler one, it is to be preferred.[18]

The point I wish to make here is this. Dahrendorf is well aware that the powerful will try to create consensus in society by creating ideologies to integrate the powerless. But his robust view of man means that he is not worried by this since he thinks that the underclass will not swallow them. Thus those who argue that Dahrendorf is no better than Parsons since he talks about positions of authority (i.e. the critics presume, of legitimate authority) but also expects authority to breed conflict, miss the point: for Dahrendorf *no* authority will be completely legitimate.[19]

This last point is especially clear in the second terminological matter. In his own theory of conflict Dahrendorf characteristically chooses to replace the distinction between 'objective' and 'subjective' class-consciousness since the latter gives the impression that class is more than a sociological concern and thus makes room for a revolutionary party to ginger up the workers.

Dahrendorf proposes that we use the terms 'latent' and 'manifest' interest; these are to be seen as purely objective, non-psychological categories, and the move from one to the other is held, as we shall see, to depend upon certain conditions. Naturally enough, many have wondered whether this is really an improvement at all: is not Dahrendorf, too, in the position of telling the workers who fail to recognise their latent interest that they are lax and lazy?[20] This impression is heightened by Dahrendorf's declaration that those who do not recognise their interests should be considered a psychological 'case', indeed perhaps a psychotic one![21] But the interesting thing, again, is that Dahrendorf clearly thinks that there will be few such psychotics around; his view is thus, if anything, *more* crude than Marx's (which is not to say that its relative brutality does not give it considerable power, especially when compared to the more fantastic moments of idealist sociologies).

Let me spell out Dahrendorf's positon a little further. So far he has argued that it is a social fact that conflict always occurs since the warrior ethic is deeply ingrained in human nature. But implicit in this is a second judgement: conflict is 'good for you'. Why is this? Dahrendorf offers two types of argument to support the claim, the second of which, that the suppression of conflict leads to disasters, we can defer discussing until later in this section. However, the first argument in favour of conflict is directly drawn from Popper and is expressed in Dahrendorf's 'Uncertainty, Science and Democracy'. The human condition is one of uncertainty, Dahrendorf tells us, since we can never, to use Popper's own example, actually know anything: the famous black swan may appear tomorrow to upset our jealously guarded 'law'. In consequence:

> The only adequate response to the human condition of uncertainty, and thus the supreme moral consequence of our assumption of the principle of uncertainty, is the necessity of maintaining a plurality of decision patterns, and an opportunity for them to interact and compete, in all spheres for which the assumption of uncertainty holds. Uncertainty demands variety and competition. From the assumption of a fundamental uncertainty about what is right, there follows the necessity of conflict.[22]

This ethic must be applied to political and social life. Democracy may be able to prevent the building up of revolutionary situations precisely because conflict will force the rulers to pay attention, to use a phrase of the Webbs, to where the shoe of the citizen fits.

Having examined the assumptions and aims of Dahrendorf's theory of class, we can now look at some of its details. The theory attempts to include the findings of Marx within a more general framework and does so by looking at both class formation and class conflict—'class' being understood here in terms of power, i.e. ruling classes have power whilst underclasses do not. Class formation is held to be relatively unproblematic. It depends upon three factors. First, certain technical conditions have to be satisfied before a class can emerge: the most important of these are the presence of leaders and of ideologies. Secondly, Dahrendorf notes that certain political conditions must be fulfilled:

> The totalitarian state is probably the most unambiguous illustration of a social situation in which these conditions are not fulfilled, and in which therefore at least oppositional interest groups cannot emerge despite the presence of quasi-groups and latent interests.[23]

Finally, certain social conditions are necessary for classes to emerge. Dahrendorf cites Marx's analysis of the French peasantry as an example of a limiting social condition, since the cell-like structure of the peasantry prevented the levels of communication necessary for class conflict.[24] Providing these conditions are fulfilled, interests which are latent will become manifest or, to use another of his expressions, quasi-groups will become conflict groups.

The analysis of the degrees of conflict that can be expected on the basis of these conditions is the most interesting part of the book. Conflict is likely to become violent when attempts are made to suppress it, but providing this is not the case three factors will be responsible for varying its intensity. It will be intense, firstly, when one conflict is superimposed on top of another. We have already seen Daniel Bell arguing that such a super-imposition has often occurred in Europe by virtue of religious divisions coinciding with class divisions. Another example of the same point is provided by the marked difference in levels of conflict at the end of the nineteenth century in Britain and Germany. Historians of the period now inform us that the relatively minor levels of violence in England were consequent on conflict occurring only over economic issues; in contrast the German anti-socialist laws superimposed a political conflict on top of the economic struggles, with results that Dahrendorf's theory has led us to expect.[25] The second factor regulating the intensity of social conflict is the level of social mobility in a society:

> A class composed of individuals whose social position is not an inherited and inescapable fate, but merely one of a plurality of social roles, is not likely to be as powerful a historical force as the closed class Marx had in mind. Where mobility within and between generations is a regular occurrence, and therefore a legitimate expectation of many people, conflict groups are not likely to have either the permanence or the dead seriousness of caste-like classes composed of hopelessly alienated men. And as the instability of classes grows, the intensity of class conflict is bound to diminish.[26]

Finally, Dahrendorf suggests that conflict may be less intense when it is recognised. In this vein he gives vent to the optimistic Popperian views that conflict is beneficial:

> It seems to me that the London *Economist* was well advised when it 'reproached British unions for their "moderation" which it declared is part responsible for the stagnation and low productivity of British capitalism; it compared their policies unfavourably with the more aggressive policies of American unions whose constant pressure for higher wages has kept the American economy dynamic'.[27]

Two final points need to be noted to complete this account of Dahrendorf's theory. Firstly, Dahrendorf devotes quite considerable attention to the Eastern European situation. He does so because he is surprised that the superimposition of conflicts in that society has not in fact led to anything more than minor outbreaks. The explanation offered for this is that these societies have invented new ways of gaining some of the information usually yielded only by conflict, and thus are able to avoid head-on collisions. In particular, Dahrendorf stresses the role that endless discussion plays as both solvent and source of information.[28] Secondly, Dahrendorf is also slightly ill-at-ease when discussing bureaucracy. He insists that a model of class must distinguish only two groups, the powerful and the powerless, and he argues that such a division allows a useful distinction to be drawn amongst the new middle classes:

> It seems to me that a fairly clear as well as significant line can be drawn between salaried employees who occupy positions that are part of a bureaucratic hierarchy and salaried employees in positions that are not ... I suggest that the ruling class theory applies without exception to the social position of bureaucrats, and the working class theory equally generally to the social position of white collar workers.[29]

It seems rather forced to include junior civil servants as part of the ruling class, but this is not in fact Dahrendorf's worry. Rather bureaucracies as a whole, in a sense, refuse to think as classes:

> Although they always *belong* to the ruling class, because bureaucratic roles are roles of dominance, bureaucracies as such never *are* the ruling class. Their latent interests aim at the maintenance of what exists; but what it is that exists is not decided by bureaucracies but given to them.[30]

Such bureaucracies, Dahrendorf feels, have been correctly described by Karl Renner as 'a service class', and we shall hear much more of his unease about their role and character.

We can fill out Dahrendorf's rather abstract picture, and present further evidence on the benefits of conflict, by considering the disastrous consequences that followed from the attempts to abolish conflict in German society. Dahrendorf demonstrates that even seemingly virtuous reforms in Germany often have the aim of trying to create a false harmony. He feels that this is true of the social policy created by the state to integrate the workers. Whereas British workers often resisted and resented the state taking control over social policy affairs, Germans willingly accepted the idea.[31] A second area in which to create harmony was in the work place, especially by means of 'participation'. Dahrendorf is quick to point to the unfortunate side effects resulting from any suppression of conflict in the work place:

> Thus we find instead of work disputes, individual actions whose connection with social conflicts is barely recognisable at first sight. Sinking work morale, growing fluctuation, indeed even sickness and accident rates, may be indicators of such redirections of industrial conflict.[32]

Most importantly, Dahrendorf offers a remarkable critique of the Social Democratic Party (SPD) which his father had served. He attempts to convince us that the party chose to place order, harmony, morality and the state, in which these virtues were supposedly enshrined, above social conflict. This attitude proved disastrous in Weimar:

> ...the Social Democrats 'saved the state' by joining forces with military and paramilitary groups of the right against the extremism of the left and thus continued a conservative policy that repressed social forces in the name of the state. Indeed, nowhere did the predictive justice of Lassalle's praise of the state become as apparent in Prussia, the largest province of Germany and governed by Social Democrats throughout the Weimar Republic: the nature of the state is always moral; not even the

hated 'princes and Junker' of Imperial Germany could alter this basic fact; this higher truth shone through even their worst errors.[33]

It was this inability to withstand conflict that led Germany to seek harmony and consensus under a dictator. Dahrendorf loathes this. He is proud of his career in German politics because he helped to replace the 'great coalition' of Christian Democrats (CDU) and Social Democrats (SPD) with the 'little coalition' of Liberal Democrats (FDP) and Social Democrats.[34] A continuation of the 'great coalition' would have led to frustration amongst those at the bottom who were no longer able to have an instrument to realise their changes; such feelings are the result of superimposed conflict, and can lead all too easily to cynicism about the whole system. This advocacy of conflict still runs strong when Dahrendorf writes about Germany.

The warrior ethic that underlies so much of Dahrendorf's work has now been outlined at some length. Full assessment of his sociology must wait, but we can ask at this stage, what should we make of the warrior ethic? An initial, seemingly academic, but crucial point to be made is that Dahrendorf has little sense of history. His arguments as to the universality of domination lead him to underplay a vitally important factor: although all systems are based on differential power, in some societies there is, as it were, less power around. One should distinguish between power or command systems and those that are liberal. He also underplays the importance of accident in allowing Western societies to be at once industrial and democratic. We do not yet understand how this combination was possible in the European case, but several much-cited factors seem to have been crucial: as no one knew what an industrial society was like it was useless in Western Europe to centralise power to achieve it quickly (this is no longer the case in the rest of the world); this in turn allowed the process to occur over centuries, thus allowing certain native liberal traditions, notably the tradition of parliamentarianism, to survive; industrialisation was small, initially, so that the powerful did not seek immediately to use it for their own ends; for a peculiar combination of reasons, the leading industrial nation was characterised socially by a diffusion of power, albeit between different groups at different periods, which again allowed liberal institutions to survive; and, finally, the doctrine of *laissez-faire* encouraged the economy to run separate from politics—the wealthy, in other words, did not turn their money into private armies.[35]

The warrior ethic is wrong. Many social orders that had vast disparities of power have remained stable so long as they remained capable of, above all, fulfilling certain basic human necessities. Thus the Roman Empire collapsed less because people became fed up with centralised power and far more because that power could no longer provide the conditions for economic activity, i.e. peace, and because its very functioning came to depend upon its taking the basics, rather than just the surplus, from the countryside.[36] We need not be surprised at stability in Eastern Europe: *if* such countries can make their economies work reasonably efficiently, there is no reason to believe that they will not be able to gain loyalty through the means that, after all, worked so well in the West in the post-war period—increasing the size of the cake. Dahrendorf has recently argued that *Class and Class Conflict* had some failings in this respect:

> The most obvious gap is that in *Class and Class Conflict*, where the analysis of conflict remains highly formal and little is said either about the substance of conflict or the direction of change... By introducing the concept of life chances as the subject matter of human social development, it may be possible to go some way towards remedying this deficiency. Social conflicts are about more life chances...[37]

This is very guarded, for we are not clearly told what comprises a life chance. I am arguing that the full-blown warrior ethic suggests, as it were, that liberty is in the soul of every man. I would not of course wish to deny that some social conflicts are motivated by 'a visceral desire for freedom', but as a general rule this seems to me untrue: if sociology is to base itself on an image of man, let it be Hobbesian rather than Popperian. But this disagreement need not worry us too much since Dahrendorf's less abstract sociology in fact bases itself on a fairly earthy view of human interests.

However, it is worth noting that—unfortunately—Dahrendorf weds himself to essentially a psychological argument rather than, as is necessary, showing how different groups in different circumstances conceive their interests (ideational and material) differently. This recalls to mind an earlier point, namely that Dahrendorf's warrior ethic served for him as an explanation of the origins of social conflict, i.e. it saved him from trying to explain how a particular type of society creates a particular balance between a particular set of forces. This is not to say that Dahrendorf is wrong to insist that conflict will always characterise society and that the political is one core issue of human life; but to insist on this does not mean that the analysis of the social infrastructure of power becomes any the less necessary. In a nutshell, the lack of historical examples in his work is not accidental; it results logically from taking the warrior too much to heart. As noted, this is a great pity since his refutation of Marx would have been more firmly based had he extended his range in this manner. However, perhaps too much should not be made of this. For underlying his formal analysis is a conception of the way one society generated a particular set of groups: Dahrendorf accepts Marx's description of classical capitalism, but wishes to argue that social changes have now destroyed the relevance of his analysis.

A Necessary Popperian Interlude

As yet we only understand one side of Dahrendorf's vision. On the face of it, the theory of class conflict is open to an even more brutal objection than those raised against it above. Is it really the case, one might ask, that conflict, i.e. murder, war, rape, pillage and loot, is attractive and a sign of high civilisation? At times Dahrendorf's language does encourage this sort of criticism: it is, for example, on the face of it manifestly odd to say that Weimar Germany did not have enough conflict when that society was in fact torn apart by warring groups! Dahrendorf's position must be, and indeed is, more complex and 'civilised' than this, and we will shortly turn to ways in which he manages to build in some restraints. The analysis of such restraints can be preceded by a brief look at the source of Dahrendorf's difficulty in the matter as a whole, the philosophy of his mentor Karl Popper. It is well known that Popper's warrior code has led him to dismiss with contempt all scientists who solve minor puzzles. Such men, pictured by Thomas Kuhn as working within a paradigm, are time-servers and our admiration should be reserved for those who create new ways of thinking, i.e. new paradigms. In Popper's words:

> These 'normal' scientists want a framework, a routine, a common and an exclusive language of their trade. But it is the non-normal scientist, the daring scientist, the critical scientist, who breaks through the barrier of normality, who opens the windows and lets in the fresh air; who does not think about the impression he makes, but tries to be well understood.
> The growth of normal science, which is linked to the growth of Big Science, is likely to prevent, or even destroy, the growth of knowledge, the growth of great science.[38]

The warrior ethic could not be stated more clearly. Yet, as many have noted, it is very strange that Popper should be against revolutions in society and advocate piecemeal social engineering in their place. In the same article from which the above quotation was taken, Popper notes:

If the method of rational critical discussion should establish itself, then this should make the use of violence obsolete: *critical reason is the only alternative to violence so far discovered.*

It seems to me clear that is the obvious duty of all intellectuals to work for *this* revolution...[39]

The crucial concept here is that we need only *one* social revolution. It seems almost as if we do have some certainty about our social forms, and that uncertainty is reserved for our knowledge.

It would be possible to add to the list of dilemmas inherent in the Popperian view of science—above all by emphasising the plausibility of the Kuhnian perspective and by noting that a scientific revolution does not in fact mean we take down our bridges—but this is no longer necessary since a clarification of Popper's philosophy can immediately be adopted. This has been provided by Ernest Gellner, and its place in his own thought will concern us later; here, we wish to place Popper so as to advance our understanding of Dahrendorf. Gellner's argument is that there is a 'big divide' which separates pre-industrial from industrial societies. If we consider only liberal industrial societies, it becomes possible to understand Popper's seemingly contradictory position. Popper is indeed right to argue that in social matters there is a vast difference between societies which do not allow gradual change and those that do. Revolutions are often very necessary to make the transition from the one to the other.

Equally, to follow Gellner, a revolution is required before the criticism that is perhaps a universal human characteristic can breed high-powered cognitive science. This revolution consists in empiricism or, in Habermasian terms, in the institutionalisation of the discourse of the experimental sciences. The change from Newton to Einstein is not really an affair of the barricades but, cognitively speaking, a prime example of piecemeal engineering.[40] This placing of Popper applies to Dahrendorf's total endorsement of the Popperian philosophy of science. But more important is the argument by analogy: Dahrendorf is not in fact arguing for any sort of conflict but only for the civilised conflict that benefits mankind.

Les Règles du Jeu

In *Society and Democracy* Dahrendorf qualified the warrior code thus:

...it is true that the notion of conflict presupposes a common context of the contestants. It is also true that this context includes more than a physical territory; it means two things: agreed-upon rules of the game of conflict and a structure of authority within which this takes place. Thus conflict implies both social contracts: the contract of association to domesticate the war of all against all by accepted rules of the game, and the contract of government to tie together the common context by an authority invested with power.[41]

Following from this, Dahrendorf draws a distinction between social integration (judged desirable) and social harmony (a dangerous utopian illusion). This is to say, in effect, that conflict about the rules of the game in a society which allows for peaceful change is more or less illicit. And the necessity for such agreement can be seen from the disastrous history of the German elite. Dahrendorf, naturally, asks who gained by the suppression of conflict in Imperial Germany. He provides an answer to this in the most original and striking part of his work, an analysis of the changing character of the German elite. Theoretically, he argues that elites are best seen as either established or not (i.e. how united in terms of social background and interest) and as either monopolistic or not (i.e. possessed or not of more than a single political ideology). This leads him to construct this four-fold table:[42]

Table 6. Types of Social Elite according to Dahrendorf.

| | | Political Ideology | |
		Monopolistic	Pluralist
	Established	Authoritarian	Liberal
Social Type			
	Not established	Totalitarian	Cartel of Anxiety

The archetype of a liberal elite is that of Great Britain. This is worth highlighting. The warrior ethic might have led us to expect that the non-established/pluralist elite would correspond to his wishes since it would seem to allow for most conflict; that this is not in fact the case we shall see in a moment. Nevertheless, the liberal elite encouraging conflict within the rules of the game of an established set of actors does eliminate certain possibilities. Thus Dahrendorf's admiration for the English legal system and for English public schools which have bred leaders for Conservative and Labour Parties is not perhaps shared by those who argue that it is the nature of the establishment as a whole that needs to be put into question. This example shows, of course, that Dahrendorf's radical reputation is, strictly speaking, undeserved: he is radical in wishing to establish a liberal society but he is essentially conservative in wishing to defend that order and no other.

These theoretical points are used by Dahrendorf in an historical reconstruction of the crises of leadership in German society. His argument is that the elite of Imperial Germany—made up of the Junkers themselves, but also of their bureaucrats—was irreparably damaged by the catastrophe of 1918. However, the various contending leaders of Weimar Germany could not find anything in common that would make their conflict fruitful. A cartel arose which, especially in the case of the service class, was riven by anxiety. The effects were disastrous:

> If the political class is an abstract [i.e. non-established] entity, if it lacks those ties that transcend the common share in the exercise of power, then political conflict always involves the fear and danger of jeopardising the system of the constitution itself. Under these conditions, it tends to assume either of two forms, apparently divergent, yet pointing in the same direction socially and politically. Either conflict is suspended altogether on the grounds of the allegedly destructive effects of strife, and thereby repressed and transformed into a dangerous potential of revolution; or it takes the form of a fundamental scepticism concerning the rules of the game of what is often called 'the system'—both conditions that are clearly not very helpful for the constitution of liberty . . . Social homogeneity promotes fruitful conflict.[43]

The historical consequence of this situation was, in Dahrendorf's eyes, that the cartel of anxiety, unable to agree amongst itself, either turned to, or at least offered no resistance to, the rise of the Nazis.[44] And one further point should be stressed. Dahrendorf considers that the intelligentsia makes up one element of the elite in any country, and he demonstrates that intellectuals, too, did little to rally around Weimar. On the contrary, the German intelligentsia tended to be split between total criticism of the system and—in part influenced by their position as *Beamte*—supine acquiescence in a new order.[45]

Dahrendorf is as interested as Daniel Bell in the establishment of the elite since he too feels that the people are not so full of virtue as to make greater democratisation a sensible alternative.[46] But this does not mean that he is no liberal—on the contrary, his interest is in how a liberal, meritocratic elite can be created that will prove socially acceptable. This can only be done if there is equal opportunity to enter institutions from which the establishment leaders are drawn. (The fact that this is not the case with the English public schools is what makes one start slightly at Dahrendorf's presentation, initially.) In other words, an establishment must not be a ruling class, and for this not to be the case it is necessary for other rules of the game to be in existence. We can turn to these by noting the social changes that Dahrendorf feels are responsible for turning capitalism into post-capitalism. Three such changes are crucial.

(1) The most important change of all is that capital is said to have 'decomposed'. By this Dahrendorf means that a separation has occurred between the ownership of property and the actual exercise of control at the workplace. Dahrendorf regards the rise of the professional manager as a clear refutation of Marx. He notes, correctly in my view, that Marx, always keen to see the seeds of a new order in the old, held high hopes that the joint stock company represented the emergence of non-capitalist, functionalist industry. Dahrendorf argues that it is indeed the case that the manager will seek to gain legitimacy in new ways since 'never has the imputation of a profit motive been further from the real motives of men than it is for modern bureaucratic managers'.[47] And managers will gain their positions in the future as a result of their professional qualifications.

Dahrendorf of course insists that Marx was quite wrong to presume that this change would remove all causes for conflict—insofar as power relations remain, conflict will always occur. But such changes are held to change the character and intensity of conflict. Ownership and control represents the superimposition of one sort of conflict upon another and this raises the stakes of struggle. In contrast:

> If incumbents of positions of subjection enjoy the countervailing gratification of a relatively high socioeconomic status, they are unlikely to invest as much energy in class conflicts arising out of the authority structure of associations as they would if they were deprived of both authority and socioeconomic status. Dominant groups are correspondingly not so likely to be as involved in the defence of their authority rules unless their high socioeconomic status is simultaneously involved.[48]

The picture being presented to us is one in which, moreover, not only is there a distinction between issues inside the organisation, but one in which conflicts do not spill over from one institutional sphere to another. There is, in other words, a separation of industrial and political conflict:

> Increasingly, the social relations of industry, including industrial conflict, do not dominate the whole of society but remain confined in their patterns and problems to the sphere of industry. Industry and industrial conflict are, in post-capitalist society, institutionally isolated, i.e. confined within the borders of their proper realm and robbed of their influence on other spheres of society. In post-capitalist society, the industrial enterprise is no longer the model after which all other relations are fashioned.[49]

(2) We have already noted the argument that increasing social mobility is likely to diminish the intensity of class conflict. Dahrendorf's review of the social mobility literature convinced him that:

> Social mobility has become one of the crucial elements of the structure of industrial societies, and one would be tempted to predict its 'breakdown' if the process of mobility were ever seriously impeded.[50]

Dahrendorf confidently envisages, in true liberal vein, nothing less than full equality of opportunity—and sees, moreover, no reason why this should not become a reality:

> When Marx wrote his books, he assumed that the position an individual occupies in society is determined by his family origin and the position of his parents... But since then a new pattern of role allocation has become institutionalised in industrial societies. Today the allocation of social positions is increasingly the task of the educational system... there are still numerous obstacles and barriers in the way of complete equality of educational opportunity, but it is the stubborn tendency of modern societies to institutionalise intergeneration mobility by making a person's social position dependent on his educational achievement. Where this is the case, no social stratum, group, or class can remain completely stable for more than one generation. Social mobility, which, for Marx, was the exception that confirmed the rule of class closure, is built into the structure of post-capitalist society and has therefore become a factor to be reckoned within all analyses of conflict and change.[51]

(3) The chances of social mobility via education depend, of course, upon the institutionalising of citizenship rights. In this matter Dahrendorf follows T. H. Marshall very closely, arguing that the eighteenth century sees the establishment of equal rights before the law, the nineteenth equal political rights, and the twentieth the creation of social rights that allow the citizen to make the most of his opportunities. Dahrendorf's period in German politics was largely spent arguing for the full realisation of these rights so as to include women, catholics and *Gastarbeiter*. Such rights need to be extended to provide a floor below which the citizenry cannot fall; and such a floor is held—and this must be stressed—to diminish the intensity of conflict.[52]

Dahrendorf is thus suggesting that these changes will create a consensus sufficient to 'regulate' conflict within reasonable bounds. This acceptance of the system depends less on shared values than on simpler calculations that the society is open enough to further self-interested action. In a nutshell, Dahrendorf offers a 'material' rather than an 'ideal' consensus. But Dahrendorf's view is not without an ambivalence that has been skillfully pointed out by Giddens. Logically, Dahrendorf's views should result in a sort of total pluralism since power relations exist in chess clubs as much as factories. Nevertheless, Dahrendorf in fact concentrates upon the divisions inside *state and industry*:

> But this obviously presumes some criterion whereby such organisations are recognised as more 'significant' for class analysis than others; and this in turn takes us back to certain elements in the more traditional concepts of class which Dahrendorf claimed to have abandoned. In Marx's writings such criteria are established by the general theoretical framework within which the concept of class is employed: namely, that which analyses the fundamental role of the economic relationships in conditioning the rest of the social and political structure.[53]

This is indeed a just criticism of Dahrendorf, but I believe that he is aware of the problem and that we can make sense of his writings in this matter. To do so we must distinguish between conflict to create post-capitalism and conflict inside post-capitalism itself. Dahrendorf does depend upon Marxist-type factors to create alliances between groups so that the 'structure change' to post-capitalism may be achieved. But in an amendment to *Class and Class Conflict* he directly argues that conflict inside post-capitalism is unlikely to take the form of conflict between large blocs of alliances; he is, in other words, accepting the logic of his theory. This amendment is contained in 'Conflict after Class'. In Popperian guise, Dahrendorf here attempts to improve his theory since he feels it misleads in four respects.

(1) Dahrendorf is clearly uneasy that the lack of socialism in America consequent on greater avenues (whether real or felt to be real being a much disputed question) of social mobility is a social reality almost, as it were, explained away as abnormal by this theory.

(2) The inevitability of violent conflict in Eastern Europe that might be expected from the broad outlines of his theory seems less and less likely to be the case. Repression can perhaps work, Dahrendorf remarks; for reasons already noted this need not surprise us.

(3) His theory did not sufficiently highlight the fact that the service class occupies the ruling positions but refuses to consider itself in class terms. These are the cowards in Dahrendorf's eyes who fail to stand up and be counted. This was especially the case with the service class of Weimar Germany, brilliantly characterised by

Theodor Geiger, in words that echo ceaselessly in Dahrendorf's mind:

> A class denies with disgust that it is a class and conducts a bitter class struggle against the reality and idea of the class struggle.[54]

(4)   He is very reluctant to accept the findings of the then recent, affluent worker studies that argued that the social base for a clearly structured political division between socialist and capitalist remained:

> The attempt to prove that the blackcoated are after all also workers by market position and class affiliation, or that the affluent worker continues to vote for socialist parties sounds desperately like the truth, nothing but the truth, yet anything but the whole truth. Too many other facts stand in its way: the riddle of Orpington man between racism and liberalism, the development of 'people's parties' appealing to all social groups all over the Western world, the corresponding *rapprochement* of party platforms in many areas, the apparent growth of the floating vote in several democratic countries, the conflict of technocrats and ideologists and the generalised sympathies for 'scientific politics'.[55]

This is slightly vague but the general point Dahrendorf is trying to make is clear, namely that the permanence of certain structures plus such changes as citizenship rights give politics a very different feel.

On the basis of these points, Dahrendorf spells out a change in his theory. He argues that class conflict is but a special case of the much more general social force of contest:

> Class conflict is that form of contest which becomes necessary if large numbers of individuals cannot realise their interests by individual endeavours. The conditions under which this is the case can be specified: if, for example, one group monopolises the distribution of chances of participation over a lengthy period of time, then groups with widely divergent interests are compelled to join forces and try their strength by collective action. This then is how classes in the sense of inclusive social and political conflict groups come about; which means that class societies cannot be open societies, or, in less absolute terms, to the extent to which class societies open up, conflicts lose their solidary, i.e. class, character.[56]

Dahrendorf has vacillated somewhat in his evaluation of contest rather than class politics. In a splendid 1964 essay, 'Recent Changes in the Class Structure of the European Societies', he showed great alarm at contest politics:

> In the service class society, however, this social basis of

representative government is giving way... In the absence of a progressive force [based on large representative blocs] the powers that be, and above all the inert force of bureaucracy, keep things running without ever changing them... In the service class societies of Europe, the political situation is often not unlike that described so brilliantly by Marx in his *Eighteenth Brumaire of Louis Bonaparte*: there are large numbers of individuals who cannot form solid political groups and represent themselves. They have to be represented, and they love the man who pretends to do so without actually hurting what few concerns and interests they have.[57]

But recently, Dahrendorf has abandoned the idea that structure change per se, as compared to the structure change creating liberal societies in the first place, is always to be desired. He now openly argues that the individualistic type of contest is to be preferred to the creation of blocs searching for structure change. In 1977, for example, he told Australian audiences that the future lay in following the American open society rather than in repeating old and dated European social conflicts.[58] We shall hear more of the rationale for this view and of the alternative ways by means of which bureaucracy can be controlled.

Dahrendorf's social democracy veers much closer to classic liberalism than it does to democratic socialism. Although this has recently become much more obvious, Dahrendorf was always fairly specific about his views. In 'Equality and Liberty', his liberalism is clearly seen in his insistence that, once basic citizenship rights have been established, liberty should take precedence over equality:

> In a word, if the minimum status guaranteed all citizens is put as high as possible, this does not constitute a threat to the chance of liberty, so long as there remains above this minimum space enough for many different levels and kinds of education, authority, prestige and income. Anyone who places a high value on liberty should do his best to see that the minimum social status of all citizens is set high rather than low, but at the same time to make sure that the space between the floor and the ceiling of the status hierarchy does not become too narrow.[59]

Dahrendorf explains very precisely what is implied here. He argues that the status of citizens is not—except in special cases, much to be deplored—any longer arbitrarily decided for them by inheritance or educational advantages. But a much greater check on the chances of liberty resides in differential access to power. It is the very crux of his theory that power cannot be equalised, but he nevertheless argues that it can be controlled:

> Where everyone has access to the chance of power and to a voice in legitimating power (politically, to active and passive suffrage),

ruling and serving both lose their arbitrary character and become compatible with the equal chance of liberty for all. It is from this point of view, I think, that the relationship between liberty and equality of social status must be judged. If I am right, all power that is not rationally legitimated must be abolished before there can be equal chances of liberty for all. In economic terms, legitimation by property is not sufficient without a measure of consent on the part of the unpropertied; i.e. group conflicts must be recognised. In political terms, power based strictly on economic power is illegitimate and must be eliminated; i.e. there must be institutional pluralism.[60]

In 'Market and Plan' Dahrendorf suggests that there are two alternative ideal-types of rationality, only one of which truly allies itself with liberalism. As one might expect, market rationality is favoured for reasons of democracy (the citizens' preferences count), politics (plan rationality requires excessive centralisation of power) and efficiency (market capitalism, for all its failings, is unquestionably far more productive). Dahrendorf's admiration for market rationality has something of the fervour of Herbert Spencer about it, and it takes him to quite considerable lengths. He argues, for example, that certain 'rules of the game' essential to market rationality have been codified as social norms, i.e. participation in market rationality has necessitated the granting of citizenship rights. Dahrendorf's espousal of liberalism is such as to allow him to question the virtues of the ways in which this was achieved:

> ...it may be argued that the methods chosen to provide this security, namely special legislation, presupposed economic conditions very different from those of the 'affluent society', i.e. of a post-cyclical economy in a permanent state of expansion. In the affluent society, measures that were once a condition of the market-rational rules of the game strengthen the state without evident need, and thereby make it more plan-rational.[61]

This is a good moment at which to assess the sociological perspective that Dahrendorf is offering. Some comments can be offered in turn on his theory of post-capitalist society and of his view of German history.

I have sought to argue that the air of radicalism about Dahrendorf's work is unjustified since he is a stalwart defender of a particular 'good' society. It would perhaps have been better had he spelled this out more clearly from the start rather than introducing his message rather covertly. In this case, it would not have been necessary later on to have to clear up several important points, such as his admission that conflict could lead to a replacement of the status quo in politics, not in industry.[62] More importantly,

Dahrendorf is not always correct in his observations of social changes since Marx. He is wrong to say that the rise of professional managers 'decomposes' capitalism: such managers share class background and, to a degree, self-interest with traditional capitalists, and their activity is in any case strictly curtailed by the strategic control of shareholder blocs, so that the maximisation of profit remains an overriding objective.[63]

Secondly, he is wrong to believe that equal opportunity has been achieved. The social mobility that has characterised the last quarter century is more the product of changes in the occupational structure, than the result of a massive increase in the openness of the social fabric. The privileged still have better life chances than those at the bottom of society.[64] In any case, I suspect (but certainly cannot prove) that a greater degree of social mobility might not, in fact, lessen solidary action by the disadvantaged or diminish the intensity of conflict. Might it not rather be the case that the presence of a member of one's family in a higher social class would increase one's reference point whilst the logic of the situation would still encourage solidary action? However, Dahrendorf seems to me right to stress that certain citizenship rights have been established in Western liberal societies; and this creates that mixture between social inequality and democracy responsible for making Western societies subject to internal conflicts that are not perhaps designed at 'structure change' but which nevertheless cause systemic problems. Bluntly, the pressure of the underprivileged cannot be bought off when economic growth has been slowed down by inflation.

Frank Parkin has recently suggested that there are a number of underlying structural tendencies that increase the effectiveness of economic action taken by working-class groups. The most important are the increasing complexity of the economy, the capital-intensive nature of production and the increasing dependence on foreign trade.[65] So Dahrendorf, as was Bell, must be criticised for leading us to expect that modern society would run smoothly when in fact it harbours internal problems perhaps sufficient to put that order in question. Dahrendorf's most recent work recognises this potential instability, and addresses it. We can anticipate his later position by saying that, ironically, it is one in which the warrior ethic is discredited, and consensus held to depend upon, in the final analysis, a change in social values. But discussion of the return of Parsons's ghost must, however, be left until a little later.

Dahrendorf's view of German history has so far not been discussed directly, and some drawing together is needed before an assessment can be offered. Dahrendorf suggests that there is a 'constitution of liberty' made up of citizenship rights, an acceptance of social conflict, the presence of an established elite and the prevalence of public virtues. He implies that this 'constitution' is the end product of history, the natural birthright, as it were, of all societies. This assumption is evident in the very terms of the analysis Dahrendorf presents: Germany is seen to be not properly modern, or stuck on the way to modernity, and 'faulted' because of this. The essential reason for this peculiarity is attributed to the fact that German industrialisation occurred late and fast; this allowed the traditional ruling class to maintain its position in an industrial society.

Dahrendorf's analysis of the famous marriage of Corn and Iron essentially follows Veblen's *Imperial Germany and the Industrial Revolution*. But he uses slightly different terminology from Veblen's: German development is seen as being non-capitalist in the size of its industrial enterprises and in the role played by the state in both investment and social welfare. This background made it difficult for the four pillars of the liberal society to be founded. Firstly, citizenship rights were not spread, the service class finds ways of reproducing itself and manages to keep the population pacific by welfare measures given not as rights but by benefit of the state.[66] Secondly, conflict is avoided. This shunning of conflict infected the important service element of the German elite and made it suspicious of the conflicts of Weimar Germany; and, thirdly, this factor itself contributed to the creation of a non-established but diverse elite in Weimar Germany, all too ready to bow before a dictator. The fourth pillar of liberty is that of social character and will concern us in the next section.

Society and Democracy offers a striking account of German development, particularly in its portrait of the German elite and of German political culture. Some of Dahrendorf's judgements are harsh. Perhaps the Social Democrats did 'save the state', but it remains the case that a deeper structural reason for the collapse of Weimar lies in the fact that too many other groups had a vested interest in opposing the artificially created Weimer constitution: the blame lay less with the SPD than with the traditional ruling elements in Germany who virtually sabotaged the state. More important, however, are two major faults at work in *Society and Democracy*. Firstly, Dahrendorf's 'constitution of liberty' implies what is best termed a theory of 'political modernisation'. This theory is extraordinarily optimistic since it views liberty—because of the warrior ethic—as the characteristic of developed societies. This theory seems to me quite wrong. Rapid industrialisation almost certainly depends upon centralising power to such an extent as to rule out the possibility of democracy. In the course of world history, it is Britain which is exceptional, and Germany which is the carrier of the norm.

Secondly, Dahrendorf does not really offer any explanation as to why the authoritarian Germany of Bismarck should turn into the fascist Germany of the Nazi party. The fear of the ruling classes, in the form of Von Papen, introduced the Nazis to the stage, but this does not serve as an explanation of fascism in its own right. The Marxist theory, in contrast, sees a fascist party as a functional necessity acting for monopoly capitalism; it is an agent designed to suppress the unions and the communist party. But the Marxist theory is certainly wrong. German capitalists were not pillars of Weimar but, with the single exception of Fritz Thyssen, they did not support Hitler until he was very nearly a winner in his own right; and in power the Nazis scarcely acted on behalf of capitalists. And this theory cannot even begin to explain why fascism should have arisen in essentially agricultural countries such as Rumania. So the Marxist view does not really explain the character of fascism either. But such an explanation is not impossible.

Industrialisation involves forcing people from enclosed and traditional communities into the abstract urban life of industrial society. It is impossible to exaggerate the social costs involved in making—especially *quickly*—the human material for modern society. In more general terms, it can be said that the transition from agrarian to industrial society is made possible because the stick of coercion is alleviated by the hope, insisted upon by all self-conscious modernising ideologies, that the people will eventually benefit from affluence. However, this transition is by no means always negotiated. Those in Germany who suffered from massive social change and inflation, who had fought in the war and felt betrayed by Versailles, were naturally drawn to a party which emphasised the enclosed, millenarian dreams of pre-industrial society. Significantly, such large scale 'regressive' ideologies were no part of the general memory in Great Britain and had never been a part of the American self-image; this fact helped to prevent these capitalist countries becoming moved by fascism. But the faster, forced modernisation in Germany had left many such dreams intact; and the success of the Nazis put such dreams in charge of a rejuvenated industrial machine. Fascism, in other words, is best seen as a pathology of modernisation. Though the future is perhaps unlikely to see Dahrendorf's theory of *political* modernisation being proved correct (for once power is centralised, it rarely becomes decentralised again), we have strong reason to hope that countries which have industrialised will be saved from the millenarian dreams that characterised Nazism.

Character and Society

Dahrendorf has really only produced occasional essays on character and society, but they are of considerable interest. Our central interest is in delineating the requisite character type for an open society, and we can do so by looking at the dangers that Dahrendorf has described in both undersocialised and oversocialised character types. But attention must initially be paid to Dahrendorf's theoretical statement on such matters, namely *Homo sociologicus*; and some brief comments at the end of this section on the social role of the sociologists follow naturally from his views of the role sociology is beginning to play in modern America—to which Dahrendorf has devoted a book[67] that has attracted little attention and been undervalued.

Homo sociologicus argues that the central concept of sociology is that of role. Roles are seen as expected behaviour of holders of particular positions; such behaviour is the result, on the one hand, of constraints of various types and, on the other hand, of what might be called inducements, i.e. socialisation and reference groups. On the face of it this approach sees man as completely determined and absolutely social. This is a position of little comfort to a liberal, and Dahrendorf makes two arguments against it. Firstly, he observes that *Homo sociologicus* does not conjure up a brave new world:

> In reality, however, although we are in fact unable to separate Herr Schmidt from the role player Schmidt, after all his roles are taken into account he retains a residual range of choice that escapes calculation and control. It is not easy to define this range of choice... There is not only the freedom that every role leaves its player by not pronouncing on certain matters... but also a freedom *within* role expectations arising from the fact that they are largely defined by exclusion rather than determined positively. Few role expectations are all encompassing prescriptions; most take the form of a range of permitted deviations.[68]

This argument seems to me very unconvincing since it fails to ask—as a more serious analyst of role distance, Erving Goffman, does not—whether there are certain circumstances that *explain* the character of variations.[69] The second argument for liberals is more interesting:

> Ordinarily, we do not much care that the table, the roast, and the wine of the scientist are paradoxically different from the table, the

roast and the wine of our everyday experience. If we want to put down a glass or write a letter, a table seems a suitable support. It is smooth, solid, and even, and a physicist would scarcely disturb us by observing that the table is 'in reality' a most unsolid beehive of nuclear particles.[70]

We shall see later that Gellner will wish to argue that this is quite wrong. Dahrendorf's point is in fact similar to Habermas's, i.e. what happens in the technical world does not affect our self-image. But his defence of humanity is far simpler than Habermas's elaborate reconstructive sciences. Thus he does not even think that the application of science to man himself can 'disenchant us'. This is held to be impossible since scientific knowledge—in this case of *Homo sociologicus*—and moral theory are strictly separable.

> Every man has an empirical character, and this character is strictly determined: in studying it, 'we are simply observing [man], and in the manner of anthropology seeking to explore the motive causes of his actions physiologically'. In addition, and at the same time, every man has an intelligible character, a practical reason that makes him a free and moral being...there is no plausible reason to reject Kant's conclusion that the two characters 'may exist independently of each other and undisturbed by each other'. Although the free, integral individual is not accessible to empirical research and cannot be, we know about him in ourselves and in others.[71]

Perhaps for temperamental reasons I am not *so* certain about the freedom of my inner life. More importantly, Dahrendorf's use of this Kantian distinction is perhaps over generous: Kant was well aware of the claims of empirical knowledge and bounded moral man far more strictly than Dahrendorf appears to. Again we shall hear more of this from Gellner. There is something of a contradiction in *Homo sociologicus* itself between arguing that moral man is separate from the role player and yet exhorting sociologists to serve moral man. Why, we may ask, is this necessary if the two spheres do not touch at all? More importantly, we shall see in a moment that Dahrendorf's charge against 'other directed' men is that they are indeed *homines sociologici*. His confidence is thus less than it appears.

The substantive analysis of the relation between character and politics has, as it were, two parts. The first of these is contained in *Society and Democracy* in which Dahrendorf argues that the fourth pillar of the constitution of liberty is that provided by the public virtues:

> The predominance of public virtues may be described in terms of the values of sport, particularly of team sport. He who is virtuous

in this sense is 'a good sport'; he is 'fair'. He thus adheres to those rules whose rationale is to promote and at the same time domesticate the competitive effort of sports.... Perhaps the single maxim that best characterises public virtues is 'Keep smiling': make things easy for others, even if this is hard for you![72]

Dahrendorf approves of this attitude, which he considers particularly British, essentially because it manages, as it were, to combine the moral character with *homo sociologicus*. Men are aware that they have social roles and do their best to play them smoothly, but the very consciousness of 'playing a role' that this involves allows some sort of inner freedom to remain. In a nutshell, Dahrendorf is in favour of masks consciously used both in the interests of facilitating social intercourse and of allowing the individual room to breathe.[73]

All this is held to contrast absolutely with the German emphasis on the private virtues of truthfulness to one's soul or, in a different terminology, of respect for one's authentic being. These attitudes are held to result from the particular style of German family life which encourages the individual to ignore the claims of the social since 'true being' results from 'inner' and 'private' activity.[74] The consequence of this was, in Dahrendorf's eyes, disastrous for Germany. Most obviously, this attitude undermines the legitimacy of political life, and thus counteracts the high levels of actual voting. The unpolitical German was relieved to accept a dictator and did not concern himself too much with the Final Solution and other public scandals.[75]

But in the final analysis Dahrendorf is fairly optimistic about the spread of public virtues in Germany. Private virtues depend upon a relatively static society, and the Nazis in Germany, ironically, are held to have finally abolished this by turning a series of regions into a national community for the first time. But if the private virtues cannot hold out against modernity, a greater threat may be discovered when the public virtues are pushed too far, when, in other words, the injunction 'keep smiling' begins to enter into man himself and not just into his mask. To understand why Dahrendorf should feel that this is possible, we must turn to his account of the changes in American society that breed this danger. In 'European Sociology and the American Self-Image' his view of such changes is neatly summed up by reference to the changing popularity of various social theorists in American culture. The social world envisioned in different ways by Tocqueville and Spencer, a world in which the individual—by virtue of his religion for Tocqueville— would feel strong enough to stand apart from the state, has fallen before a more integrated, communal vision represented by

Malinowski and Parsons. Such a change naturally allows little room for more questioning concepts and theories to emerge in American social thought, and Dahrendorf shows how little impact the potentially critical concepts of elite, class, revolution and intellectual have had on the American self-image. Dahrendorf's hatred of utopia leads him to criticise very strongly the rather significant impact that he feels the sociologists of integration— amongst their number, in the last analysis, Bell—have had on American life:

> American sociologists have, apart from a small 'intellectual' minority marginal to the group, failed to absorb those ideas of European sociologists which threatened the undisputed accept- ance of the values of their society. They have thereby rendered their society the dubious service of apparently protecting it from some of the more unsettling ideas of modern times.[76]

The character type resulting from an integrated, communally conscious society is held to be that made famous by David Riesman as the 'other-directed' man. In a careful analysis of Riesman's work, Dahrendorf tries to analyse the dangers of the man so socialised that he has no inner resistance to the crowd, exactly the opposite fear, ironically, to Daniel Bell's nightmare of the inner man pulsating with libido. Dahrendorf feels that such 'other-directed' cowards will all too easily accept dictators:

> Democracy means conflict; but other-directed man does not like conflict. He wants to be liked, not opposed. Democracy means that people articulate their interests, even if they are self-interests. But other-directed man is not supposed to have any self-interests; his radar equipment perpetually skims the horizon in search of the ideas, attitudes and interests of others.[77]

It is clearly this that underlay Dahrendorf's fear that a society based on contest might eventually stagnate. The fear expressed is, in other words, that the service class of the future may not be so much authoritarian as other-directed.[78] But even in the mid-sixties, Dahrendorf insisted that American society remained very open, and he has since made very little of this particular nightmarish scenario.

Before offering some general conclusions about Dahrendorf's view on character and society, it is as well to draw together his *en passant* remarks on the social role of the sociologist. The crux of Dahren- dorf's position is that there is a systematic relationship between theory and practice; the sociologist should, in other words, take full cognisance of the moral impact his own research can have on society. Thus he rejects the Popperian-inspired view that sociology should simply solve social problems just as much as he opposes the view, attributed to Helmut Schelsky, according to which the sociologist has no effect and simply tries to explain the world after the event. His position draws him close to Habermas in spirit, although they would doubtless argue for very different versions of the open society.[79] It is interesting to note that his arguments about the role of the sociologist suffer from an ambivalence familiar to us from the discussion of Habermas, namely that a certain tension exists between trying to scare us (sociology is very powerful, and can be misapplied and to encourage us (sociology is not at all powerful, and premature approaches to the powerful ruins the advance of knowledge). Certainly, Dahrendorf does seem to think that the integrationist ethic of American society is cognitively powerful, but we are not told how this is to be reconciled with the stark statement that 'so far the much scorned empirical-analytical science of sociology consists at best of approaches, and often enough of mere programmes'.[80]

The Twilight of Modernity?

Dahrendorf's recent work is based on the assumption that 'the subject of history' has changed, a change dramatically marked, in his eyes, by the first oil crisis of 1973. Does this mean that we are leaving modernity, or merely that we must find a new political theory designed to help us retain the benefits of the open society in changed circumstances? As yet, Dahrendorf has no final answer to this question, but the two short volumes on this general theme—*The New Liberty* and *Life Chances*—suggests that he wishes to endorse the latter of these propositions.

The explanation for the problems of Western society depends less upon the analysis of social character than upon a series of 'contradictions of modernity'. Each of these demonstrates that when the benefits of modern society are asked for too insistently, new and impersonal forces come to rule our lives. Some of these contradictions need to be spelled out.

(1)   Inscribed almost in the very concept of liberal modernity is the insistence that the citizen has the chance to participate in his social world. Dahrendorf's championing of citizenship rights, of course, expressed his own firm endorsement of this value. But he now tells us that there is a limit. If everybody seeks to, or—as in the new schemes for co-partnership in industry—is allowed to, participate then organised change will become impossible. This worries Dahrendorf immensely since he regards a stalemate of vested interests as conducive in the long run to revolutionary politics.[81]

(2)   Egalitarianism too can apparently become self-defeating. No

reference is intended here to character types, but to institutional and logical facts of life. As regards the former, Dahrendorf has come to believe that, for example, the urge to establish equality in education has already in part resulted (and will do so completely if public schools are abolished) in the establishment of equality of performance; the desire to liberate us has, in other words, removed the opportunities of the gifted few. This levelling is occurring, we are told, in intellectual and artistic affairs, and even in respect of sexual differences.[82] Dahrendorf has recently latched onto Hirsch's *Social Limits to Growth* so as to argue that there are logical limits to what egalitarianism can achieve. *Class and Class Conflict* can be seen as a Hirschian book in its argument that few positions of command exist, and that not everyone can hold them; egalitarianism is thus impossible. But Dahrendorf seems to be attracted to Hirsch now, since he can argue, by process of analogy, that egalitarianism is impossible not only with regard to power but in matters of status and income or wealth. The argument that certain goods are positional, i.e. that only one person *can* by definition enjoy an isolated hut by a lakeside, is used by Dahrendorf to support his contention that equalisation of incomes is a chimera. We shall return to this point in our later criticism of Dahrendorf since it significantly ignores more positive elements in Hirsch's very complex analysis.[83]

(3) Dahrendorf has come to make very great use of Weber's fears that bureaucracy would create a 'cage of bondage' for modern man. His argument here is already familiar to us in the form of his earlier imprecations against the service class. If governments are asked to achieve more and more, particularly in terms of social policy, then more and more rules will be laid down, diminishing the space within which the citizen can act. Dahrendorf's earlier uneasiness about the welfare state has thus grown, and he has recently told us (in a manner similar to Daniel Bell) that he remains in favour of high government expenditure but is more firmly than ever resistant to the idea that the government should be responsible for actually spending the money.[84] In this, he suggests that the control of bureaucracy must be a prime target of any progressive politics.[85]

(4) A final contradiction that interests Dahrendorf greatly is based on his own personal experience. He suggests that the pursuit of modernity in terms of economic growth can be self-defeating, and he tries to argue this point by reference to the standard of living in the two countries he knows best, Britain and Germany. The German economic miracle, he suggests, may well have increased the options, i.e. the ability to go on foreign holidays, move geographically and so

on, at a considerable cost. That modernity may have costs is a new idea for Dahrendorf, and it needs spelling out. Costs are seen here in terms of the destruction of 'connections', or 'ligatures', which bind the individual to his fellows and to his community, and which consequently give his life meaning.

Dahrendorf now argues that total destruction of such ligatures would lead to an anomic, purely instrumental world in which men would not know what to do with the options before them. But a more usual reaction to the loss of some connections is a half-conscious awareness that the modern world is somehow out of joint, and Dahrendorf argues that this feeling underlies phenomena as diverse as Glistrup's anti-welfare party in Denmark, demands to protect the environment, and the student movement. The novelty of this point can be emphasised by saying that it presumes a rather different view of man from that which Dahrendorf had presented to us beforehand. Tradition now seems to have a place that the warrior code would surely not have contemplated. Dahrendorf might perhaps reply to this, in the vein of Habermas, that the preservation of tradition is in itself rational and can be done consciously. However, if this is really so, I doubt very much whether 'rational ligatures' will give men the sense of identity he seems to be recommending. Certainly the examples that illustrate his case, such as the monarchy in Great Britain, do not seem to stress this rational element.[86]

On the basis of these observations, Dahrendorf offers us a sociology of modern politics which both explains how the situation could arrive, and begins to allow us to see that much of his liberalism is nevertheless extant. Modern politics are seen as becoming increasingly polarised. The problems of Western society have led to a motley crew made up of believers in innate intelligence (Jensen and his followers), political scientists who think that democracy is ungovernable (Samuel Huntington) and Spenglerian forecasters (Robert Heilbroner) who argue that the West must have greater central authority if it is to survive. Dahrendorf is a liberal through and through, and he resists such moves to return the world to some imagined pre-1914 state of innocence.[87] But Dahrendorf is equally opposed to social democracy. Indeed, his contradictions of modernity are basically blamed on social democrats, and his recent refusal to endorse a British 'centre party' of all good social democrats represents the logical fulfilment of the unease he has always shown about social democracy.[88]

Dahrendorf offers us instead a third way, and it is not surprising to discover that the goals to which this way leads are familiar. This third way is designed to show that Western societies can improve even though they might well have to manage without growth; life-chances can, in other words, be extended even now, and must be so extended if our societies are to survive. Dahrendorf, in other words, has not yet joined the ranks of the doomsters and, if anything, he may be criticised for retaining far too much of his early optimism. The improvements he envisages as possible certainly include some of the following points:

(1) Most importantly, Dahrendorf now stresses even more strongly that, once the floor of citizenship has been established, the ceiling of what the individual can achieve by himself must scarcely be limited at all. Hope and progress depend upon stressing opportunity:

> Diffusion of responsibility, taxation, and the welfare state have all conspired to make initiative less likely. There is something right and good in all these developments. But the time has come to turn in the other direction. Unless incentive is provided by our tax systems, one is not likely to find much enthusiasm for individual initiative. Unless basic security is coupled with encouragement for personal initiative, it will be difficult to motivate those who have responsibility. And unless structures of authority allow people to make mistakes, one is not likely to find people who advance good ideas and put them into practice. A society without participation may be unpleasant, but a society without initiative is dead...[89]

And from his consideration of Hirsch, Dahrendorf feels it necessary to add that this structure of inequalities cannot somehow be escaped by economic growth, even if this were still possible. It is time, instead, to recognise that, so long as equal opportunity is assured, the structure ought to be accepted as it stands.[90]

(2) Dahrendorf suggests that in the long run such acceptance will be aided to a great extent by more flexibility in the division of labour. Men's lives should no longer be measured entirely by the job they hold. Instead, much more time and money should be spent on education. There is much to be said, Dahrendorf suggests, for changing tax laws so as to allow men to hold two jobs if they so wish. Finally, he criticises the inhumanity of forcing people to retire when they wish to carry on working. An improving society, in other words, can create life chances by imaginatively removing many of the causes of alienation.[91]

(3) This reform of the division of labour is really Dahrendorf's most substantial proposal, albeit it is not really worked out at any length (and, certainly, it fits badly with the possibility, of which he is aware, that structural unemployment may be on the increase). But he has also offered proposals on more immediate matters. In

'Conflict and Contract' he suggests that the British system of industrial politics needs to be changed. Here, lessons can be learnt from Germany. One latent function of co-partnership, Dahrendorf now assures us, was that it educated trade union leaders into the economic realities of their firms. Conflict, in other words, came to take place within a contract of all to produce economic growth. We are not told exactly whether this implies an advocacy of Lord Bullock's proposals on industrial democracy. But Dahrendorf does suggest that the Social Contract between government, unions and employers current at the time of his lecture may have similar benefits.[92] This whole argument is far removed in spirit from *Class and Class Conflict* and it is with amazement that one finds Dahrendorf advocating that workers in those services essential to the community no longer be allowed to strike.[93]

(4) Another proposal that could scarcely have been predicted from Dahrendorf's earlier work is one that he made much of during a lecture tour in Australia in 1977. Unemployment could be handled, he suggested, by a measure—in any case beneficial to the society—namely, that every citizen be required, probably between the ages of eighteen and thirty, to undertake a year's service to the community. Dahrendorf has not to my knowledge spoken further about this proposal, which raises very considerable and obvious difficulties: it would almost certainly be opposed by trade unions, whilst it would require considerable funding.[94]

(5) Dahrendorf, very much to his credit, has begun to pay much more systematic attention to the sociology of the developing world. *Society and Democracy* contained the implicit theory that all societies were advancing towards a condition of modernity modelled after the British experience. His new awareness of the importance of ligatures has made him question this model:

> ... I believe that it is becoming increasingly evident that the First and the Second Worlds are going through a phase in which the traditional values by which people have lived in Europe, America and similar countries no longer help us to solve problems. In many ways the traditional prescriptions create more difficulties than they resolve...[95]

In consequence:

> I think we are going to get a change in human attitudes and that this change would make a lot of sense certainly in the developing countries I happen to know. It is a change of attitude which, transposed to India, for instance, would mean not forced industrialisation but concentration on employment in villages and village development and so on. And I would, therefore, say that it

is just conceivable to me that the time in which people look for quick results, quick modernisation, is over.[96]

Whilst Dahrendorf's insistence on the importance of North-South politics is convincing, every general consideration weighs against this argument. One must hope that India can develop democratically—indeed, this is crucial—but it is very unlikely that the developing world in general will accept his advice, namely, to maintain their own ligatures rather than to force industrialism. Unfortunately, the pressures of poverty are just too great to make this a realistic proposal. And I, for one, feel slightly alarmed at encouraging Third World countries to express their native traditions: I remain unconvinced of the virtues of Shi'ite Islam. And disagreement on this point is totally unimportant since the Third World looks like managing without the advice of Dahrendorf or myself. But this is a side issue. What are we to make of the general argument that we are moving into a post-modern age? And how does this relate to the early conception of post-capitalism?

The best way to answer these points is by looking at the question of theory and practice. Dahrendorf's early position connected theory and practice rather coherently: the good society was morally desirable and it was realistic to expect it to be achieved. Man the warrior would try and create the open society, and once in it he would come to accept its rules since the reality of equal opportunity would make him realise that chances existed for all. This dream did not come true, Dahrendorf is now telling us, because many social democrats were misguided enough to think that full equality could be achieved. This is an illusion, and therefore we must return to more realistic aims. These aims are supposed to be post-modern, but they are in fact exactly the ones that lie at the heart of the earlier liberal creed. Has, then, nothing changed? He still wishes to see men as moved by their experience; a certain change in values is held to be occurring since disillusionment is following the inability of social democracy to fulfil the hopes it has raised. But, whilst he would thus argue that the subject of change exists as before, he would—I think—have to admit that this subject is far more confused than was the actor imbued with the warrior ethic. Maximising life chances is difficult—it is, for example, extremely hard to decide whether private transport is more economical than public transport in the long run. The complexity has led Dahrendorf to become slightly more elitist in his ideas than he was before. Whereas men imbued with the warrior ethic would establish the open society without benefit of intellectuals, this is less true of post-modern man. Here

Dahrendorf has much in common with Daniel Bell. Centres for technology assessment need to be set up, with governments taking much greater interest in modern science (this is seen to be especially important by Dahrendorf, who feels that governments may, in ways unexpected by Bell, come to ignore modern science).[97]

At the European Commission, Dahrendorf set up a 'Europe plus Thirty' research organisation that could almost have been manned by Bell's own 'Commission on the Year 2000'; at the LSE he tried to establish a policy centre, able to provide the sorts of advice that governments need, and again one can imagine that Dahrendorf would willingly recruit a young Daniel Bell to such a centre. But there remains a difference. Dahrendorf's period in politics has led him to place a very great emphasis on people, like himself, who understand, as Weber stressed, that science and politics work on different ethics and to different deadlines. This group of 'straddlers is beginning to be large enough to develop its own consciousness'.[98] I think we can take this to mean that Dahrendorf's own ambitions, intellectually and politically, are far from fulfilled. If he and others like him are successful, Dahrendorf assures us that our future may yet be bright.

There is a still more important change between Dahrendorf's earlier and later work. As noted, Dahrendorf claims to be building on his earlier views. Thus the praise for a 'contract' in industrial relations 'develops' the earlier concern with the contract of society that was needed to give bounds to conflict and make it beneficial. Dahrendorf tries to make us believe that men will choose the new liberty because they feel so frustrated by the new bondage of social-democratic-inspired bureaucracy: men are, in other words, seen to be responding on the basis of their interests. I think that we should not be persuaded by Dahrendorf's pleas of continuity here. He does not really explain why the social democratic bloc is able to survive the social changes since Marx that he analysed.

In my view, an explanation is not at all hard to find. The changes in Western society have not established equal opportunity; life chances are, in other words, still structured unfairly, and Dahrendorf's perfectly accurate account of the contradictions of total participation cannot alter this fact. If this is so, then it may be possible to catch Dahrendorf with a type of Hobson's choice. On the one hand, if it is true—as I think it is—that men's values resonate with their experience, then there is no reason to expect a change of values that will leave social democracy and, much more important-ly, the social roots of inflation, out in the cold. Alternatively, Dahrendorf must accept that his programme depends upon changing his view of man in a remarkable way—advocating a change in men's values *against* their immediate experience. This would surely fuel the fires of those who claim that hatred shows hidden love; for such a change would amount to taking over Parsons, wholesale. Instead of the 'material consensus' offered earlier, Dahrendorf would then be advocating an 'ideal consensus'. As Dahrendorf's critique of Parsonian Platonism seems a powerful one, I regard this point as amounting to a criticism.

There are at least four other critical points that Dahrendorf will have to deal with if his post-modern theory is to seem more convincing. Firstly, the distinction between ligatures and options is—and this is a strange charge to bring against Dahrendorf—politically unusable. The affluent workers studied by Goldthorpe in the 1960s left craft jobs in order to increase their incomes, and Dahrendorf would no doubt consider this a move from ligature to option. But they made this move because they wanted the money to spend on their families; in other words, increased money allowed a development in a connection. Secondly, Dahrendorf seems to have lost his sense of social structure. Even if sociologists, students, intellectuals and media men are more or less aware of the contradictions of modernity other institutions and groups, most obviously trade unions, remain far more central. Dahrendorf thinks that change can come from such allies against both business and unions.[99] This is a fantasy.

Thirdly, we need to be very suspicious indeed of Dahrendorf's belief that economic growth is outmoded. It is true that he allows a place for controlled growth, but he nevertheless gives it a very secondary place indeed. This is a mistake for a whole host of reasons. Most obviously, to create the 'improving' society that Dahrendorf wishes requires money; ecologists, for example, are already aware that most conservation depends upon spending resources. And it is almost certainly the case that Hirsch's argument, recently made much of by Dahrendorf, to the effect that growth cannot extend some benefits since they are by definition scarce, should be taken with a pinch of salt. In Gershuny's words:

> Higher productivity and wider distribution of material goods is what growth is all about. Certainly, to the rich, this growth in material productivity means a double loss: they can no longer afford servants, and they must themselves work to provide their own services. And certainly the poor cannot expect, as a result of growth, to employ servants: but they can expect to enjoy services which they could not have done previously. The rich lose and the poor gain. A judgement of whether growth is a bad or a good thing depends on which side of the divide you stand.[100]

This point can be made more forcefully. Dahrendorf may be right in believing that a single cottage by a lake is a positional good (see page 149). But if we must have five cottages beside a lake, so be it, for a more general sharing of something still very desirable may be defended on many versions of the felicific calculus. But most importantly, growth has served as a solvent of social pressures, and I am sufficiently sceptical about the possibility of creating shared legitimation in non-authoritarian industrial societies to wish to see every effort made to revert to the easy path of increasing, to use the classic metaphor, the size of the cake. Of course, this may not be possible and this makes it very regrettable—finally—that Dahrendorf's proposed solutions are not, as he believes, very imaginative. This can be seen especially clearly in his use of Hirsch to argue that there are very strict limits on our political capabilities. It is perfectly true that Hirsch does make much of the nature of 'positional goods', but there is another more creative side to his analysis. This is, that we should try to use the market imaginatively; in particular we should try and dissociate status and wealth. As noted, this strategy may perhaps be inoperable, but it is far reaching, and something of such range may well yet be needed.

Conclusion

I have the greatest admiration for Dahrendorf's resolute championing of liberal values as a politician and in his work. In the latter, however, his hopes run some way ahead of his analysis: specifically, the constitution of liberty is harder to achieve than Dahrendorf thinks since men are not the warriors for freedom he led us to believe them to be. Although he is sceptical of some of Bell's post-industrialism theories, in the last analysis his thought overlaps, and does so increasingly, with that of the American. Both thinkers have always seen Western society as 'post-capitalist', and both now assert that the stability of that society depends upon a consensus of values. I have tried to argue that this analysis mis-describes our societies and is unlikely to lead to successful politics.

6 Raymond Aron

The Peloponnesian War of the Twentieth Century?

Only in 1970 at the age of sixty-five did Raymond Aron receive the highest accolade of French academic life, election to the Collège de France. The recognition probably took so long because Aron had very publicly and, given the character of French academia, bravely rejected the intellectual approach of his teachers. He explained in his inaugural lecture to the Collège how the events of the 1930s made the optimistic sociological determinism of the later Durkheimians seem naive. In one evocative passage he recalled that:

> Beginning in 1930 . . . . . I felt, almost physically, the approach of historical storms. *History is again on the move*, in the words of Arnold Toynbee. I am still marked by this experience, which inclined me toward an active pessimism. Once and for all, I ceased to believe that history automatically obeys the dictates of reason or the desires of men of good will. I lost faith and held on, not without effort, to hope. I discovered the enemy that I as well do not tire of pursuing—totalitarianism, an enemy no less insidious than Malthusianism. In any form of fanaticism, even one inspired by idealism, I suspect a new incarnation of the monster.
>
> The rise of National Socialism in pre-Hitler Germany and the revelation of politics in its diabolical essence forced me to argue against myself, against my intimate preferences; it inspired in me a sort of revolt against the instruction I had received at the university, against the spirituality of philosophers, and against the tendency of certain sociologists to misconstrue the impact of regimes with the pretext of focusing on permanent and deep realities. How superficial were parliamentary developments when Hitler's advent to power foreshadowed a world war! How secondary were economic mechanisms when the Great Depression, with its millions of unemployed, was prolonged because of mistakes that today's students, even before graduating in political economy, could easily discern. . . . The mood of my generation was ill-adapted to this attitude, both resigned and confident, and still susceptible to the positivism of Auguste Comte: the acceptance of social determinism, comparable to a natural determinism, and an ineradicable optimism concerning long-range outcomes.[1]

Aron is here referring to the period between 1930 and 1933 which he spent in Germany reading Kant and the neo-Kantians, and becoming acquainted with the *Geisteswissenschaften*, on the one hand,

and witnessing the first ceremonial Nazi book burnings on the other. It was no wonder that a Frenchman of Jewish origins should reject the optimism of his teachers and become a disciple of Max Weber, albeit, as we shall see, Aron tried to remain loyal to their liberal values. In 1938 he presented as his doctoral thesis *The Introduction to the Philosophy of History* which was meant, and was received, as an attack on the academic establishment.[2]

I have cited this conflict, the substance of which is examined below, for a simple reason: Aron is a thinker moulded by the historical events to which he remains a witness, and he has agonised long and hard over difficult questions of political choice. It would be easy to cite other events which have marked his biography: the period of exile in London during the war, at which time he edited *La France Libre* and so acquired his remarkable journalistic skills; the friendship with de Gaulle which gave him such a firm sense of the politically possible;[3] the debates with Sartre,[4] pre and post-war; the stand for Algerian independence;[5] and, most recently, the reasoned but firm criticism of the student movement of 1968.[6] However, it is not my intention here to write a biography of Aron; I think that the most appropriate way in which his engagement with our history can be seen is through describing the way in which he has come to see twentieth century European history. His analysis of that history is scattered throughout his work, but *The Century of Total War, Le Grande Schisme*[7] and *Penser la guerre, Clausewitz* (Vol 2)[8] contain the main lines of his analysis. The keynote of that analysis is simple: Europe in the twentieth century is held to have torn itself to pieces somewhat in the manner of Greece and Sparta in the Peloponnesian war.

The 'total wars' of twentieth century Europe began in 1914, and it is not surprising to find that Aron has devoted much attention to the origins of the First World War. It is perhaps best to begin by describing his rebuttal of the one theory that offers a relatively simple explanation of that war, namely that of the Marxists. Lenin's *Imperialism, the Highest Stage of Capitalism* suggested that the war was the inevitable result of the logic of capitalism. More particularly, the development of monopolies forced capitalist nations to find new markets through colonising Africa and India; the inability of each nation to gain its fair share in this imperialist venture created the pressure that eventually exploded in the European theatre. Rosa Luxembourg's argument differed from Lenin's only in stressing that imperialism resulted from the need to have new areas in which to invest excess capital.[9] Aron cannot accept either argument as an accurate account either of imperialism or of the origins of the First World War.

Aron does not dispute that arguments over empire had occurred, and notes that the rules of the European state system had been covertly broken in the case of Morocco in that Germany's position as a great power had not been duly recognised in tangible rewards.[10] But the acceptance of this and of many of the factors that Lenin noted (especially industrial concentration) does not lead Aron to the view that a European war was necessary. Most obviously, he considers that the Marxist theory fails to pay attention to obvious facts that do not fit its theory. The excess capital of France, for example, found outlets in South America and Russia quite easily. France was generally unwilling to invest significantly in the North African colonies, which were not a great source of profit. This does not surprise Aron who notes that the economic justification for colonialisation offered by Jules Ferry was necessary for a bourgeois democracy.[11] More importantly, Aron knows enough economics to disagree profoundly on Keynesian grounds with the Marxist insistence that capitalism's endemic over-production necessitated colonial expansion.

Aron clearly considers that there is no reason why capitalism cannot expand indefinitely through the growth of the home market, and he believes that this route has been followed since 1945. More particularly, Aron tries to refute the Marxist position by the banal, but obvious argument that capitalism is not dependent upon foreign markets secured through colonial conquest since decolonialisation has been associated with fantastic economic growth. This growth is dependent in very large part upon trade between advanced countries; thus Aron dismisses the newer notion that the Western world 'underdevelops' poor countries, although he is quite prepared to recognise that raw materials may be extracted from such countries in ways that obviously go against their interests.[12]

Aron is not content to simply rebut the Marxist theory; he offers us his own characterisation of imperialism in its place. Imperialism is judged to be essentially a political phenomenon. In a world in which states face each other in rivalry, a state can, according to Aron, entirely rationally judge the pursuit of prestige to be worthwhile and sensible. This explains why France, afraid of losing its status as a great power to Germany, took the scramble for Africa so seriously. Objective facts such as population decline should have encouraged a passive attitude on the part of the French, but these were overruled as a result of political calculation. And this political theory of imperialism explains the fact that politicians rather than capitalists set the pace for the scramble for Africa—in Germany and England as well as in France. This theory is magisterially invoked in Aron's recent analytic history of American involvement in Vietnam.[13]

The same essential characteristic of international relations—that states rival one another, and find war an acceptable form of behaviour—is used by Aron to explain the origins of the First World War. In a detailed account whose broad outline would probably gain endorsement from most historians, Aron describes the diplomatic manoeuvring that led to the war, placing some blame for hostilities on Germany and Austria.[14] But if Aron's argument is that the war itself was a normal phenomenon of inter-state relations, he wishes nevertheless to insist that its 'total' character represented something new. Two reasons are cited for the 'escalation to extremes' in the First World War. Firstly, the 'technical surprise' of industry applied to armaments meant that a very great escalation became almost inevitable. Politicians became the servants of the war effort and it was symbolic that Lloyd George moved from the Ministry of Munitions to take office as a Prime Minister with a brief for total war.[15]

Secondly, Aron has stressed that the progress of democracy tended to carry with it the insistence that adult males should serve their country militarily. This had been most obvious in France where the one clear lesson learned from the defeats of 1870 had been that Germany had triumphed, at least in part, because of conscription. Although conscription, in itself, meant an escalation of the conflict, Aron suggests that its impact had a deeper, hidden significance. The classic eighteenth century European wars had been fought over dynastic claims of one sort or another, and had often been resolved by the ceding of a minor piece of territory. Bismarck's wars had been essentially of the same type, according to Aron, but this style was already being regarded as old-fashioned. The fact that a whole nation now had to be mobilised to fight a war meant that war had to be justified in terms acceptable to the masses, that is, their suffering had to be justified.[16] The popular anger directed at Bismarck's restrained treatment of France in 1870 was a portent of the 'war for democracy' or 'war to end wars' of 1914–18.

Aron's explanation for the character of the First World War can be put in other terms. Total war was the consequence of the two major (and interrelated) factors of the modern age, namely industry and the entry of the people onto the political and social stage. Aron's argument is, then, that war, as it were, ran out of control. He has in mind here Clausewitz's final, trinitarian definition of war which he encapsulates thus:

> War, considered in its concrete totality, is composed of a strange trinity: the *original violence* of its element, the hatred and hostility that must be considered as a blind natural tendency; *the play of probabilities and chance* which make it a free activity of the soul; and the subordinate nature of a *political instrument* by which it belongs purely to the *understanding*. The first of these terms is related mainly to the people; the second, to the military commander (*Feldherr*) and the third, to the *government*.[17]

We shall hear more of this high valuation of leadership, and some assessment of the argument will be offered later. But Aron's thesis about the First World War is thus that politicians failed to exercise their function in the First World War, and allowed themselves to become appendages to an ill-defined war. This loss of control was almost inevitable, but Aron nevertheless considers that the politicians failed in their duty—in part because they succumbed to a false doctrine whereby peace could only be conceived as a result of destruction.[18] In particular, the Allied politicians in 1917 refused to take the risk of opening peace negotiations at a time when the intervention of America must have convinced them that victory would be theirs in the long run.

The consequences of war escalating to extremes beyond the control of politicians are held by Aron to be very great. Most obviously the Russian Revolution was made possible by the turmoil consequent on defeats at the Front. The implication of this is that revolutions depend on political circumstances quite as much as upon economic ones. And this point is generalised by Aron when arguing that the Revolution, made before Russia could be considered bourgeois, goes to prove that politics have a certain autonomy of their own:

> I should add that the most striking proof of the autonomy of the political order in relation to social conflicts is the Russian Revolution of 1917, when a group of men, by seizing the state as Louis Bonaparte did but more violently, was able to transform the entire structure of Russian society and even, if you will, to establish socialism, not on the basis of a minority proletariat but on the basis of the omnipotence of the state machine.[19]

However, as long as Russia was not an industrial power, state socialism mattered little to the balance of power. More immediately disastrous was the effect of the Versailles Treaty upon Germany. This made the terrible mistake of alienating Germany when it should have been realised that a strong Germany was necessary if a

European balance of power was to be achieved. This alienation was affected by making Germany admit to a war guilt which she did not feel. And perhaps equally important was the fact that normal Germans tended very naturally—if incorrectly[20]—to blame the Depression that came later upon the reparation clauses in the Treaty. In this way was Hitler given his cards, although Aron was quite prepared to admit that the democracies gave him every help in his manner of playing them.

Nazi Germany, for Aron, is partly a direct consequence of the way in which the First World War was conducted. But, in occasional essays describing how intelligible the regime appeared in the 1930s, Aron has pointed to three factors explaining the rise of fascism.[21] Firstly, Weimar democracy became 'corrupted' because of the inability of the parties to agree on a means of tackling the economic problem. Secondly, a considerable body of the population, especially state employees, felt that it would lose by a socialist revolution and so leaned heavily in an anti-communist direction. Thirdly, Aron notes that the success of fascism probably depends upon the aid of elements of the ruling class. In Germany this aid was symbolised by Von Papen, and it seems that Aron lays much of the blame for the success of Nazism on the irresponsibilities of the German aristocracy.

All these circumstances make the rise of a fascist demagogue comprehensible. But the character of fascism is fully revealed by its actions in power. Most immediately, fascism was able, as Hitler proved, to 'solve' the economic problem through state direction of public works. A corollary of this, in Aron's view, is that fascism naturally becomes imperialist: its fear of rival powers combines with central planning in the call for the conquest of areas which contain vital natural resources. Fascism is thus considered as imperialist and ideological, rather than nationalist, since its 'secular religion' gives it a sense of mission that makes it difficult for its leaders to survive without spectacular conquests. It was this sort of analysis that made Aron believe that war was inevitable the day Hitler came to power.

Aron observed the war from exile in London. This enforced inactivity drove him to reflect, in long articles in *La France Libre*,[22] on the extraordinary conflict between the two great twentieth-century revolutions, Nazism and Communism. Aron has recently insisted vehemently that disastrous misjudgements were made by the Americans at the end of the war that allowed Russia to solidify its share of the victory against Hitler into an empire in Eastern Europe. Roosevelt is harshly criticised for combining idealism about Russian intentions with an unwarranted view that the Western countries would retain their colonies.[23] The details of his account of the origins of the Cold War do not concern us. But the crux of his argument is clear: the war, and in particular the way in which it was conducted, was responsible for the spread of socialism to Eastern Europe. There was, in other words, no inevitable logic to history whereby this could have been predicted, and Aron is very harsh to those who write about Eastern Europe without a sufficient sense of the intangibility of the history involved.[24]

It was not immediately apparent to Aron on his return from England that 'total war' had led to 'the great divide' between East and West. For a year or two he co-operated in a mood of euphoria with Sartre and others on the left, and became a co-founder of *Les Temps Modernes*. But Aron soon began to argue that the division between East and West was fundamental, and that it was necessary to make one's choice for one or other version of industrial society.[25] Aron 'chose the West', and became an advocate of national reconstruction. It is important to point out here that he considered his position to be an essentially liberal one. He wrote polemics against both left and right, arguing that a progressive industrial society could be established which would allow the West to combine democracy with a measure of social justice. His justification for this position will be explained later, but the position as a whole can be characterised here. Despite deeply regretting the lessening of European influence as the result of its internal wars, Aron still holds fast to the hope that European liberal ideals will come to have great influence. It is for this reason that I have felt it appropriate to put a question-mark behind the heading to this section.

Aron is thus a very European thinker—although he has not, of course, ignored the patterns of development in the rest of the world. But underlying the chronicle of events are systematic themes in his thought. One reason for his studying and teaching in Germany in the early 1930s was to enable him to justify his own political beliefs. He insists that:

> This critique consisted, and still consists, of two elements: a comparison of the historical perspectives opened by the Marxism of Marx with the actual development of modern society; and an exploration of the relation between history and the historian, between society and the one who interprets it, between the historicity of collective institutions and that of the individual.[26]

The critique of Marxism has two parts to it that have been mentioned already, and which will be treated separately, below. Firstly, Aron's emphasis on the very considerable impact of inter-state rivalries implies a deeper criticism of Marx than has hitherto been considered. Historical evolution, he believes, seems to have as its end product nation states. This is immensely important since Marx saw, as Michael Mann has emphasised, both class and capital as transnational factors.[27] Aron's 'sociology of states' is thus designed to fill a gap in traditional social theory.

Secondly, Aron wishes to argue that the crucial characteristic of our age is that of industrialism, and that 'capitalism' and 'socialism' are best seen as alternative ways of making industrial societies work. Neither method is held to accord with Marx's expectations of them, and the difference between them is judged to rest on political rather than economic grounds. Significantly, Aron's critique of Marx cannot be separated from his views of man, and of proper sociological method. His arguments in this area are convoluted and cannot be easily summarised, but two intentions are clear: he refuses to accept (as Marx did in his cruder moments) that action is directed to the realisation of economic interests alone; and his awareness of the history of our time makes him wish to conceive social structure or system in looser terms than either Marx or the later Durkheimians.

Although the same themes run throughout all Aron's work, it is useful—heuristically—to introduce some distinctions. His sociology of states will be treated first, as this provides a concrete introduction to his very abstract views on man and method which are considered immediately afterwards. A discussion of his sociology of East and West follows the analysis of his conception of method.

Inter-State Rivalry

Aron's most systematic work, *Peace and War*, is over 800 pages long and one suspects that it is more quoted than read. The book is justly celebrated for its massive learning, range of historical reference and insistence on drawing necessary conceptual distinctions. If potential readers are put off the book it is because of these qualities, which is doubly unfortunate; for on the one hand there is no question that the book is valuable, but also—paradoxically—its basic idea is extremely simple. Aron sees himself as a descendant of Hobbes and Machiavelli in considering the prime characteristic of inter-state relations to be that they take place in a state of nature under no higher law. It is not surprising to find Hobbes being quoted approvingly:

> ...yet in all time Kings, and Persons of Soveraign authority, because of their independency, are in continuable jealousies, and in the state and posture of Gladiators; having their weapons pointing, and their eyes fixed on one another; that is, their Forts,

Garrisons, and Guns, upon the Frontiers of their Kingdoms; and continuable Spyes upon their neighbours; which is a posture of war...[28]

In other words, states, jealously guard their independence and regard the resort to war as a natural option always open to them.

It is, of course, the case that many thinkers—among them Hobbes, Sartre, Pareto—have claimed that violence dominates every sphere of life or, more precisely, dominates the inside of states quite as much as their external behaviour. Aron is deeply opposed to this idea. A society is something which at best can allow a community to participate in some conception of the good life; socialisation into such an entity is to be profoundly welcomed since it represents, simply, the chance of civilisation. Aron has made this point very forcefully, recently, in a criticism of the theory of Pierre Bourdieu that socialisation itself is a form of 'symbolic violence':

> A curious vocabulary because it no longer enables one to distinguish between different modes of socialisation: on the one hand, the inevitable and diffuse *influence* on individuals of the social group which tends to reproduce itself, on the other hand, *constraint* which presupposes resistance, whether conscious or not, on the part of those who feel the pressure of social milieu and authority. Violence only retains a specific meaning when it designates a relationship between men which comprises the use of physical force or the threat to use physical force.[29]

This is a very typical passage and shows Aron's high valuation of the duties due to the societies which give men their very humanity. The absence of this common socialisation defines the character of international relations.

The basic argument of the book, then, sees war as a normal state of affairs given the independence of separate states. But one other point must be grasped for the character of Aron's work in this and in other areas to be appreciated. Aron chooses as a legend to his book the observation of Montesquieu that:

> International law is based by nature upon this principle: that the various nations ought to do, in peace, the most good to each other and, in war, the least harm possible, without detriment to their genuine interests.[30]

This might seek a very paradoxical statement given Aron's general realism but it is characteristic of his thought in two ways. Firstly, Aron's rejection of sociological determinism was not so complete that he rejected liberal values. So his thought constantly oscillates between his hopes and his awareness of reality. It is, of course very much to his credit that the two virtually never intermingle—that Aron does not declare that the cunning of reason will in some mysterious manner realise the world he desires.

In the second place, he wishes to argue that the observation of the maxim is in the long term interest of states themselves. He makes this especially clear when discussing Clausewitz, demonstrating that Clausewitz's early admiration for the 'total' war waged by Napoleon, i.e. an admiration for war seen as the maximising of power at all costs, became more and more circumscribed. In particular, Clausewitz realised that the blind ascension to extremes practised by Napoleon had, in the end, accomplished less than Frederick the Great's calculated and limited wars, which had been small enough to avoid a general alliance against him. Aron even suggests that more time might have allowed Clausewitz to have finally chosen between Napoleon and Frederick, the two war leaders he so greatly admired. Had he done so, Aron argues, he might not have been misinterpreted in Germany as an advocate of total war at all costs, a doctrine which, as we have seen, falsely elevated military leaders above politicians:

> Had death not prevented Clausewitz from elaborating his thesis on the two types of war...perhaps instead of interpreting Frederick II's strategy in the light of Buonaparte's, the German command would have recognised Frederick's true greatness in the light of Napoleon's catastrophic defeat.[31]

Aron's own sociology of international relations attempts to perform a similar task to Clausewitz's for modern conditions. The weapons of war are now capable of destruction on a vast scale, and the central fact of international relations is the opposition between two powers which represent different principles. In these circumstances, what chance is there for the observance of Montesquieu's maxim? Aron's answer is Clausewitzian in spirit. It depends upon four kinds of analysis, those of theory, sociology, history and praxeology—in other words, a necessary conceptual language, social forces, history and arguments as to what should be done. Aron's analysis of each of these is lengthy and discriminating, but some conception of his argument can be given.

Aron insists that international relations cannot produce anything like a closed field of study and that, consequently, it is foolish to expect finality from anything that is dubbed theoretical. This is true to some extent in economics, where no theory can legislate whether we should maximise at the moment or restrain ourselves in favour of future generations. But Aron argues that the area of uncertainty is very much smaller in economics as a result of the considerable sway that a single objective, the maximisation of economic resources, has over behaviour. International relations theory cannot be anything like as closed as this because no single aim can be ascribed to state behaviour. This essential equivocacy evident in reality underlies Aron's criticisms of two theories that falsely ascribe to inter-state behaviour a single aim. The first of these suggests that states act in the national interest. The weakness of this theory is its vacuousness, as national interest can be defined in different ways:

> ...whatever the diplomacy of a state may be, nothing prevents one from asserting after the fact that it was dictated by considerations of 'national interest', as long as 'national interest' has not been strictly defined.
> Indeed, the so-called theory of 'national interest' either suggests an idea as undeniable as it is vague—that each actor thinks first of itself—or else tries to oppose itself to other pseudo-theories, for example that the foreign policy of states is dictated by political ideology or moral principles. Each of these pseudo-theories means something only in connection with the other. To say that the Soviet Union conducts its foreign affairs on the basis of its 'national interest' means that it is not guided exclusively by ideological consideration, by its ambition to spread Communism. Such a proposition is undeniable, but to conclude from it that the rulers of a non-Communist Russia would have had the same diplomatic policy between 1917 and 1967 is simply absurd. The purpose of the empirical study of international relations consists precisely in determining the historical perceptions that control the behaviour of collective actors and the decisions of the rulers of these actors.[32]

The second pseudo-theory that Aron himself has remorselessly criticised, as we shall see, is related to this in that it argues that states are concerned to maximise only one end, namely, their power. Aron's initial objection to this is simply that power is a means, which may or may not be embraced, towards different objectives which can include a simple search for independent glory, for empire or for the sway of an ideology. The second objection to this pseudo-theory is that it leads to a false praxis which fails to take account of historical specificity. The failure on the part of American strategic thinking over Vietnam will be illustrated in a moment, but it can be stressed here that Aron objects on the general grounds that the falsely rationalist definition of 'the search for power' tends to suggest, against Clausewitz, that peace is but an interruption to wars and not the aim and end of war.

The purpose of Aron's theory now becomes obvious. The fact that certainty is impossible does not mean that we cannot have the conceptual tools necessary to 'think war' in all its diversity. This Kantian search for the proper conceptual apparatus was most fully undertaken by Clausewitz, the freshness of whose *On War* can be seen, in part with the aid of Aron's own recent commentary. Aron's conceptual tools in *Peace and War* might well have been sharper if he had at that time known Clausewitz better. This is especially true of the definition of war; his book would have had greater impact had Aron been more familiar with Clausewitz's trinitarian definition of war. As it is, Aron bases his concepts around the simpler definition of war as a 'continuation of politics by other means'. This allows him to introduce the figures of strategist and diplomatist, and to characterise force as a means of foreign policy. To this, Aron adds that international systems can be bipolar, as today, or multipolar, as in the eighteenth century; and this variable must be considered in relationship with another, namely that of the heterogeneity or homogeneity of culture of the states involved. All these factors lead to a certain rapport of forces between the contending states. This in itself would lead to re-emphasising that the management of strategic relations is more of an art than a science, something in which Aron has come to follow Clausewitz closely. The number of factors involved in a duel between opponents means that rigid calculation is beyond scientific powers; as in chess, judgement alone can be taught and this remains capable of beating chess computers.[33]

Aron attempts his own demonstration of the essential uncertainty involved in international affairs in one of the key chapters of the book that deals with the goals of foreign politics. Here he shows that states can choose goals that go beyond mere security, and, characteristically, emphasises that such choices, given the intentional state of anarchy, are felt to be, and often indeed are, sensible and rational. A clear example of the dangers of mere security was experienced by Aron himself, when France refused to consider military action against Hitler when he occupied the Rhineland. The search for security at all costs proved self-defeating.[34] And Aron goes further in adding an essential indeterminacy, namely that states sometimes choose to participate in power for its own sake, and so prefer to take risks rather than to lead a secure and peaceful life:

> Even the desire for revenge is not more irrational than the will to power. Political units are in competition: the satisfactions of *amour-propre*, victory or prestige, are no less real than the so-called material satisfactions, such as the gain of a province or a population.
>
> Not only are the historical objectives of political units not deducible from the relation of forces, but the ultimate objectives of such units are legitimately equivocal. Security, power, glory, idea are essentially heterogenous objectives which can be reduced to a

single term only by distorting the human meaning of diplomatic-strategic action. If the rivalry of states is comparable to a game, what is 'at stake' cannot be designated by a single concept, valid for all civilisations at all periods. Diplomacy is a game in which the players sometimes risk losing their lives, sometimes prefer victory itself to the advantages that would result from it.[35]

One apposite example of this has been offered by Aron very recently. Where Western nations abandoned their colonies when they became more expensive than they were worth, Aron insists that Russia has retained her interest in Eastern Europe although in the process she is damaging her own standard of living.[36]

The conceptual tools offered by Aron help us to 'think' war in any society. But Aron of course is aware that social circumstances change the character of war, and we have already noted his arguments about industry and the participation of the people. However, in his section on sociology Aron wishes to examine whether there are any fixed social determinants of war the removal of which would allow us to hope for a reign of peace. Aron's thought on this matter is particularly rich; he rejects social factors as universal determinants, but recognises that such factors can be the cause of particular wars and can certainly change its character.

Aron has no difficulty in dismissing three material factors often considered as determinants of war. The first is that the search for space, or the character of space possessed, exercises a profound influence on war. This theory is perhaps a peculiarly French one, and it is treated kindly, possibly out of respect for Montesquieu. But Aron's conclusion is characteristic: space provides a circumstance to which men must react, but there is no certainty that they will react in the same manner. Poor soil can depress, but can also encourage, trade; and, another example, the hills around the Mediterranean Basin have produced dissimilar cultures. A second social factor often considered as a determinant is population. Whilst Aron is quick to note that overpopulation can provide an all too rational excuse for war, he nevertheless insists that not all wars are due to population factors. The French empire, for example, was gained at a time when the population was actually falling.

The third factor stresses economics. This interests Aron the most since it is the Marxist view. In 'War and Industrial Society', Aron makes clear that industrialism, for the first time, makes many wars not obviously rational since sufficient welfare can be created without them. But the burden of his realism nevertheless made him observe in his usual banal but forceful way that the actual effect of industry has simply been to escalate the size of conflicts. There is no evidence, pace Comte, Veblen and Schumpeter, that industrial societies are less belligerent than military societies,[37] but, as we have seen, Aron rejects the argument that capitalism inexorably leads to imperialism and conquest.

The most important chapter concerned with specifically social causes examines whether the quality of regimes and the fact of nationalism can be considered as causes of war. Aron's thought constantly oscillates on the question of how important is the type of regime in certain circumstances. There is no doubt in his mind that the shared faith of the Soviet Union and China made the split between them especially venomous; but the split itself does not surprise him given the natural rivalry between states. Similarly, Aron is prepared to admit that the conflict between Russia and America is exacerbated by heterogeneity, but he seems increasingly drawn to the view that the more fundamental cause of the conflict is again the sheer fact of rivalry.[38] Aron's position in regard to nationalism is much more tolerant, as we might expect in view of his high valuation of a national society as the potential bearer of a specific way of life. He is well aware that nationalism proceeds hand in hand with industrialism, and he specifically points out that an educated native minority will try to wage anti-colonial wars:

> It is an irony of history, but an intelligible one, that Algerians who had received a French education headed the nationalist move-ment, just as it was those about to become French who were the ones who wished most to remain Algerian. This is readily explained; they understood that they were the victims of an inferior status imposed upon them by the French minority, and they had everything to gain by establishing a state in which they would become part of the ruling group by virtue of the removal of French competitors with comparable training.[39]

The national principle will, Aron adds, very likely lead to further wars designed to keep together states artificially drawn up by colonisers. But he does not consider that the fact of increased numbers of states is itself responsible for burgeoning hatred and war. The First World War was not inevitable, while the Second War had an imperialist and ideological character rather than a national one. Moreover, Aron argues that the course of realism is to learn to deal with nation states since he sees no evidence that national collectivities are losing their hold over the loyalty of their citizens.

Social facts condition but do not determine war. Consequently, it becomes necessary to consider the particular historical diversity of diplomatic-strategic conduct in the contemporary world. His analysis centres on the superpowers and their relations with the

Third World, and something can be said about his views in both areas. The concept of superpower arises from the destructive capability possessed by only two states. The necessity for a second strike capacity means that an effective nuclear force is at present beyond small powers. Aron accepts the force of the American strategists' argument that small powers seeking to have a nuclear force are unreasonable as they could inflict little damage unless they strike first, and they thereby court the possibility of prior total destruction; but he does not consider such action absolutely irrational since there is a type of 'nuclear illusion' which gives prestige to any state with such weapons.[40] Aron's main interest, however, is in American nuclear strategy.

The Great Debate chronicles how the horror at the doctrine of total reprisals led to the development of sophisticated nuclear strategy modelled on the theory of games. The basic argument was that a series of steps should be placed between regular war and total reprisal each of which should be taken in turn; this slow escalation would allow stakes to be publicised and mistakes to be avoided. The most immediate impact of this policy was to insist that the traditional NATO army be sufficiently strong to fight a long delaying action either to avoid defeat or to give contestants time to signal to each other their exact intentions. This strategy undoubtedly met with some approval with Aron who has nevertheless always been careful to point out that there is no certainty that the strategy has been adopted by the Russians. But insofar as nuclear war has been avoided, he feels it right to talk of the superpowers as 'enemy partners',[41] at the same time noting ambiguities in the American theory both in theoretical and practical terms.

The theoretical ambiguity is one that Aron thinks cannot be solved. Basically, this is that there exists a contradiction between, on the one hand, a taboo on any nuclear war ever and, on the other, the expectation that the possibility of war will act as a deterrent. It is this that makes him understand the fears of Europe far more than do American strategists. Germany's fear that America might not actually launch a nuclear attack on behalf of Berlin that would put all its own cities at risk is all too comprehensible. More importantly, Aron is aware that European powers are none too happy at the prospect of being involved in an American nuclear war that they cannot control. It is probably because he shares these views that he has always been a firm proponent of independent European defence.

The event that convinced Aron of the necessity of 'steps' of traditional war *inside* a nuclear world was Korea. The simple fact of a near nuclear monopoly did not cow China or the Soviet Union.

This was, however, a traditional war fought for most of the time for limited purposes, and not equivalent to a direct confrontation between the superpowers. The Cuban Missile Crisis, in contrast, was a direct confrontation, and Aron initially accepted the American argument that the strategy of escalation had proved its worth. He is no longer sure of this, however, and prefers now to suggest that Russia was deterred much less by the possibility of nuclear war than by the massive traditional forces that America would have been able to bring to bear on Cuba.[42]

Aron presents no clear conclusions about the strategic relations between the superpowers. He has claimed that he never totally believed in the likelihood of massive retaliation but neither does he completely accept the optimistic view that nuclear was is now impossible.[43] He does seem to place some faith in the fact of a nuclear taboo, and has recently become almost optimistic, given the possibilities of satellite observation, about armaments control.[44] But he stresses that the issue is an open one that depends upon human vigilance. More particularly, he considers the successful situation one that is a 'wager upon reason'; as always, he argues for reason but is constantly aware of its fragility.

One of the most curious facts about the creation of superpowers is that the very size of the means of destruction has made it difficult to control the developing world. This can be seen in the case of, say, Egypt, which is prepared to bargain with both major powers for maximum advantage. The inability to control allies is also apparent in America's failure to prevent India fighting Pakistan, and so establishing the new nation of Bangladesh. This war is judged by Aron to have been a classical one in that it was waged with all available means (unlike Korea, where America felt unable to use all its means and came to realise that the preservation of the status quo was an appropriate political aim). Aron has considerable praise for Mrs Gandhi's handling of the war. He argues moreover that the war probably prevented greater killing and that an accurate calculation was made between forces available and the goal to be achieved. His views in this matter contrast strongly with his sad analysis of the Middle East situation. In 1967 Aron instantly realised that the classical victory of Israeli arms meant little:

> Israel could have lost the shooting war, she cannot win it. She has won *a* military victory, but not *the* victory. A State of two and a half million inhabitants has not got the wherewithal to force the Arab countries as a whole to capitulate. She has destroyed two armies, but she has not destroyed either the States or the populations against which she was fighting.

This lack of symmetry partly explains the course of events; it also contains lessons for the future. Whether in the short or the long term, the only true victory for Israel would be peace.[45]

Another element of Aron's understanding of relationships with the developing world can be seen in his conception of praxeology. In the last fifteen years he has become a harsh critic of the mechanical, and thus false, conception of theory that guided American practice, archetypically in Vietnam. His very impressive analysis of the Vietnam débâcle stresses that the Americans made the fearful mistake of trying to treat the Vietnamese situation under the aegis of a strategic theory designed to deal with a superpower. But no theory can take the place of examining local geographical and physical conditions; the failure to do so in this case led to the sending of the wrong sort of army and—crucially—to a lack of awareness that the 'stake' involved was not perceived in similar terms on both sides. The ability of the Vietcong to endure bombing attacks has led many to declare that America had to lose the war as it was, in its essence, a war of liberation. Aron refuses such outright conclusions and prefers to think that the war was lost basically through mistakes. The Vietcong were 'partisans of a regime' rather than 'national liberators', and the Americans, had they been wise, might have been able to create national feeling in South Vietnam as they did in South Korea. The guerilla wars of this century do not, contrary to popular opinion, tell us of the inevitability of victory for guerillas. Indeed, in an interesting recent aside, Aron has argued that the Cuban revolution is very much the exception to the rule in South America, and that no inevitable link between revolution and peasantries exists.[46]

Another point that needs to be stressed about Aron's conception of praxeology is its firmly statist character. Two related points are at issue here. Firstly, Aron places his hopes on political leaders becoming sufficiently wise to act as the 'personified intelligence of the state'.[47] This is not, of course, to say that he believes political leaders always do act in this manner, and he has been particularly critical of the tendency of American foreign policy to veer between widely differing alternatives.[48] Naturally there is a whole literature on the making of foreign policy, and I would not wish to rule out of court the arguments of those, for example, who demand less secrecy in foreign policy so that 'special interests' may be properly controlled; nevertheless, Aron puts up a formidable case for his position. He convinces both in his demonstration that imperialism is in essence a political phenomenon, i.e. not the product of the capitalist interest, and in his insistence that leaders control the masses. He insists upon the latter point not just because of the 'hatred' engendered by war—although in this matter Aron, unlike Bell, has both evidence and plausibility on his side—but also as a result of the sheer complexity of nuclear strategy ruling out participation in foreign policy.

The second point to be made here—and more important for Aron—is the question of the continuation of states themselves. In an exceptionally lucid and striking analysis of the Marxist (especially Maoist) hope that a transnational struggle between classes will take the place of inter-state rivalry, Aron makes clear his belief that nation states in fact offer us the greatest chance of peace. He rejects the Marxist position since he believes that it would encourage an endless war of partisans. Similarly he refuses, after long and careful deliberation, to place his hopes in the emergence of any new world organisation capable of outlawing war. The impracticality of such organisations strikes him forcefully, but ultimately he does not embrace this position because his own experience has overwhelmingly convinced him that wars can still be just:

> Tomorrow, other men will live by different passions. French, of Jewish origin, how could I forget that France owes her liberation to the strength of her allies, Israel her existence to her arms, a chance of survival to her resolve, and to the resolve of the Americans to fight, if need be.
>
> Before feeling guilty, I will wait until a tribunal decides who, between the Israelis and the Palestinians, has the proper claim to the land which is holy for the three religions of the Book.[49]

Between Hedgehog and Fox

The *Introduction to the Philosophy of History* is directed against 'the great systems of the beginning of the nineteenth century, so discredited today',[50] and it was taken by many contemporaries, rightly, as a defence of history in the face of over-confident sociological determinism. This defence of history, resulting from contingency, makes Aron, in the famous words of Sir Isaiah Berlin, a fox. But it is important to realise that he is a reluctant fox, and that the book is written against his immediate intellectual background. That background might well have made him a hedgehog along the lines of his teacher, Brunschvig, whose books analysed the progress of reason in the West in Kantian guise. There is, in other words, a tension at the heart of Aron's philosophy that we have already encountered in the conflict between his realism and his hopes. This tension can be seen most obviously, here, in the fact that Aron gives, not always clearly, two meanings to 'history'. On the one hand, history is the recording of facts and so the record of contingency. But on the other hand, Aron suggests that history is *our* history, and that it can become constitutive of its own object.

As noted, Aron's writing in this area is exceptionally complicated and convoluted. Consequently, in the interests of clarity, I will first describe the formal, methodological arguments that he offers. The abstractness of these can, however, be alleviated by—secondly—highlighting the view of history at work in Aron's analysis. Aron's formal argument is presented as a phenomenology, and is thus at times difficult to understand—a difficulty compounded by the feeling that certain passages represent a private dialogue with Sartre. Nevertheless, the main purpose of his argument is clear. His indebtedness to the *Geisteswissenschaften* is seen clearly in his insistence that historical reason, and therefore sociology, cannot be objective in the same sense as natural science. He might have embraced Dilthey and Heidegger so completely as to argue that a separate historical reason was appropriate for the moral sciences; this extreme position is, however, not taken up and Aron seeks a middle way between scientism and pure hermeneutics. He attempts this by arguing that interpretative and causal analysis are both necessary and partially flawed; a final section, 'History and Truth', attempts, in very Hegelian manner, to offer some sort of synthesis.

Interpretative sociology is held to be necessary for the standard reason that men possess consciousness and are thus different in kind from inert atoms. Aron begins his analysis of the effect this has on historical reason in Sartrean style by asking how the individual ego understands his own past action. Understanding is held to be difficult even here, since one can never be sure that former actions are not being seen in the light of present circumstances. What in fact the individual does is to reconstruct what his past motives must have been, and it is such a process of rational reconstruction that Aron believes the historian or sociologist must undertake. This understanding of others presents certain difficulties. The main problem considered is that the intentionality of the other is not the subject of any sort of memory; the reconstruction cannot be based on empathy but must instead be more of the character of a Freudian-style imputation of probable motive. This is balanced, however, by two considerations that help the investigator. The first advantage is that:

> The historian, as distinguished from the contemporary, knows the whole of the individual life. What might have become of the individual he definitely does not know. But he knows completely what he did do.[51]

Secondly, Aron knew Durkheim too well to conceive of the individual as socially isolated. However, he chooses to emphasise the presence of an 'objective mind' by making use of the work of Schutz:

> One fact is for us fundamental: the common feeling created in each individual by the priority of the objective mind over the individual mind is the historically and concretely primary datum. Men arrive at consciousness by assimilating, unconsciously, a certain way of thinking, judging, and feeling which belongs to an epoch and which characterises a nation or a class.[52]

This position has led others to Platonism. Aron refuses to go so far since he considers that 'the objective mind is multiple, incoherent, without definite unity or certain limits'.[53] It is presumably this that allows him to note that:

> In historical movements it is true that individuals, cut adrift from their habits, become subject again to the most varying impulses, to the call of prophets, to the suggestions of propaganda rather than to the calculations of self-interest.[54]

In other words, Aron is saying that the theory of action he proposes—for that is what rational reconstruction amounts to—must be based on a realisation that men's interests are more than economic. This makes him especially resistant to the notion of determinism. He insists that any visible pattern perceived by the historian could be the result of a consciously-taken decision. We do not imagine our own future as completely determined, and we would therefore falsify the position if we presumed that historical actors were so determined. The view of men acting in history is symbolised for him by a battle:

> A battle has the same structure as history in its totality. Made up at once of reasonable intentions, unpredictable encounters, and material forces, it appears by turns intelligible, like human behaviour or work, and absurd or at least determined like the stone's falling or the struggle between animals. It is understandable or not, depending on the level from which it is viewed. The incoherence of individual motions is followed—thanks to the discipline of the troops or the perspective of the observer—by the ordered vision of the commander or of the historian. But these events, already organised, do not steadily unfold according to a plan; accidents still occur, and in the final analysis men meet in combat, and courage, material means, or Fortune decide the outcome. Of course there is still a logic at this level. But at times order dissolves into chaos, panic seizes the crowd. And one wonders whether the microscopic facts and accidents, overlooked in favour of the overall pattern, do not constitute the true and effective reality.[55]

Aron thus considers that the historian must often give an

'ideal-typical' coherence to random events. This position leads him to follow Weber in arguing that reality is so rich as to allow for a 'plurality of interpretations' by which we approach it. Aron offers three glosses on this, the first directed against Weberian views that evaluation need play no part in social science. Aron characterises the position thus:

> Every event, even spiritual, would in the last analysis be of a psychological nature, and history would forbid itself any appreciation, either moral or aesthetic, and would attain a universally valid truth. One would establish the causes of a work of art provided that no attention be paid to its beauty.[56]

Aron considers this silly: the ideas of Kant are worth studying whilst many others are not, especially as Kant's ideas have had a great historical impact. Morever, to pretend to proceed without some understanding of value would be senseless, as it might lead to denying one obvious character of social reality, namely that men *do* value particular ideas or phenomena. Aron's remaining two glosses on the 'plurality of interpretations' argument are designed to resist attempts to make the consequences of this seem less serious. For example, Dilthey in his later work suggested that social *science* might be based on a powerful psychology. Aron doubts whether this can make much difference in the past since there is no way in which the paucity of information can be increased.

More importantly, however, he notes that most action depends upon mundane motives that are easily comprehensible; consequently, a cognitively powerful psychology could teach us little. Finally, Aron notes that an attempt to undermine the plurality of interpretations is unwittingly contained in Weber's suggestion that the actual conduct of an investigation can be objective, although the selection of subject matter is 'value-relevant'. Aron considers this view unduly optimistic as he believes that any value-relevance involved is likely to translate itself into the manner in which a piece of research is done.[57] This absolute endorsement of the 'plurality of interpretations' does not mean, as we shall see, that Aron is unaware of some of the dangerous consequences of this essentially relativistic epistemology.

In the 1930s many thinkers shared Aron's distrust of universal systems which blithely ignored the true nature of the political: that men choose to live by different gods. But where an Isaiah Berlin could rest content with this discovery, Aron's sense of reality was sufficiently strong to lead him to ask about causal processes as well. We have already seen that he considers causal factors important, but not determining, in international relations and his argument here seeks to establish this. Once again he makes good use of Max Weber. Firstly, he endorses Weber by arguing that the historical or sociological investigator need not necessarily involve himself in a naive sociologism which ignores the specificity of events. Aron suggests that Weber describes correct historical procedure when he insists that a sense of social structure is necessary for the historian; for the historian can only describe an action as responsible for an event if he has sufficient sense of structure to argue that it made a crucial difference.[58] The historian is thus permanently engaged in constructing a series of 'might have beens' in order to understand what did happen.

In the second place, Aron keenly embraces Weber's idea of elective affinities between situation and action since this covering phrase neatly conveys his own views that men are not passive dopes but are engaged in a creative response to circumstances. This in itself scarcely solves any problems, and it is not surprising to find that Aron's formulations are abstract and vague:

> Common sense suggests—and reflection confirms—that the margin of uncertainty is neither always fixed, nor always unlimited. Of course, in all periods certain eventualities are excluded; there is no retrogression from big industry to craftsmanship, and political power shows the force of certain features to which submission is inevitable. In this sense it can be said that there are limits within which Fortune rules, but those limits are vague and indeterminate. One could not say, from the outset, that chance events play no other role than to speed up or slow down an immutable fate spelled out in advance. In times of crisis it seems that possibilities multiply, each quite different from the others....[59]

Aron is arguing, in other words, that faced with an objective situation men respond in ways that make sense to them; and this necessitates diversity since the gamut of human response is, as we have already seen in the goals aimed at in state policy, so very large. The generality of his statement should not surprise us as it is a call to get on with understanding social reality.

Aron offers us very subtle readings of Durkheim and Marx on the basis of this general approach. His most immediate criticism of Durkheim is that he does not actually describe the method he uses in his empirical work. Thus Aron considers that Durkheim did, despite himself, engage in interpretative sociology, and believes that this can be seen in the typology of suicides Durkheim proposed.[60] He also dismisses Durkheim's claim to have provided complete causal explanations. Aron accepts that Durkeim offers a sensible analysis of why men respond to certain circumstances by suicide, but argues that his account overrates itself when it talks of 'suicidogenic currents'.[61] And Aron's very subtle reading of the relations of superstructure and substructure lead him to seek to reduce the 'absolute' quality of causal explanation often implied by Marxism:

> But whatever the starting point, the conclusions are negative rather than positive: a given economic system excludes a given political regime (for example, a planned economy excludes formal democracy) or else the conclusions are stated in terms of trends: a given economy favours a certain type of government. In proportion as one reaches out for more distant phenomena, the tendencies become more vague.[62]

The first two sections of Aron's work suggest, then, that both understanding and cause are flawed in themselves, but that the two must be combined in analysing the social world. This is essentially unexceptionable, although the manner in which Aron avoids the extremes of either pole is impressive. But Aron is aware that his acceptance of the 'plurality of positions' might seem to lead to relativism. He states the problem in a way which leaves no doubt of his own dislike of relativism:

> Neither the discovery of the primitive, nor of other cultures, aroused scepticism or anarchy so long as the normative, normal so to speak, significance of contemporary society was maintained. The crisis which is shaking the foundations of our civilisation is more formidable than the empirical investigation. Evolutionism became historism on the day when the two values on which the confidence of the nineteenth century, positivist science and democracy—that is, basically, rationalism—lost their prestige and authority.
> Irrationalism brought on pessimism. History has no goal since man has no destination and since he is always the same and vainly creates ephemeral works.[63]

Aron naturally rejects this. Most immediately he argues that human reflection on the meaning of life, and therefore the study of history, is a universal attribute of man. In this spirit he notes that logical thought is universal although some societies may not yet have embraced it:

> But when we submit ourselves to the rules of truth, the results at which we arrive are universally imperative. In a different but comparable way, reflection, logically, does not express the imprisoned consciousness, and claims universality. For example, reflection on the conditions under which we know history is not essentially relative.[64]

More importantly, however, Aron argues that men may come to

learn from their history. His language here is exceptionally difficult to follow, but we can disentangle his arguments once we realise that they are directed against Sartre. In a fascinating passage he suggests that the ethical position to be derived from his work is one that calls for a type of reasoned commitment:

> Fidelity could not consist of feigning sentiments which no longer exist. Even lasting love is not fixed. One follows its inevitable development as soon as one has the courage to observe the true experiences instead of clinging to words or to a complacent representation of oneself. Not that it is reduced to the rare moments when one experiences its reality (between these moments there still exists the receptivity to joy or pain), but it would decompose into attitudes and contradictory impressions unless the will upheld the actual unity of it. When the affections have died out, one can still show by one's conduct that one has neither forgotten nor repudiated. Between the sincerity which desires instability and the constancy of obstinacy or blindness, there is still room for the double effort of sincerity and genuiness.[65]

Aron clearly objects to a Sartrean-style doctrine where free decisions could lead to acting simply at the behest of passion; he seems to suggest that man learns from his history in so far as he exerts his willpower:

> Because he is at once both brute and spirit, man must be capable of overcoming minor fatalities, those of the passions by willpower, that of blind impulse by consciousness, that of vague thought by decision. In this way, freedom at each instant, puts everything at stake again, and asserts itself in action in which man is reunited with himself.[66]

Aron has recently dubbed his general argument 'ontic' rather than 'ontological'; the crucial meaning of this is that man is seen to be inevitably limited by his social being and his place in time. Aron places his hope on the growing mastery of the passions in international relations as much as in morality, but he does not think that any such growth can somehow remove the fact that man's consciousness is not pure, but historical. Aron's whole methodology is one that insists on reconstructing the actor's intelligible motives, and it is consequently one that argues for tolerance in social life:

> As long as there remains room for discussion, it is better, indeed, to remember that no humanity is possible without tolerance, and that the possession of total truth is granted to no one. But it is enough that there should come extreme situations, wars or revolutions, for wisdom to become powerless and for the fundamental disagreement again to arise. As his historical task, man must assume the risk which for him carries everything with it.[67]

In the aftermath of the war, for example, he was completely at odds with extensive reprisals against collaborators since he was aware—as he has recently stressed in a very moving analysis—how comprehensible it must have been for many to choose to support Pétain's government.[68] His views are perhaps most fully expressed in his careful and subtle analysis of Sartre's *Critique of Dialectical Reason*. Here, he argues that 'understanding' should not be so exaggerated as to suggest that only a special 'dialectical' reason based somehow on the ontology of freedom can comprehend social life. Aron rejects this since he feels that Sartre's phenomenology of consciousness is mistaken:

> I have quite another experience that I too call freedom. Each of us is born with his chromosome heritage and into the family milieu that is already half-determined or is being half-determined before we reach a thetic self-consciousness. I put the effort of liberation not in the spontaneity of the pure for-itself but in the reflective decision, taken on the basis of a me-object who is and is not *I*, and of whom I am not the unconditional master.[69]

Aron argues, interestingly, that the combination of ontological freedom and ignorance of social conditions leads—as in some of Sartre's comments on colonisers—to a call for 'commitment' that is (and this no light charge on Aron's part) akin to the fascist emphasis on will.[70] It is better, we are told, to choose a more tolerant way that accepts that men make their decisions with imperfect knowledge and in situations not entirely of their own choosing.

These methodological views of Aron's have not changed very greatly since 1938. For example, his discovery that a facile relativism can result from a total and automatic endorsement of the 'plurality of positions' argument has not led him to abandon epistemological relativism but only to insist that rigorous argument concerning the selection of facts and the nature of definitions can help to ensure that relativism is a last, rather than a first, resort.[71] But rather than examine in detail the way in which Aron tries to illustrate this distinction, we can turn instead to some comments on his view of history.

The starting point of Aron's reflections was a strong dislike for naive and optimistic Durkheimian or Marxist determinism. One criticism of these views was examined in the previous section. This was that inter-state relations take place in an open rather than a closed system, and thus inevitably involve an element of uncertainty. This does not mean that Aron is unable to offer us interesting generalisations about the place of man and its effects in the world today but rather that it is always dangerous to talk of a rational logic to social life since wars can upset the best laid plans. Another argument against naive social determinism is present in Aron's careful analysis of the concept of social structure. The burden of this analysis is that while, for example, a particular form of production may rule out certain possibilities, it does not rule out all of them. There is, in other words, considerable freedom left for various options. It is on the basis of this sort of view that Aron dissents from the rather crude Marxism he encountered in his youth which, perhaps unlike Marx himself, paid little attention to the autonomy of the political and to the fact that men's interests must be understood in more than merely instrumental terms.

These two arguments seem to me very strong, and two things should be noted about them. Firstly, it is important to stress that they do not imply that Aron lacks a sense of social structure; on the contrary, his analyses of various societies are quite brilliant at finding how a particular belief has an elective affinity with certain social conditions. Secondly, this search for ways in which beliefs are engendered by particular circumstances underlies Aron's long and valuable reflections on the relations of theory and practice. The burden of these reflections is, as we have seen, simple: 'theory' must not become so abstract that it fails to understand local conditions— as was the case with Vietnam.

Readers will recall that in the introduction to this work it was suggested that the ideologies that have so characterised the twentieth century could be seen as either consequence or cause of historical change; and we can go a little further in analysing Aron if we try and see him in relation to this distinction. There can be no doubt about the importance of the question since Aron's whole life has been concerned to warn us of the dangers of total ideologies which can so easily justify human bestiality. But does he see such ideologies as the consequence of particular circumstances, or are they rather, as Bell believes, the breakthrough of the irrational? It is worth stressing that if the latter position is held, no real generalisations about historical development are possible. The sociologist would be reduced to trying to understand such outbursts, albeit an understanding of social structure might prove important in explaining the ways in which such charismatic movements are routinised.

The crucial point to be made is that Aron does not clearly place himself within the terms of this distinction, and would perhaps resent anyone else doing so. However, it seems to me that his thought as a whole entitles us to infer that he sees belief as the consequence of particular circumstances. In the *Introduction to the Philosophy of History*, for example, he speaks of the appeal of ideologies being to men 'cut adrift from their habits'.[72] More importantly, his hope that the industrial age would permit an 'end to ideologies' suggests that there are general circumstances which explain the emergence of what he came to call 'secular religions'. We shall see Gellner offering us a theory as to the nature of those general circumstances in the next chapter. All this could be summarised by saying that Aron is, in the last analysis, an optimist about the chances for industrial society since he does not, as we shall see, feel that it need succumb to crises that engender total ideologies:

> .... in spite of my reputation, I am in a certain sense an irrepressible optimist. I cannot help believing that in the long run an evolution in the direction of reason is more probable than an evolution toward madness and catastrophe. When I think about it, I see no reasonable reason to believe in my own optimism.[73]

This reservation suggests the other side of the picture, and explains why Aron cannot, as it were, formally endorse the more optimistic position. He is a witness to his time, and cannot forget that the crises of the 1930s were at first dubbed 'an aberration' by social theorists. He remains cautious, unwilling ever to allow us off our guard. One special reason for respecting Aron's position is that his caution is usually free from the crudities evidenced in Bell's view of the demonic. For Aron what is important is the reconstruction of apparently irrational action so that we can understand why it felt sensible to the actor. But I shall argue below that in recent years Aron has changed somewhat so that his views have at times become less subtle than formerly.

The Sociology of Modern Civilisation

Aron's most lasting contribution to sociology probably remains his comparative sociology of East and West. The basic conception underlying this is simple, intuitively convincing and brilliantly executed. He argues that the crucial characteristic of our time is the fact of industrialism, which he sees as comprising four elements: the enterprise is separated from family control; the division of labour becomes ever more specialised; capital must be accumulated for investment; and the whole is based upon a system of rational calculations.[74] Such a definition allows for the developments described as 'post-industrial' to be considered as but the logical fulfilment of industrialism.

The industrial age is held to characterise both East and West, but the brilliance of Aron's analysis depends upon creating ideal types of both systems based upon a threefold analysis of economy, class structure and policy. His analysis of each of these dimensions was published in a separate book, and the full force of his argument has, unfortunately, never been appreciated in the English speaking world since the middle volume, *La Lutte de Classes*, has not been translated. I shall outline the two ideal types in a moment, but three preliminary remarks are called for. Aron's analysis of market and command systems is straightforward, as is that of the class structure, inevitably engendered, for Aron, by the need of industrialism for hierarchy. But it is important to stress that he draws a distinction between the full emergence of classes in the West and the manner in which this emergence is curtailed by the political system in the East. This is to say that the crucial element distinguishing the two regimes is held to be the polity, and the volume in which this is discussed, *Democracy and Totalitarianism*, is Aron's masterpiece.

The second preliminary point is that Aron structures his discussion with reference to the competing theories of Marx and Tocqueville. The main point made against Marx is simply that we should understand industrialism as a 'mode of production' in its own right demanding stratification and 'exploitation', i.e. the retention of surplus for investment, yet capable of supporting different political regimes. A second argument against Marx is that there is in fact no reason why the liberal class societies of the market economy should collapse. Both these points would seem to imply that Aron is unreservedly endorsing Tocqueville's view of our position. But for all his reverence for the great sociologist of liberty, Aron is not in fact uncritical of Tocqueville. Most obviously, he feels that Tocqueville's analysis of increasing equality failed to pay proper attention to the inevitable hierarchy of an industrial world. Aron sees the modern social order, in other words, as being made of a dialectic of industrial hierarchy and the urge for equality. He feels that Tocqueville is also at fault, as is Marx, in perhaps a more important matter:

> For Tocqueville, the major fact was the disappearance of distinctions, for Marx it was the conflict between the proletariat and the entrepreneurs. But I am inclined to believe that for us the major fact, which is found as much in Soviet industrial societies as in Western industrial societies, is the growth in productivity, the increased value produced by the whole collectivity and by each individual within it.[75]

The third and final preliminary point is that the abstract quality of the ideal types we shall be discussing should not let us forget Aron's view of the nation as—at the moment, at least—the end product of social evolution. More precisely, socialism creates, where it can, i.e. outside Eastern Europe, new nations rather than a new transnational reality. Aron became convinced of this as a result of the break between China and the USSR, and he was not for a moment surprised at the war between Peking and Hanoi. Inter-state rivalry remains the rule in East and West.

The command economy, or Soviet model, is one in which a particular type of growth can be successfully achieved. Its peculiarity lies in its insistence on investment in heavy industry at the expense of providing consumer goods. This obsession with heavy industry is seen to be the result of Russia's desire to be a great power, and of Lenin's having based his economic arguments on the war economies of the First World War. What judgements does Aron offer about this model? In general he is typically circumspect and prefers to leave the exact balance of certain factors open to empirical investigation. He admits the success of the Soviet model but qualified this in certain ways. The actual growth rate achieved was not in the final analysis really so much higher than that achieved in the industrialisation of, say, the United States, and Aron refuses to believe that this model was the only one appropriate for Russia. In this respect he notes that Tsarist Russia itself might have been capable of continuing the industrialisation it had begun but for the accident of war. In general, however, this possiblity is discounted as Aron recognises that a centralised administration has a special advantage in dealing with the social tensions created by industrialisation. He does suggest, however, that forced collectivisation was not necessary. Indeed, he argues that this was in fact counterproductive since the kulaks' resistance only led to famine.

Aron feels that there are strict limits to the applicability of the Soviet model, and he suggests that when applied in the wrong circumstances (i.e. when the population is much larger than Russia's and when agriculture is not very productive) disastrous famine can result.[76] This point could be made in another way by saying that Aron considers that the forced collectivisation of agriculture exhibits the power of ideology over a more obviously 'easy' alternative. He is not prepared to say exactly how much Marxism guides action, but he opposes those who say that it plays no part at all.[77] It is when arguing thus that he resists those who consider forced industrialisation as being motivated by the search for power alone:

> This interpretation seems to me too simple. The Communist philosophy is one of abundance. At the present time the Communists are in many ways concerned for the welfare of their populations. It would be absurd to declare that the Soviet planners have consciously and cynically sought for power at any

price. The Soviet economy has successfully carried out the job of industrialisation without foreign capital; the growth of the Russian economy before 1914 involved a considerable contribution of foreign capital, as did the American economy in its phase of rapid industrialisation. Soviet industrialisation took place at a time and with an ideology which made the planners fear foreign aggression. The Soviets have always devoted to war or the preparation of war much greater resources than did Western countries during comparable stages.[78]

It would be hard to find more sympathetic understanding of the Russian case. The massive investment in heavy industry undertaken by the Soviet model necessitates centralised political power. Similarly, the need to serve the industrial machine requires that the state have sufficient power to control the conflicts that may arise from social stratification. Aron insists that there is nothing in Marxism that per se rules out unequal reward, and he has always kept an interested eye on the question of income distribution in Eastern Europe. However, his analysis of stratification essentially follows Eastern European sociologists and ideologists in distinguishing intellectuals, peasants and workers as objective groups. Aron does not doubt that each of these groups has some measure of subjective identity, but considers that this cannot develop into pure class feeling. For such class feeling is dependent upon opposition and this is formally banned. Equally importantly, intellectuals, the purveyors of creeds that build up a sense of opposition, are not allowed to spread ideologies that present society in class terms. This is not to say that Aron is arguing that conflict cannot occur in the East. Very much to the contrary, Aron insists that a mere strike, as in Poland in 1980, can be such as to call the whole regime in question—although he does not therefore go so far as to say that in consequence Eastern Europe is permanently lacking in social stability.

Command economies that limit class conflict are held to be ruled over by a united or 'monopolistic' elite. Aron clearly has in mind here the Bolshevik party, although his analysis is designed to apply to all one-party states. His argument is very subtle, paying, due regard to the monopolistic regimes. In particular, he takes great care to stress that it is only at certain, abnormal, moments that such regimes descend into totalitarianism. This development is seen as a permanent possibility, given that a single man may come to dominate the party, but it is one that Aron considers to have been fully embraced only by Hitler's Germany and Stalin's Russia. He also goes to great lengths to distinguish authoritarian regimes from those dominated by an active monopolistic party inside an industrial country.[79] Most importantly, perhaps, he recognises that a monopolistic regime is exceptionally good at managing the social strains engendered by forced industrialisation. The possibility that the Eastern model as a whole may prove reasonably successful leads Aron to contemplate the possibility that a monopolistic regime might liberalise itself:

> What seems to me decisive is to know to what extent the governed are dissatisfied with their rulers. If in distributing the national resources 35 per cent of the total is kept for military expenditure or investment, it is obviously preferable not to have several parties disputing for power, since at least one of them will claim that too much is being spent on defence. If planning is directed to hastening industrialisation it is undoubtedly difficult to combine party rivalry with planning. On the other hand, if one thinks of a planned economy with a very high level of productivity and a very high level of general wealth, and if the controversies are concerned with allocating 10 per cent more or less to the various social groups, it is not inconceivable to have at the same time a planned economy and competition between parties for the exercise of power.[80]

Whilst this refusal to close down possibilities is typical of Aron, it is nevertheless true that he argues that the reverse side of the success of industrialisation is in fact far more gloomy. He notes quite correctly that it is becoming apparent that one party regimes are far less good at managing the economy once industrialisation has been completed. Agriculture remains chronically inefficient, and—in the Soviet Union, at least—large amounts of food have to be grown on the very small plots that the peasants are allowed for their private use. This has resulted in the necessity of buying wheat imports as planners' targets fail to be met year after year. Equally importantly, Aron knows that the growth rate of the Russian economy has now slipped noticeably and is unlikely to be improved so long as low productivity (in itself perhaps a source of political stability since it tames unemployment) cannot somehow be removed. All this leads to a terrible dilemma for the monopolistic party:

> Either the single party does not have an ideology and it is a question then of a minority which holds power, forbidding those whom they govern to debate the problems of government; or it is a question of a single party, armed with an ideology, with the will radically to transform the whole society. But a party which justifies the exclusion of other parties by its will to revolution is faced with an alternative: either permanent revolution or, if it renounces permanent revolution, traditional stabilization or technocracy.[81]

It is increasingly Aron's belief that the party is unlikely to liberalise the regime since any concession can easily lead to the questioning of the party's supreme role.[82] Aron has not treated the Prague Spring of 1968 in any detail, but one imagines that what might impress him here was that the Russians apparently objected far more to the questioning of the party than they did to various plans to decentralise the economy.

Four points are held to distinguish between market economies and command economies:

(1) Present day capitalist economic systems exhibit great diversity in the types of property, in particular the maintenance of family ownership in commerce and agriculture.
(2) Capitalist systems are incompatible with the radical separation of the national economy from the world economy and must conform to the requirements of external trade.
(3) The influence of consumers over the allocation of national resources is dominant in the long run.
(4) Trade unions are not directed or controlled by the state.[83]

As noted, Aron argues that both East and West 'exploit' labour, but he does not think that capitalism per se is therefore automatically invalidated:

If capitalists receive large profits and use them to buy luxuries, the capitalist system becomes detestable. But if most of the income going to capitalists is reinvested, it does not matter much that the incomes are received by individuals and only later returned to the various sectors of production. The first problem, therefore, is to discover the proportion of the surplus value which is consumed by the privileged class. The second is to determine the relative efficiency of the system of private production and the collective system. The third problem is to decide whether the planned distribution of investment is better or worse than the distribution of investment by the capital market.[84]

It is, effectively, upon the last two of these points, i.e. upon the ability of capitalism to achieve growth, that Aron's case most firmly rests. He refuses to accept a whole series of Marxist arguments asserting various economic contradictions of capitalism. Thus he refuses to accept the underconsumptionist argument of John Hobson and others who consider that capitalism is weakened by its inability to create demand. Aron has always believed that trade unions would be powerful enough to increase spending, and he was an early reader of Keynes. It is very typical to find him ahead of old orthodoxies in his recent argument that the economic problems of the West since 1973 can be seen as the product of excessive demand.[85] Moreover, as we have seen, Aron does not think that the

West's capital will necessarily fail to find further sources of investment since the insatiability of human demand when combined with technological progress makes new industries possible. Finally, it is argued that the simple fact of private ownership is not enough to make the capitalist economies inflexibly anarchic. Aron considers that the possibility of nationalisation has changed the character of private property. He is probably also Keynesian enough to note that the government now has so many more means of directing the economy at its disposal as to make the last argument very dated.[86]

The weakness of these arguments stating an inevitable decline does not prevent Aron from asking whether particular factors do not develop as a result of the progress of capitalism that may not help or hinder the regime. Aron suggests that no static balance can be drawn up between these sets of factors, but he felt in the 1950s a measure of optimism was justified: the habit of economic calculation would spread, purchasing power would be better distributed, a measure of socialisation of the regimes in matters of welfare would lower social resentment, and science and education would be able to provide a constant source of renewal for the economy. These factors were judged to be powerful enough to outweigh the poorer investment possibilities, the necessary spread of some non-productive tertiary activities and the difficulty in establishing new industries. But Aron has always been aware of a certain political problem that may affect the economy, which we will examine later. Beforehand, we need to say something about his view of Western stratification.

Aron approaches stratification in Western societies with a series of interesting qualifications to the effect that class is virtually as equivocal a facet of social life as inter-state rivalry. This equivocacy is evidenced for Aron in the different numbers of classes located by different sociologists, and it is judged to be irremediable. But an even more interesting general point is made about class. Aron has always had a very healthy scepticism about the possibility of the proletariat acting as a universal class capable of bringing history, or perhaps pre-history, to an end. He refuses to believe that the proletariat is the bearer, in the Weberian sense, of a new industrial principle—as he believes that the bourgeois, in opposition to the aristocrat, most certainly was. This suggests to Aron that the conflict between bourgeois and worker may prove to be less total than Marx had imagined, especially as both might cooperate together in the creation of a high growth economy:

> The common interest of both sides .... is the prosperity of the firm and the economy, that is, growth whose necessary conditions

correspond to the simultaneous interest of wage earner and managers.[87]

This logical argument is followed by Aron's analysis of the tendencies of social evolution in industrial society. He suggests that such societies are likely to urbanise, create a salariat, differentiate further and allow for a proportion of the population to become bourgeois. It is not entirely clear exactly what Aron means by this last factor (Is embourgeoisement a phenomenon he considers to take place inter- or intro-generationally?), and it might seem as if he is adopting the naive view of Bell and Dahrendorf of an increasingly harmonious society.

Aron is in fact very far indeed from doing this, and argues instead that these tendencies will tend to be translated into social reality as a lessening of passivity and an increase in acrimony amongst the population:

> Often the directors of capitalist companies have noted with regret that the workers of other civilisations have, when they have achieved a certain income, judged they had enough and have stopped working, indifferent to any further increase. This attitude, reasonable from many viewpoints in a different social system, is that which all industrial societies wish to eliminate. One cannot teach French people to desire more without pushing them at the same time to demanding more . . . one can say that there will be more and more claims, more and more opportunities to claim, more and more individuals and organised groups who, aware of the relation between their own income and that of their neighbour, protest, whether against a cut or whether against an insufficient increase, at least in comparison with that received by another. Making demands cannot be separated from the drawing of comparisons. The essence of democracy, combined with industrial civilisation, is a state of constant agitation.[88]

Aron considers that modern Western society is likely to lead to a condition of 'querulous satisfaction'. Constant disputes will not, it is argued, typically become violent although this is always possible. Violence will arise if a group feels itself to be excluded from the national culture, has a strong group identity and is prepared to use force. But Aron feels that these conditions, quite often satisfied with peasantries, are less and less likely to occur inside the working class. For growth permits a rise in income which is sufficient to buy social peace. And to this can be added a certain lessening in objective social distance and in status that makes us all members of one, much more conflictual, community. On the basis of these remarks, Aron undertakes some of his most succinct essays on national solutions to stratification problems, and offers a very relevant analysis of the difficulties associated with the concept of social mobility. He seems to suggest that mobility will at once weaken mass protest but considerably increase acrimony as standards of comparison change.[89] He is also evidently aware that Britain was once able, for a short time, to combine the provision of social services with the authority of the establishment. But Aron, unlike Dahrendorf, considered this an inherently unstable association. He may be seen as charting a typical *via media* when he notes that conflict must have a basis in consensus for the Western system to work:

> As far as rivalry between politicians is concerned, it must be understood that a multi-party system only functions well to the degree that the struggle, however genuine it may be, camouflages a certain agreement.[90]

This point is developed in his analysis of the polity so as to suggest that there may be a political, rather than an economic, difficulty facing Western society.

The comparative political sociology that Aron offers us represents an attempt to integrate Pareto's insistence on the necessity of analysing elites into the mainstream of sociology. Yet Aron's analysis of the West departs from Pareto in two ways. In the first place he bitterly criticises the reductive style of Paretian analysis which sees internal politics as concerned only with the struggle for power:

> Instead of a philosophy of sense it puts forward a philosophy of nonsense according to which the meaning of politics is the struggle and not the search for a justified authority.[91]

Secondly, Aron argues that the elite of Western society is open rather than closed or, precisely, 'constitutional-pluralistic' rather than monopolistic. Power, in other words, is held to be very definitely—in part due to the exigencies of industrialism—centralised in the hands of politicians, administrators, trade union leaders and capitalists, although each of these groups is considered to be in some measure distinct. Aron's exceptionally rich analysis of Western regimes which, unfortunately, we cannot do justice to here, revolves around the four particular problems that can confront the Western system, demagogy, tyranny, oligarchy and anarchy. The last two breed the former and exhibit the most important conclusions reached by Aron.

Aron's answer to those who argue that democracy is ruled by oligarchies is to admit that this is and must remain so in a complex society; democracy can only, in the industrial age, have the merit of 'circulating' elites and offering some opportunity for participation.

This said, Aron opposes the Marxist insistence that any such circulation is habitually dictated by the hidden hand of capitalists (although he is far too realistic to deny that such attempts can be made or that democracy can, in a South American situation, become a mere game behind which vested interests are at work). Aron's own experience of Western capitalists has convinced him that they are not dedicated enough to manage much at all:

> One of my disappointments has been to realise that those who, according to the communist picture of the world, determine the course of events are very often men without political ideas; it is impossible to say what the French capitalists (by this I mean the middle classes) wanted on most of the great questions discussed in France in the last ten years.[92]

Aron takes far more seriously the possibility of the corruption of the regimes through the central power becoming powerless as the representative of the community in the face of organised pressure groups. Writing about the market economy, he says:

> In a democratic regime there is a danger that electors will usually be more concerned with the immediate future than with the long term, and that they will tend to prefer a low rate of investment at the risk of slowing down growth. This raises doubt about the compatibility between political democracy and rapid growth.[93]

The matter is really more serious than this since a democratic government, for reasons of popularity, may choose the line of least resistance and thus refuse to act in terms of economic rationality in matters such as pre-election budgets, closing down factories and in restraining wage competition. Aron does not actually prophesy that this political contradiction will lead to desperate problems, but his own experience of the collapse of the Fourth Republic has convinced him that the thread of legality is slender and fragile.

This comparative sociology shows that both Eastern and Western systems have advantages and disadvantages, and it is to that extent the most distinguished piece of work produced by any thinker involved in the 'end of ideology' debate. But for all that, Aron's own preferences are clear:

> Among the freedoms which Marx called formal, two, protection from the despotism of the police and in the intellectual realm the limitation of the principle of authority, seem to me to correspond to irrepressible needs of human nature. Never will the despotism of the police force or a state orthodoxy appear to either the man in the street or the intellectual as a form of freedom with a capital 'f', regardless of the subtleties of the dialectic. In this respect the

word does not have two meanings, one in the West, the other in the East....[94]

Aron has recently stressed how very remarkable it is to have liberal societies at all, suggesting that their very possibility depends upon the traditional governing classes managing to liberalise and thus avoid a revolution that would finally centralise power.[95] This view stands in marked contrast to that of Dahrendorf, and is far more realistic, but it raises a problem. Aron's account is so historical, so aware that history is made in imperfect circumstances, that it raises the question of the degree of freedom involved in each of his models. Are all the elements in each model *necessarily* related to each other?

Aron's views of the East are very pessimistic here, and need detain us only a moment. The monopolistic power of the party is such that it is exceptionally unlikely that liberalisation will occur—especially, as noted, since the economy does not seem likely to improve. This view means that Aron does not really address the question that has exercised others, namely whether Eastern European liberalisation can occur on the basis of the pluralism of groups bred by more complex industrialism, or whether only the restoration of greater social inequalities can sufficiently decentralise power.

Comparable questions can, of course, be raised about Western society. Aron considers the defining character of these regimes to be, again, political, and has stressed the view that not all state behaviour in the West is dependent upon, or in the interests of, capitalism. But does the society as a whole rest necessarily upon private property, i.e. upon capitalism as a means of differential reward, or is a third, social democratic, way possible between Western and Eastern systems? Very regrettably, space prevents a full exploration of Aron's careful analyses of various national attempts to 'socialise' capitalism. He has, however, never ruled out the possibility of social democratic development, and would possibly welcome it since he only ever considered rights of property justifiable on functional grounds. Generally, however, he has become less optimistic about the possibilities of finding such a third way, and it is thus appropriate to say in the final analysis that he is offering us a defence of liberal capitalist society.

The reason for this increasing awareness of, as it were, the logical links between a market economy and a liberal polity is in no way similar to those offered by thinkers of the right such as Hayek or Friedman. All that Aron does is to point out the terrible difficulties involved in trying to go beyond the socialising of capitalism by means of the welfare state, some social mobility, citizenship rights and so on, to the creation of a liberal socialist state. It must be stressed again that Aron does not rule out the possibility *per se*; but several considerations—the impossibility of trying socialism in the West in 'fair' conditions since it would require a siege economy[96], the near impossibility (and perhaps injustice) of removing all privilege without attacking the family as such (something that might well require centralised power and thus the creation of new privileges) and, more particularly, the untrustworthiness of one chosen instrument of such a move, French Eurocommunism—make him sceptical of the dream of a free, affluent, centrally-planned and propertyless democracy. He remains willing to listen and to consider, and he rejects only on pragmatic grounds.

This is a good moment to pause briefly and to compare Aron's view of the West with that offered by Dahrendorf and Bell. Following Parkin,[97] it is possible to distinguish three 'defences' for Western society as it stands: that it is just, that it produces economic growth, and that the continuing conflict between the forces of labour and capital is desirable since this alone—rather than the creation of a meritocratic and complex society—makes pluralism real. It has already been noted that Aron gives us a proper sense of what it is about Western society, namely its liberalism, or balance of power between different social classes, that is worth defending in the first place. He never believed that Western society was 'post-capitalist', i.e. a pure and just meritocracy, and this has saved him from the rather question-begging theoretical development of Bell and Dahrendorf. Instead, Aron emphasised from the start the ability of Western societies to increase productivity so as to raise the general standard of living.

Aron's view is interesting and realistic. He stresses not so much the necessity for high rewards for wealth creators as the ability of the price mechanism to prevent the blockages so characteristic of central planning. But his endorsement of the market does not mean that he is unaware of the Keynesian responsibilities that have accrued to governments since the war. This makes his thought exceptionally lucid in another manner. While he would probably endorse Parkin's view that the conflict between labour and capital is the keynote to pluralism, at the same time his thought allows us to see how difficult it is to combine democracy with social inequality—especially at those times when economic growth cannot be secured. I have argued above that this is a systematic contradiction in Western societies, and that novel methods are necessary to deal with it. But what is Aron's position in this matter?

Aron does not unreservedly accept that it is this contradiction that is causing the economic difficulties of the West. He continues to try and discriminate, although some of his arguments—that Britain's economic problems are due to too great an investment in the tertiary sector, for example—are probably flawed.[98] But insofar as he does accept this sort of analysis, he has become exceptionally pessimistic. This pessimism can only be understood, I believe, with reference to Aron's extreme hostility to what he regarded as the self-indulgent, facile neo-anarchism of the 'jeunesse dorée' of the 1968 events. Aron produced an interesting book on the events of May in which, especially when trying to draw morals from animal behaviour in crowded situations, he comes close to viewing man as more or less irrational.[99] This is unfortunate since it has given his most recent 'plea for the West' a slightly rigid tone. He now seems to very much regret his use of the phrase 'the end of ideologies' since he feels that it gave the impression that the West could survive by means of economic growth alone rather than as a result of a positive endorsement of a common way of life. This is not to say that the great ideologies are held to have become plausible after all, merely that there is 'a proper use of ideologies' in assessing a reasoned goal worth striving for.[100]

Although this demand for a 'value consensus' is shared with Bell and the later Dahrendorf, Aron differs from them in his view of that consensus. He does not propose any revival of religion, and goes some way beyond the straightforward hope that liberty will come to be embraced for its own sake. Aron has always been exceptionally sceptical about the transnational ideals of the European Community but he, interestingly, sees some hope for a Europe once more prepared to play an historic role. If American troops were to be withdrawn from NATO, Aron feels that a measure of consensus might be achieved in Europe through the simple fact of having to undertake the traditional responsibility for self-defence.[101] This is an interesting idea, and breathes political realities in way that the recent proposals of Bell and Dahrendorf do not, but in the end I doubt whether Aron's ideas are much more practical. Later, I shall argue that a more creative approach to the domestic scene of Western societies is necessary.

Conclusion

Aron is the greatest 'sociologist of the middle range' of our time. Perhaps his greatest legacy has been to maintain interest in problems of social and historical development amidst more conceptual fashions. This interest in events combines with the essentially 'open' nature of his thought in a way that, unfortunately, makes some of Aron's work date rather fast. But his work is much more than the sociological journalism of which he is also a master; his attempts to 'think' international politics, industrialism and the regimes of East and West remain contributions of the highest order. As a philosopher of social science, in contrast, Aron is less impressive. Toward the end of his life Scott Fitzgerald, writing about his 'crack-up', observed:

> Before I go on with this short history, let me make a general observation—the test of a first-rate intelligence is the ability to hold two opposed ideas in the mind at the same time, and still retain the ability to function.[102]

What is finally impressive about Aron's methodology is the way in which he manages to combine, in a fruitful manner, positions that are often separated. It is, perhaps, this ability, above all, that most characterises his thought as a whole—even more than his constant concern with the question of human rationality. He is quite clear that social life does not hide any secret code that guarantees increased human rationality. We can, however, place 'a wager on reason' in international politics, whilst there is always the hope that men will choose to consider their circumstances and realise that the industrial age does not actually call for human bestiality. The intellectual has the responsibility of combining hope with an awareness of reality that dispels facile illusions, and this is what Aron has sought to do. He has remained a witness to the world of the concentration camps, but has sought to show us that a better way is possible. The ability to remain a witness without becoming a cynic is the achievement not just of a sociologist, nor even of a very fine intelligence, but of a very great humanity.

7 Ernest Gellner

The New Social Contract

No one is quite sure what to make of Ernest Gellner. He has no easy niche in English intellectual life, being of Czech origin and having intellectual horizons that are European rather than English. Moreover, he is at once philosopher, sociologist and anthropologist—in which capacity he has a specialist reputation amongst Africanists. But I suspect that people find him a discomforting figure because of his style. This is celebrated for its wit and fire, and it would be a foolish man who wilfully brought a Gellnerite diatribe on his own head. The *bons mots* and the jokes, however, have misled many into neglecting the seriousness of purpose in Gellner's work. This mistake should never have been made since a deeper characteristic of the style is irony. This irony is seen in Gellner savagely mocking, above all, those who do not seek to understand and explain the social world in systematic terms. This chapter is designed to show Gellner's own simple but far-reaching understanding of our current philosophical and social scene.

There is certainly nothing unclear about the new social contract that Gellner claims is the central feature of modern life. This contract, described in *Thought and Change*, is based on two principles that do and should legitimate social orders in our age. A society will be and should be considered legitimate if it provides affluence and leadership co-cultural with the rest of society; these principles are designed to satisfy the conditions of industrialisation and nationalism.[1]

Gellner is quite prepared to entertain the naturalistic fallacy and to suggest that our ethics and morals must be made relevant to a process that is quite inevitable; jumping on the historical bandwagon is justified on this occasion by the absolute certainty that affluence, in particular, is something which poor countries will not be content to do without. The emergence of 'bourgeois rational capitalism in the West' was probably a unique process, as Weber suggested, and it consequently had little appeal for the rest of the world. But the effective industrialisation of Russia and Japan changed the picture; industrialisation became a general possibility, and for Gellner the very concept of industrialisation represents the fact that, in this at least, the whole world is or shortly will be, at one in demanding the affluence that the greater cognitive powers of (originally) Western science are capable of achieving.

Gellner does not, in fact, consider that he is committing the naturalistic fallacy since he sees affluence as desirable in its own right. He is not at all surprised to find that whole populations are voting with their feet to escape a cruel, brutish life torn by poverty and disease. His views on the matter are summarised in a gloss on Pascal's celebrated observation that the human condition resembles that of a condemned man:

> Human life is totally unlike this. The end may be certain, but not its date or manner. In the meantime, there is constant opportunity, indeed necessity, for seeking postponement of the verdict and for improving one's condition. These activities do *not* concentrate one's mind marvellously at all.... These ends—postponement, improvement—can or could however only be attained at the cost of other men. So, if we must have a comparison, it cannot be the condemned cell.... but something like Auschwitz: you can live a little longer and a little better, provided you are very lucky and are willing to participate in the degradation and extinction of your fellows.[2]

Affluence thus offers humanity the very chance of humane behaviour that had been obviated all too often in the past by physical scarcity. Gellner's argument, it can be noted, is blunt and forthright, and the harsh tone of some of his polemics against other thinkers is the result of his amazement that they have not recognised this revolution, let alone placed it, as he does, at the centre of his thought.

Some limitations of Gellner's view must be stressed. When he refers to the achievement of affluence as 'the great transition' or as a doctrine of 'truncated evolution', he is not asserting that the transition is to do with anything other than technical and material factors. Indeed, *Thought and Change* opens with a remorseless attack on the idea of progress, especially as seen in evolutionary garb. According to theorists of this school, such as Hobhouse, evolution would lead not merely to industrialism but to democracy, and in the distant future to world government. Gellner is quite free from such illusions and, as we shall see, explicitly suggests that the course of industrialisation is often such as to *debar* greater democracy. But it is worth noting that this realism is not embraced gladly. Gellner's thought would not make sense were we to believe he *really* thinks that affluence and nationalism alone make a social order praiseworthy; he is at one with his evolutionist-minded predecessors at the London School of Economics, Hobhouse and Ginsberg, in considering liberty the highest value of them all.[3] That he is unable to 'anchor' it socially as they felt they had done is a source of regret to him as well as an incentive to investigate the possibilities of liberty in the modern world.

The fact that the industrial order does not come into being without great disturbance brings us to a consideration of the second principle of the social contract. It is important to realise that Gellner wishes to *explain* nationalism, i.e. he rejects explicitly the view associated with Elie Kedourie according to which nationalism is somehow a natural, even atavist longing. We are told that it is, on the contrary, an invention: 'Nationalism is not the awakening of nations to self consciousness: it invents nations where they do not exist....'[4] There are two strands to the explanation of nationalism. The first points to certain characterists of industrial society that make some level above that of the tribe a present necessity. In primitive societies the structural necessities of daily life mean that a common or national culture is not really called for—thus Lévi-Strauss once observed a society of Brazilian Indians in which two separate languages were spoken.[5]

But modern industrial life is not similarly formed by the fight against an omnipresent nature. On the contrary, industrialism depends upon the ability to work together with the benefit of the division of labour. This cooperation depends upon the ability to communicate at higher levels or, technically, upon the ability to sustain more abstract relationships:

> ....a very large proportion of one's relationships and encounters—in fact, there *are* more frequently encounters than relationships—are ephemeral, non-repetitive and optional. This has an important consequence: communication, the symbols, language (in the literal or in the extended sense) that is employed, become crucial. The burden of comprehension is shifted from the context to the communication itself.... the message must itself become intelligible—it is no longer understood, as was the case in traditional society, before it was even articulated...[6]

The ability to sustain abstract interaction depends upon making people able to communicate, by the written as well as the spoken word, in a single language. And this, Gellner insists, is something that nationalists and other 'modernisers' realise full well: the drive to universal literacy or, in other words, the turning of tribesmen into citizens, is one injunction rarely broken. But we can see at once that this process of creation, for that is what it is, is likely to cause fantastic pain. Men's lives are literally being made anew. Thus in

Algeria the 'Arabisation' of the country means an extirpation—the word is accurate—of Berber, and thus a systematic destruction of a way of life. Such extirpation can probably only be achieved under the aegis of a strong central state, and we shall hear more of the consequences of this fact below.

The first half of Gellner's argument could be summed up by saying that warm, small-scale community life cannot provide the social infrastructure for industrialism. The second half of the explanation seeks to explain why this social infrastructure could not be established by the colonial powers themselves—in other words, why North African for example, did not become literate in French and 'develop' as part of an imperial system. Gellner argues that certain social strains consequent on the uneven diffusion of industrialism made this impossible; the most important strain concerns the position of the intelligentsia. Typically, colonies worthy of the name must be controlled by representatives of the mother country. This means, however, that the natives able to become educated in the mother country, say in Paris or London, find that their chances of social mobility are blocked. The top jobs are not open to them despite their skills, simply because they can be distinguished on the basis of colour or religion. This blocked mobility naturally encourages the aggrieved local intelligentsia to turn to nationalism.

The ideology they produce is essentially fanciful in presuming that there ever was a nation (rather than a set of tribes) which is being suppressed by imperialists. But this ideology appeals to a second set of people disrupted by imperialism, namely the working class of the new towns. The intellectuals thus become leaders of a nationalist movement claiming, plausibly, that only national control will allow for the full appropriation both of local resources and of the benefits to accrue from industrialism. Such movements do not, as Aron stressed, need to gain massive support: victory can be achieved as long as support is sufficient to make the colony more expensive than it is worth.

If these are the social-structural origins of nationalism, Gellner also wishes to underline one point about what nationalism does when in power. Nationalism is caused by the uneven diffusion of industrialism, and its task in power is to so mobilise the people that modernisation can occur. It is this that makes Elie Kedourie's view of nationalism absurd in Gellner's eyes: nationalists do not, as it were, protect local cultures (the plural is crucial) but destroy them even more systematically than do imperialists. In this the intellectuals of the underdeveloped countries of the post-1945 world—to whom Gellner's theory applies most effectively[7]—are strikingly different from their Russian counterparts of the nineteenth century who often became 'westernizers' only at the expense of guilty feelings that they were turning their back on the Russian people. 'By the twentieth century,' Gellner writes, 'the dilemma hardly bothers anyone: the philosopher-kings of the "underdeveloped" world all act as westernizers, and all talk like *narodniks*'.[8]

Two final points may be noted about Gellner's account of nationalism. Firstly, he sees the nationalist route to industrialisation and affluence as one that is likely to be a successful route. He shares with Aron a considerable scepticism about theories of economic imperialism or dependency that imply that the developed world needs to—or indeed at all times can—exploit the underdeveloped world. He seems, in other words, to have little doubt that the underdeveloped countries can, and have begun to, make their way to the great transition independently. Secondly, curiously enough, Gellner, despite his endorsement of the liberal ideas of Ginsberg and Hobhouse, takes comfort from this diversifying, nationalist approach to industrialisation. Necessity makes for strange bedfellows, and Gellner's appreciation of nationalism is one that is pragmatically concerned with the defence of Western Liberalism.

His argument is based on an alternative, imagined state of affairs: had there been a world government of real effectiveness by, say, 1945 it is possible that the fight to achieve full affluence and citizenship rights might have occurred inside the existing political units. Gellner suggests that the privileged liberal and democratic minority, faced with 'the risk of being submerged by overwhelming numbers of people culturally alien to them',[9] would, in all probability, have adopted a harsh and repressive attitude, causing liberalism to go by the board. Hence he proposes that the independent routes, via nationalism, to industrialisation and affluence has two notable advantages. It has allowed Western societies themselves to retain a considerable element of democratic liberty (and he is hopeful that this example might prove to be important in the longer term); and the idea of world government has not been permanently vitiated, as it would have been had such a government had to handle the impossible problem of the spread of industrialisation throughout the globe.

Industrialism is the baseline of Gellner's sociology, and he encapsulates its significance by saying that it forms a crucial 'episode' in human affairs. 'Episode' is preferred to 'evolution', because it emphasises industrialism's accidental character, i.e. it is not a logically necessary development of reason in history. Gellner is, in effect, arguing that there are two crucial episodes in human history, the neolithic revolution and the industrial revolution, which leads him to see history in trinitarian form, as a division between pre-agrarian, agrarian and industrial eras.[10] And the word 'episode' makes clear that a new stage requires a new social order to go with it. And a new social order will be linked to new styles of cognition, a matter to which we can now turn.

The Modern Mind

Crisis

We have seen Gellner arguing that the creation of industrial society is so dramatic that it disrupts received identities. The key to understanding Gellner's more philosophic work is to note that the identities that are destroyed are as much cognitive as social. The position consequent on the removal of assured certainty is well described by Descartes:

> .... I had accepted many false opinions as being true.... but inasmuch as reason persuades me already that I must avoid believing things which are not entirely certain and indubitable, no less carefully than those things which seem manifestly false, the slightest ground for doubt that I find in any, will suffice for me to reject all of them. And.... the destruction of foundations necessarily brings down with it the rest of the edifice....[11]

The destruction of certainty, in other words, creates a situation of complete crisis in which, literally, nobody can be sure of things, let alone himself. Perhaps the best known literary exploration of this theme is the famous surrealist moment when Antoine Roquentin, the hero of Jean-Paul Sartre's *Nausea*, stares at a tree and briefly feels that the sheer facticity of its roots are such as to make the convential label 'roots' insufficient.

Crisis of this measure had historically—and indeed has now—to be avoided; the consequence of this is to make epistemology, the search for secure knowledge, the central point of modern philosophy. Gellner claims that there are two central strategies that are adopted in order to help us escape the crisis, and these are examined in *Legitimation of Belief*. The first is the Crusoe tradition which suggests that we take a point outside our world and received wisdom in order that some sort of reliable and solid ground may be discovered.[12] The second tradition is that associated above all with the name of Hegel. This school insists that it is not, of course, possible for a social creature ever to become a *tabula rasa*, free of all social influence; in other words, it is all as in the plays of

Pirandello where the characters 'search' for an author, the audience communicates with the actors and so on.[11] This criticism of the first tradition is admitted by Gellner to be entirely correct, and we shall see him drawing some consequences from this later. Nevertheless, he aligns himself with the Crusoe tradition because he feels that the cognitive strategies recommended by the Pirandello technique are feeble. They seek as a rule to examine our cognitive equipment, and to declare that, with minor improvements, they will serve.

The first type of such 're-endorsement' philosophy characterised much of nineteenth century thought, and at least has the merit of recognising that the existence of different cultures and different standards poses a problem for our thought. The presence of many liberal Christians amongst its ranks perhaps made this school unwilling either to see its own society as just one option amongst others, or to allow that man was not altogether one in his rationality.[13] The solution they proposed was simple and forceful: the different positions were allowed but they were placed within a theory of the great ascent (to industrialism, democracy and humanism). Thus, all men were the same and there was a single plan of the universe; social development would eventually allow for all to coexist at the same stage of finished perfection.

As already noted, Gellner has no objection to the values enshrined in this picture of the completed evolutionary state; rather it is with regret that he is forced to admit that the theory does not hold. Firstly, he suggests that the mere placing of things in a series does not in itself offer an explanation of evolution as such; Gellner is here following the Popperian attack on the logical impossibility of establishing historical laws from a single instance.[14] An explanation can only be had by specifying the mechanism of change between different stages, and once this is available the actual series becomes redundant. Secondly, Gellner notes that the doctrine simply does not describe the great transition properly: industrialisation does not usually occur as the result of the 'development' of a society, it is rather the creation of a society on an entirely different basis.[15]

These last comments are of course directed at social evolution, but an underlying point made against this doctrine applies—as we would expect given that societies bear cognitive styles—to the more technical matter of cognitive evolution. This is simply that evolution tends to ignore the vast mass of human history in which no progress occurs. As is well-known, the failure of even the signs of progress in Indian civilisation was sufficient to encourage one of the most famous nineteenth century evolutionists, Karl Marx, to see some justification in English imperialism if it shocked India into getting onto even the bottom rung of the evolutionary ladder. Similarly, those who believe that our cognitive equipment is bound to develop as need requires—the position Gellner feels is held by Pragmatists and, as we shall see, by the later Popper—fail to recognise how rare is cognitive growth.[16] Social learning in any sphere is far too delicate ever to justify being reconstructed, as Habermas would have us do, in terms of its inner logic.

Two other types of 're-endorsement' strategy have characterised recent thought, and these are considered to be of much less merit in that they fail to realise the sense of crisis from which modern philosophy tries to escape. Relativism's proposed solution to the breakdown of cognitive certainty is negative: that standards of judgement differ from place to place only goes to show there are no absolute standards. In other words, relativism turns what had seemed a problem into a solution: truth is what is believed locally. Gellner has two criticisms of this position. On the one hand, this doctrine all too often masquerades under false pretences. Superficially it is extremely tolerant, but at a deeper level this tolerance may not prevail. In Gellner's words, 'If nothing is really, universally true, who are you to deny local custom or the local authorities?'[17] More important, however, is the inadequacy of relativism to deal with the 'great transition'. Such strength as the doctrine had, depended on the supposed possibility of locating a particular set of practices in a particular place; the importance of the great transition is that it makes this rather silly. The advice, 'When in Rome, do as the Romans do' is now vacuous:

> What is 'Rome'? The upper class of the contemporary municipality of that name? Central Italy? The Common Market? Catholic Europe? Countless boundaries, geographic and social, vertical and horizontal, criss-cross each other in a rapidly changing world.[18]

A final strategy is termed, variously, 'carte blanche' or 'the way of residue' and it is of especial interest here since it underlies Habermas's notion of non-distorted communication. The doctrine is extremely straightforward: our cognitive equipment would be perfect but for one particular defect that prevents its smooth functioning. The specification of the single defect varies considerably, but examples include class interests, unconscious repression, and, more recently, 'misguided' use of language. Gellner is scathing about the optimism of such doctrines, and notes that the basic assumption, that truth is manifest but for the single distorting factor, is usually not even backed up with arguments. He notes:

> What these approaches have in common is that they evade the requirement of a positive specification of truth, and pass the buck, with a more or less elaborate justificatory theory for so doing. They may naively claim that once the scales have fallen off our eyes, truth is there, ready to give herself; or they may be more guarded, and merely promise that no persistent, deep obstacles will then remain; or the buck-passing may be complex, and they may merely say that the positive specification of difficult truths must be left to some other kind of agency....[19]

These approaches are dubbed 'all-too-benign'. In contrast the Crusoe tradition offers us harsher tactics; they are to use Gellner's term, 'hanging judges'. They deserve separate treatment.

Selectors
Gellner considers that there are two philosophic principles that serve as 'selectors' of reliable knowledge. These are empiricism and mechanism, and they form the pillars of judgement for his whole position. Their attraction for Gellner is at once philosophic and sociological. Philosophically, he considers these principles to be meritorious in recognising the depth of our dilemma; this recognition can be seen in their insistence that we cannot trust our received cognitive equipment at all. It is perhaps the case that inventive minds could establish a whole series of principles designed to act as selectors, and we shall later hear about the use of language as a selector. However, only mechanism and empiricism are really worthy of our attention for the crudest of reasons: these were the principles that actually did get the West out of complete cognitive chaos. In other words, Gellner is offering us a sociology of philosophic principles at work just as much as he is seeking to explain their inherent merit. This is a point of importance. Many approaches to the philosophy of science concern themselves with asking *whether* knowledge is possible. Gellner is so staggered by the powers of science, by the very great amount of certain knowledge that we now have, that he has no need to begin from a *tabula rasa*; he asks, rather, given this knowledge, '*How can we explain its working?*'

The two selectors seek to shift true knowledge from evanescent impression and opinion. The selecting device in empiricism is well known: only those things which can be sensed are judged to be real. The principle underlying mechanism is equally simple and elegant, namely that knowledge must consist of the specification of structure that can be examined and repeated at will. Gellner's full discussion of the two selectors is of the greatest sophistication, and is extremely hard to summarise with justice.[20] But two themes are quite central and must be noted, namely, his analysis of one of the ways in which the two selectors conflict and the surprising way in which they do eventually manage to work in tandem.

The conflict between the two occurs over the question of the proper explanation of human behaviour. Gellner follows Quine in suggesting that behaviourism represents the attempt to use empiricism as an explanation of human behaviour. This doctrine will literally suggest that man is the result of those experiences he has had placed before him. Gellner stresses that the self-image of this approach is that of being both practical and tough-minded; both these qualities he admires, and mentions only in order to suggest that underneath this virile veneer there lies something very different. This is made clear through a general interpretation of the work of Chomsky, and in particular Chomsky's attack on Skinner.[21] Chomsky makes two crucial points. Firstly, our linguistic powers are far greater than the behaviourist model allows; we are capable of inventing sentences, not just of reiterating ones that we have heard already. The situation is thus rather akin to that of modern chess computers. They are, as it were, model citizens of a Skinnerian world, obediently recalling all their conditioning at the flick of a switch. Unfortunately, they have only been programmed with games already played and have no talent in making new moves; the ability of humans to beat such computers represents the element of human complexity that conditioning theory does not begin to capture.

The second point is far more important. Gellner is insistent that this does not mean that Chomsky, despite his reputation as a radical, has somehow 'vindicated' human powers and placed them above explanation and beyond any chance of consequent political manipulation. For Chomsky's second objection is the actual absence of explanation offered by behaviourism. Chomsky suggests that behaviourism fails to explain, even in its own terms, *why* and *how* humans learn in this way; merely to say that men can be conditioned describes but does not explain. In other words, what is called for is a specification of the structure of the mind, its machine-like qualities; only this would truly explain. Chomsky's own work of course suggests that the human mind is extremely complex, and he does not describe the machine for us. Nevertheless, his work is seen as definitively establishing that explanation must be 'mechanical'.

The conflict between the two selectors is not, however, fatal; instead some sort of convergence can, and indeed did, occur. Logically, of course, there was no reason why British empiricism should not, especially in its utilitarian form, have encouraged mere hedonism: if nothing exists but one's sense impressions why not try to give them plenty of delights to keep them happy? That this did not in fact occur may be suggested by the unlikelihood that 'any orgy was ever graced by the body of John Stuart Mill'.[22] The reason for this, besides a covert puritanism that Gellner does not consider an explanation in the light of the seriousness of the thinkers concerned, was simply that, from the start, empiricist and mechanist visions were already working in tandem; British empiricists typically wished to establish a mechanical structure on the basis of the facts they assembled.

There are good reasons for the rapprochement. Both approaches are critical of received ideas, and in the attack on such ideas each of the two selectors can perform a different task. Mechanism must lay down the set features of necessary explanation; empiricism, however, can prove useful as a selector of data, albeit in the rather specific fashion examined below. Finally, both insist on the value of public testing of supposed knowledge. This last point is considered by Gellner to be the most significant of all. Mechanism's concern for public testing is built into its very set of rules. If explanation requires the specification of a structure, then publicness is guaranteed since everybody must, as it were, be able to assemble—as in a Lego Kit—the pieces of the structure specified. And the positivist tradition gained fame and notoriety for attacking metaphysics, public and private, on the grounds that such approaches lacked sense since they could not be confirmed by the public world of facts.

Cognitive Norms
Others would perhaps choose to highlight the same strategies as Gellner were they to undertake a similar mapping of modern philosophy, and this makes it important to underscore two novelties (one spelt out here, the other in the next section) that lend his work its importance. In a brilliant essay, Gellner notes:

No-one who writes a book on method thinks he is merely replicating the precepts of consistency, non-contradiction and so forth. So, a methodology must have some meat which is not merely logic. But if it asserts, or presupposes, something over and above the formal requirements of logic, will not that *something else*, whatever it may be, have some implications concerning *the world*? And if so, can one not imagine or construct a possible world within which those implications are false, and within which consequently those recommendations are misguided? ...But what use is a methodology which prejudges the nature of the world we are in, before we have even investigated the matter, and before we have any right to an opinion about it?[23]

This argument would naturally seem to undermine the real pursuit of methodology, but Gellner suggests that it is better understood as a proper description of what epistemology actually does. Methodological ground rules are not to be seen as somehow reflecting on the 'real' world, but as encoding norms whose use helps us to create powerful knowledge. We can see what is meant immediately by considering mechanism. It may, in fact, be the case that the external world is made up of jelly which melts or congeals at random, i.e. there may be neither structure in the real world nor any basic regularity of nature. However, we must presume that this is not the case if we are to have science at all, and although Gellner is not in possession of any proof of, for example, the regularity of nature, I think that he would allow himself to hope that our great ability to manipulate the world via mechanism signals that the world may *in fact* work on structural lines.

Much more effort must be spent on understanding how Gellner sees empiricism work as a cognitive norm. Any first-year undergraduate in the social sciences can now, regrettably, at the drop of a hat rehearse arguments against the positivist/empiricist tradition— most importantly, that facts are not pure but theory-laden, but with occasional obeisance to the old Hegelian insistence that facts are not isolable but part of a larger whole which should not be ignored. Gellner knows these criticisms, and does not try to ignore them; and for this reason his defence of empiricism is very valuable.

Gellner's charge against the critics of empiricism is that they are anthropologically naive and fail to realise that there is a vast difference between the belief systems that characterise the modern, as compared to the savage, mind. Writing of the latter Gellner argues that:

> It would be ideal in such a society to ask to have concepts separated into two camps—those which have an empirically operational role, and those whose reference is transcendent. There may be specimens of such pure types; but the interesting and characteristic examples are concepts which are, so to speak, semi-operational, which have both empirical and transcendent reference according to a locally recognised sliding scale, which is part of their very life and meaning, and the working of which dovetails neatly into the rest of local life and its ends.[24]

In contrast, modern belief systems have become habituated to recognising a boundary between their factual and their theoretical moments. The recognition that theories should not be judges in their own case permanently humbles theoretical extravagance:

> .... the really important social impact of [empiricism] is the injunction 'Be sensitive to the boundary, and impose consistency with respect to it; the secondary injunction, 'Down with the transcendent' (*Burn the books containing it* according to Hume, or *Call it technical nonsense* according to Ayer) does not matter much. If the first injunction is well observed and implemented, for all practical purposes the second is already performed and prejudged. In social contexts in which the first is well diffused and respected, it is perfectly possible to play down and, at a superficial level, ignore the second in the interests of courtesy, kindness, tact or antiquarianism. It hardly matters.[25]

Gellner's argument can be captured in part metaphorically. The sliding scale of package-deal belief-systems suggests a beauty contest in which masks, girdles and Elizabethan dress must be worn; the revolution of modern science consists, in contrast, of having all the contestants arrive more or less naked.

The movement away from belief systems that operate systematically in their own favour is achieved, Gellner argues, by virtue of accepting empiricist norms. Merely moralising that one should not do this is not enough. Only acceptance of the positivist way of seeing the world as made up of—and this is very important—granular, or atomic units allows for the emergence of the boundary between theory and fact. It is quite possible that the world is not like this. After all, this way of seeing the world is a norm rather than a guaranteed aspect of reality. Nevertheless the acceptance of such a picture of the world is essential if theories are to be sufficiently humbled to allow modern science to emerge.

Gellner does not expatiate at great length on the actual mechanism of modern science, but instead offers two considerations. On the one hand, the relative 'undress' of theories may make it possible to allow the facts, even if somewhat adulterated, some capacity to judge between theories. But on the other, and more frequently, he seems to follow some sort of Lakatosian line which stresses that refutation is not a once-and-for-all affair; science is unlike, say, the F A Cup in being subject to replays even when a fairly clear result has been obtained.[26] And perhaps even Lakatoś was too optimistic in believing that there would come a point when a research programme would be abandoned. But I am not sure that this matters as long as a paradigm continues to be sufficiently loyal to the positivist ethic by being used to investigate the world.

Gellner's view of science is subtle. His demand that we try and stand outside a particular belief system, at times, gives the impression that he hopes to find a neutral Archimedean point from which to survey the world. And his advocacy of positivism could mislead readers into thinking that he is a 'naive' positivist who believes that the facts are easily available. So it must be stressed that his argument is that, 'we choose a style of knowing and a style of society jointly'[27] or, in other words, that the nakedness of contesting theories is itself a social construct. Gellner has recently taken to encapsulating his theory by saying that 'positivism is right for Hegelian reasons'.[28] By this he means that positivism is indeed a *Weltanschauung* of its own, albeit one that can be defended. The two central reasons behind that defence can be noted after saying something about Gellner's careful analysis of the Kuhn-Popper debate, and after comparing his view with that of Habermas.

Both Kuhn and Popper are convicted of paying insufficient attention to the 'scientific revolution' as such, i.e. to the acceptance in society of the cognitive norms specified. Gellner begins his assessment of Popper by noting the justice of a familiar criticism of Popper, namely that he adulates 'revolutions' in science but dislikes revolutions in society.[29] This has led many to suggest that there is a contradiction in Popper's theories. Gellner's description of Popper is much more sophisticated, emphasising that his view on science runs entirely parallel with his views on society, but suffers from a similar weakness.

Popper's arguments for piecemeal engineering are considered by Gellner to be sensible and applicable to liberal societies which do not habitually sabotage reform; they are useless in societies in which piecemeal reforms can be suborned. Similarly, the revolutions in science Popper describes are in fact *piecemeal* changes inside a society that is characterised by basic attitudes, i.e. the acceptance of positivist norms, allowing intellectual change. What Popper misses, in other words, is any awareness of the veritable revolution that made science possible in the first place. This ignoring of the great transition to science has, in Gellner's opinion, a fatal effect on Popper's recent formulation of his approach in which criticism alone is judged to be the hallmark of science. Criticism occurs in most pre-scientific societies, but is invalidated by the ability of package-deal beliefs to explain away 'awkward' problems. So Popper's work must rest on the positivist cognitive norms if it is to work at all.

Curiously enough, Kuhn is to be convicted of similar ignorance of the importance of the great divide. Gellner suggests that Kuhn's insistence that science operates through the presence of a shared body of intellectual assumptions (a paradigm) is to be explained by the fear summoned up in his breast when working amongst social scientists at Princeton. The fear of intellectual anarchy has made Kuhn call for government at all costs; thus, 'Thomas Kuhn is the Thomas Hobbes of the philosophy of science'.[30] Gellner judges the emphasis on government by paradigm to be a poor criterion of science. The social scientist may be without a clearly defined paradigm, but there is no evidence that 'the savage mind' is in a similarly anarchic state. What is at issue rather is the *kind* of paradigm, i.e. ones which judge their own case completely and ones which recognise the great selectors. Gellner insists that Kuhn's work (or perhaps only his early work) itself suggests that the modern mind does allow intellectual change in a progressive direction; this can be clearly seen in the fact that Kuhn considers some paradigms in modern science superior to others.

It will be remembered that Habermas offers us a view of science emphasising that cognitive growth results from the consensus achieved by scientists once they have been able to raise certain validity claims, including that of the observations on which it is based, of any theory placed before them. This theory takes from Popper the idea of cognitive growth (although it notes that there was a particular 'institutionalisation' of scientific practice in the seventeenth century) and from Kuhn the idea of a community of investigators (although it ignores the argument that there are sometimes two consensual sets of paradigms at work at the same time). Curiously, Gellner is at one with this view in stressing that our mode of cognition should be seen as normative rather than somehow guaranteed, absolute and real. Beyond this, however, Gellner's position differs.

Firstly, he would surely object to the essential optimism inherent in the notion that the validity claims of modern science reside in the structure of language itself. This is to give the impression that cognitive growth is somehow on the evolutionary cards, whereas Gellner wishes to stress how unusual and accidental a set of cognitive norms was necessary for it to occur. This point can be put negatively: consensus will not lead to cognitive advance unless certain norms are accepted. Secondly, Gellner endorses positivism. It is important to realise that he eludes Habermas's polemical definition of positivism as the absence of reflection since he offers arguments as to *why* we should accept it. The most obvious of these is simply that this set of norms, by excluding circular rivals, allowed for cognitive growth. However, Gellner also offers a more subtle argument for the relatively naked world left by the empiricist ethic of cognition. He rejects, as we shall see, theories seeing the world as a

'Big Cosy Meaningful Unity'[31] in large part because he finds all that are on offer so repulsive. But here the point can be put constructively:

> The appeal underlying the closed vision [i.e. the Pirandello school]...is the moral gratification of seeing a coherent, un-'alienated' world. But this is not the only moral vision.... There is also.... the Protestant-Kantian ethic, which spurns extraneous confirmations and sanctions. We hold certain values, it says, and we do not need nature to confirm them for us. Let the facts be what they will; our norms are not at their mercy. We take no bribes—not even from the Top Management.[32]

So although we are offered reasons for a particular set of values, these reasons are not held to reside in man's basically good instincts, or in the very structure of language.

Disenchantment

Gellner's endorsement and development of the Weberian disenchantment thesis is more deeply felt than anything in his work. At different times we are offered various considerations on behalf of this theory, all of which gell together into a single argument that is at once philosophical and sociological. However, I shall, for reasons that will become apparent at the end of this chapter, deal with each type of argument separately.

The core to the disenchanting power of science is held to reside in the application of the mechanical scheme of explanation to human behaviour, that is, to our very selves. Gellner makes this clear when discussing Chomsky:

> Any explanation of human conduct or competence in terms of a genuine structure is morally offensive—for a genuine structure is impersonal, it is an 'it' not an 'I'.
>
> Chomskian structures are also known to be, in part, well hidden from consciousness; he himself lays great stress on this. If this be the correct strategy in the study of man, then the *I* is ultimately to be explained by an *it* (alas). The Freudian *id* was beastly, but, when all is said and done, it was cosily human in its un-housetrained way; at worst you could say it was all too human; it was human nature seen in the image of conscious man, but with gloves off. (Like us, but without the advantages we've had, if you know what I mean). The explanation of our unthinking, quasi-automatic competence into explanatory schemata outlining structures not normally accessible to us at all, is far more sinister. This kind of *id* is not violent sexy and murderous, it is just totally indifferent to us.[33]

Knowledge is thus a cold mistress, and Gellner describes two possible reactions to this discovery. On the one hand there is a retreat from investigation altogether; as Bob Dylan expressed it, 'The man in me will hide sometimes and keep from being seen but that's because he doesn't want to turn into some machine'.[34] This anti-intellectualism is much disliked by Gellner, as will be seen when his discussion of the sociology of 're-enchanting' creeds is examined below.

The second approach attempts to locate some specific quality of humanity that will raise it above being a mere machine. Gellner considers this approach to have a distinguished representative in Arthur Koestler. And, of course, Habermas's concern with 'knowledge and human interests' and his discussion of communicative competence is best seen as an attempt to argue that there is something special about humanity that prevents it from being tied down, i.e. explained or, properly, 'reduced' in the ways mentioned. Gellner, again with regret, does not feel that this is a viable option either. If an explanation of human uniqueness was found, the very act of discovery and thus of making it *public* would turn it into yet another piece of mechanical information. In the final analysis, it is perhaps the case that this would apply to some of the competences that Habermas wishes to analyse in 'reconstructive' terms. And in this connection it may be noted that it is perhaps doubtful whether the specification of stages buys as much immunisation from disenchantment as Habermas seems to think. The point of one joke made in the wake of the Kinsey report, after all, was that seeing one's partner mentally turning the next page of the latest sex manual and thus moving onto the next 'stage' deprived the act of spontaneity and thus enchantment.

At this point we can turn to a consideration of the more sociological side of the argument. The fact that there is not yet a mass of mechanical explanation of our inner selves perhaps makes the argument about the character of explanation, i.e. that the aim of science must be to so disenchant us, too esoteric in general social terms, however much it matters to Gellner himself. But he adds two more directly sociological considerations. Firstly, as noted, the positivist ethic, as it were, underpopulates the world with our theories; the world is no longer seen in homocentric terms. And where Habermas accepts this but yet wishes to argue against Weber by saying that *we* make science, Gellner chooses to stress that the norms of cognition, though they are indeed ours, no longer place *us* at the centre of things. Secondly, the power of modern science has a disenchanting effect on our social lives in another way. We turn to science whenever serious problems arise, and this means that the low-powered, commonsensical understandings of our daily lives are devalued. In Gellner's words:

> .... the world we live in, and the world of thought, are not the same. The *Lebenswelt* loses its status: though we must go on living in it, for we have no other, it becomes devalued, and we cannot treat it seriously. When important decisions are faced, we must seek information from more reliable sources.... [35]

How does Gellner react to this situation? He accepts that it is necessary to 'preserve our humanity' from explanation, but his model here is Kant, whom he holds to have been sparing, even miserly in his desire to save so little, albeit so reliably. [36] And he is convinced that it is quite wrong to try and produce easy formulae to protect either man or his social world from science (and we shall see him excoriating phenomenology on this point, below). All in all, our best, indeed our only, tactic is now to hold our identities ironically to act, in other words, with the awareness that we cannot make the world as we would like it. [37]

Gellner's whole position can be characterised by calling him the Proust of modern social thought. It it quite likely that he would object to this comparison on the ground that Proust showed little interest in science but the case is not so simple, for *A la recherche du temps perdu* is, in fact, a novel concerned with the hero attempting to establish his identity. Love and society are found to be illusory, and anguish results from being absolutely unable to decide which appearance is to be judged to correspond to a true reality. The novel concludes with a triumphant affirmation of the hero's new-found ability to solve (rather weakly) this epistemological problem and thus to establish a firm identity. Two points of comparison are noteworthy. Firstly, both Gellner and Proust insist on considering the absence of cognitive certainty as painful; this is a condition that has to be escaped. Secondly, the identities achieved are limited. Several things are lost as a result of the new cognitive certainty: Proust loses his belief in love and society whilst Gellner's respect for mechanism and empiricism obviates any belief that identity can be secured in any 'total' fashion.

It is likely that Gellner will add something in the future to the picture of disenchantment painted here. [38] This picture has stressed that the aims of positivism as a political movement, that of destroying false values *and* that of creating new ones, were incompatible: science destroys but cannot create. The English empiricist tradition shared its cognitive norms with positivism, but had little desire to produce a surrogate religion. However, the naturalism of British empiricism is perhaps mistaken in one dimension. The forces driving the animal man in empiricists' eyes tended to be rather benign, i.e. maximising pleasure and diminishing pain. Gellner frankly feels that the Nietzschean tradition paints a much truer picture of our inner lives, albeit he does not think that the Nietzschean ethic has had nearly such a powerful impact on larger political realities. This too, perhaps, leads to a measure of disenchantment, especially as he has little respect for the supposed 'scientising' of Nietzsche's vision by Freud. How can one be romantic about men when their inner lives are dominated by passion, envy and lust for power?

Sociology and Belief

Gellner can be an elusive writer, and this is perhaps especially the case in the analysis offered of 'our' position. This position is held to rest on four planks—empiricism, mechanism, 'ironic' identity and truncated evolution, i.e. industrialism—each of which has been examined. We must now look more closely at the relationship between this highly puritanical minimum and social life. Is it not possible to combine, as in Marxist dominated industrialism, a package-deal belief system, full of entrenched clauses, with modern science? And more important still, how can this position be reconciled to the undoubted fact, stressed so much by Habermas and Aron, that men do have beliefs? Social life is not, in other words, simply physically explicable, for men with similar genetic backgrounds produce very different societies. So what does an explanation of social behaviour look like? Finally, is Gellner in fact right that disenchantment is a fate from which modern men cannot escape?

None of these questions is far from the centre of Gellner's attention. The difficulties of running a modern society with an entrenched belief-system will be examined later. Here, we can concentrate on Gellner's approach to social life, and in particular to the question of the role and function of belief. His celebrated critique of idealism must be examined first, before his own alternative social science methodology (and consequent view of man) is underscored. Throughout, it is useful to keep in mind Gellner's debt of acknowledgement to social anthropology which:

> .... taught me how, without prejudice to its validity, one should see a set of related ideas and practices as a system of mutually supporting, and sometimes conflicting parts, and interpret it in terms of the service it performs and the conditions it requires in the social context of which it is a part.[39]

The Critique of Wittgensteinian Idealism

It has already been noted that a third selector of information has characterised the history of modern philosophy, namely that of language. Gellner has far less respect for this approach as a whole since it seems to him essentially academic.[40] However, he wishes to distinguish between two types of linguistic philosophy (and, indeed, perhaps three if Chomsky's 'mechanical' linguistics is to be considered part of 'the linguistic revolution' in modern philosophy).

The first period of linguistic philosophy bred the doctrines of Logical Atomism and Logical Positivism, and in this country was associated with the names of Russell, Ayer and the Wittgenstein of the *Tractatus*. In the crudest terms it may be said that this first general approach sought either to so refine language that it could refer immediately to the physical world or, through the analysis of logic, to damn certain doctrines or notions as meaningless: the keynote of the enterprise was to use language to transcend the boundaries of the received. As is well-known, the Wittgenstein of *Philosophical Investigations* turned against precisely this. According to this view, it is virtually a sin to try and establish any sort of ideal language that will get us closer to reality; on the contrary, reality is seen by virtue of the language that we have, and the attempt to transcend this is ridiculous, and creates endless false problems. In other words, Wittgenstein came, for Pirandellian reasons, to consider the Crusoe tradition in linguistic philosophy utterly mistaken.

The move from using language as a selector of information to re-endorsing it as a non-transcendable, and in any case smoothly functioning, system is made much of by Gellner. I am not at all sure in the light of, for example, Ayer's refusal to 're-endorse' as completely as Wittgenstein whether this move is logically necessary. This question can, however, be left to others more qualified than myself. What matters here are the sociological implications of the later Wittgenstein's view of language. These result from arguing that the carrier of a particular language is a society or 'form of life'. This creates a pure idealism of a heavily Platonic hue. Our lives are held to be structured for us by the concepts, linguistic and cultural, given to us by society. The doctrine is familiar to us from the hermeneutic tradition's insistence on 'meaning', whilst the particular Wittgensteinian version had an especially interesting forebear in Durkheim's famous arguments on the social origin of concepts.[41]

In the next section some general comments will be drawn as to the relation of Gellner's critique to the category of meaning as a whole. In this section, however, it is as well to remember that he is criticising the most rigorous versions of Wittgensteinian idealism, especially that of Peter Winch. This 'new idealism' has two particular strands that infuriate Gellner, which may be considered in turn. The first of these argues that each 'form of life' offers its own distinctive way of seeing the world, and that consequently no universal standards of judgement are available; the second strand follows from this and suggests that sociological explanation consists in understanding and describing the conceptual apparatus of another society.[42]

Gellner's discussion of the nature of 'forms of life' begins by faulting Winch's argument that cultures are, as it were, separate but equal. If it were the case that everyone, including Winch, was completely imprisoned inside the conceptual straightjacket provided by his society, then the standards of another society would surely be judged wrong, and certainly not equal. The fact that Winch argues for this equality suggests to Gellner that he in fact occupies a place somewhere above all 'forms of life' from whence he can assure us about the equality of all social forms.[43]

A second point concerning the nature of 'forms of life' is one that might by now be expected and it is the one which he makes with much force. The world is, in Gellner's eyes, daily refuting the relativism of Wittgensteinian Platonism. As noted, his own sociology centres on the transition to affluence; the fact that whole societies are choosing to become affluent argues that their own forms of life were highly defective and, more importantly, suggests their ability to see other conditions and judge them, in a universal sense, superior. The making of this choice allows Gellner to presume certain common standards of human rationality.[44]

The third objection to the primacy of 'forms of life' might be termed 'the attack on the seamless wonder theory of society'. The power of Platonism derives from its assertion that the commanding heights of our thought are controlled by a coherent set of conceptual tools we receive from society. Gellner argues that the simplest examination of any of the major literate traditions shows that this picture is vastly exaggerated. Both Christianity and Islam, for example, have contained reform movements which have sought to condemn and ban previous practices on putatively universal grounds. These traditions are thus less seamless wonders than perpetual battlegrounds. And this fact means that it is useless to expect consistent guidance from a form of life. An example of this, one of which Gellner is fond, is that of the Jansenists of seventeenth-century France who wished to place their allegiance to the Pope above that which they owed to the King, but were instructed by the Pope to obey the King. Such contradictions make the adulation of 'forms of life' rather silly. Moreover, it is of the essence of these beliefs (and not the application of them in the wrong circumstances, as Winch believes) that they contain a vision of 'the truth' that makes them have universal aspirations: thus cultural relativism, stressing equality and separateness, is belied by at least two of the major world religions.[45]

The confusion inside these traditions is, of course, only another way of describing the situation which Gellner considers to have given birth to philosophy in the first place. However, Gellner's training as an anthropologist allows him to go further than this and suggest, in effect, that it is most unlikely that even 'primitive' society operates with such conceptual economy that its 'form of life' corresponds exactly to its way of life. Gellner is more than suspicious of the extreme reliance of Winch on Evans-Pritchard's description of the Azande and notes that a careful reading of Evans-Pritchard shows that several languages (presumably containing different options of one sort or another) are spoken, and that 'Azande culture is a thing of shreds and patches'.[46] In other words, the concepts of the Azande are not so coherent and elegant that they rule out all options, and Gellner plainly believes that options are likely to exist in most 'primitive societies':

> No doubt, situations of this kind—conceptual loyalty without any option—do occur. But consider the implications of accepting this as a general criterion of traditional mentality: it means that within it there can be no syncretism, no doctrinal pluralism, no deep treason, no dramatic conversion or doctrinal oscillation, no holding of alternative belief-systems up one's sleeves, ready for the opportune moment of betrayal. Frankly, I do not believe this. Some savages may live in a unique, optionless world. Many do not.[47]

This is not, of course, to argue that there is no difference between primitive and modern society. If both types of society possess internally inconsistent conceptual standards, Gellner remains insistent that the great selectors allow inconsistency to be dealt with systematically, whereas primitive thought-systems encode muddle. In the words of Jarvie, who has sought to expand Gellner on this point: 'in fact with the Azande it is not that they cannot see any problem when they get contradictory advice, but that they possess a poor strategy for dealing with it'.[48]

It must be stressed that Gellner's general criticism of the emphasis on 'forms of life' does not mean he is uninterested in the social role and function of belief. However, his argument that behaviour is not to be explained by the supposition of a strait-jacket effect of the conceptual apparatus available leads him to look for other facts that explain how a particular approach can gain prominence. These will be considered fully in the next section, but they can already be seen in the second strand of his criticism of Wittgensteinian Platonism, namely that expounding the activity of anthropologists.

Once again, several things may be said about the argument that the proper job of anthropologists is merely to translate the different rules at work in the 'form of life' being studied. His first charge is simply that a mere conceptual account of something presumed to be 'different but equal' is liable to be highly defective. Taken to its logical extreme such an account would allow ludicrous examples. It would, for instance, be a rather unusual anthropologist who accepted as true a belief that men have no part in the procreation of children; yet total relativism would lead to a type of mere translation that should produce such results. More seriously, Gellner is reluctant to trust an approach that has a tendency to stress that a 'form of life' will provide concepts that make sense and which work. Against this 'principle of universal sympathy', Gellner stresses that the real functioning of concepts may depend upon their *not* making too much sense; it would thus rule out absurdity and ambiguity as characteristics of most society. His position is summarised thus:

> Excessive indulgence in contextual charity blinds us...to the possibility that social change may occur through the replacement of an inconsistent doctrine or ethic by a better one, or through a more consistent application of either. It equally blinds us to the possibility of, for instance, social control through the employment of absurd, ambiguous, inconsistent or unintelligible doctrines.[49]

Gellner's second point is equally simple, namely that anthropologists routinely discover a great deal more about various societies than would be possible if Platonism were taken seriously. One example of this that Gellner offers concerns kinship. In a provocative exchange with Barnes and Needham, Gellner argued that a considerable amount of anthropological knowledge is made possible by its being based on 'universal' knowledge about physical facts. Needham's original argument had been that the anthropologist had no interest in the 'physical father', merely in the role of 'social father' prescribed by society. At a later date, Barnes chose to expand this position by suggesting that anthropologists might be interested in both 'the social father' and 'the socially prescribed physical father'; however, they would neither be interested in, nor could know about, Gellner's real physical, or 'physical-physical father'. Gellner's answer to this assertion that anthropology is only interested in social not physical facts is brutally simple: unless some knowledge of the physical state of affairs is gained, there will be no possible way of establishing that either 'social father' or the 'physical father' *are* social constructs. Gellner thus argues that social understanding in large part concerns the relation between physical and social reality. And, though prepared to admit that it is at times difficult to establish firm information as to physical facts, he insists that the absence of any such information would mean that anthropology would be effectively neutered.[50]

The example of kinship shows that anthropologists gain much of their knowledge through being able to assess the role of beliefs about factually false propositions. A second, rather negative, example takes the argument one step further by noting that, even in cases where belief cannot be classified as false (notably religious belief), the anthropologist nevertheless wishes to go behind the belief to examine the social conditions that make it possible. The example concerns the disrespect shown by the tribesmen of the High Atlas (whose society was the subject of what is probably Gellner's best book, *Saints of the Atlas*) for the modern law which has recently taken the place of the traditional method of adjudication by collective oath at a sacred place. Some might think that this disrespect for the law resulted from the failure to swear at a shrine and thus make use of existing beliefs. Gellner, however, clearly prefers a structural explanation:

> In terms of transcendental belief, we might suppose that the failure to use a shrine was what makes the modern oath so feeble: but structurally what mattered was the failure to commit and implicate, with the guarantee of maximum publicity, all the people on whom the accused is normally most dependent.[51]

What Gellner is in effect saying is that men are not just concept fodder; they also make use of the concepts they are offered according to social circumstances and occasion. Thus, for example, memories of genealogies only stretch as far back as is necessary for present social placing; the basic interest is here social interest not truth—it would be disastrous to take the belief literally.[52]

Gellner makes two final subsidiary points on the practice of anthropologists. Firstly, he notes the trouble that those emphasising the 'seamless wonder' theory of society unwittingly get themselves into. The problem is simple: if a 'form of life' is, so to speak, seamless and complete then it becomes extremely hard to explain social change. Gellner argues that their awareness of this problem led Durkheim and Leach to suggest that social change was caused by the presence, within a single society, of two mutually incompatible belief-systems. He adds:

> But ironically, such a refinement is not necessary. Some social change may be accounted for precisely because *one* set of ideas has been inculcated too well, or has come to have too great a hold over the loyalties and imaginations of the members of the society in question, or because one of its subgroups has chosen to exploit the imperfect application of those ideas, and to iron out the inconsistencies and incoherencies.[53]

Gellner's own picture of less dominant and more confused conceptual apparatuses avoids this dilemma. The second point follows even more closely from some of those made above. Gellner insists that anthropologists and sociologists explain more than the conceptual tools of society. With reference to war, for instance:

> Real sociology does *not* explain warlike conduct (though both Louch and Winch are willing to do so) in terms of the implications of the *concept* of war. The concept may be there, but some soldiers will run away, some refuse to fight, and some fight. Any sociologists would look not merely at what is involved in the 'concept'.... but also at the social controls or pressures available and operative.[54]

Sociology is, in other words, concerned as much with the nature of powers that operate concepts as it is with the concepts themselves.

Gellner, quite simply, thinks that Platonism's picture of society is wildly wrong. But the bitterness of his diatribe against it has another source. He considers that it is, as it were, too kind to human beings: the emphasis on the ability of humans to create 'meaningful' words makes it possible to ignore ways in which human beings are themselves determined. And this refusal to evaluate determining factors is the more irresponsible in that it means that the options that are left open by, in particular, the 'great transition' are not fully evaluated. But before these options can be looked at it is necessary to summarise his views on the proper method for the social sciences.

Options, Structure and Reason

Gellner has not offered us a system of sociological rules, but the implied view of method, and thus of man, in his work can be culled from occasional essays. He bases himself on, and wishes to extend, the structural-functional method. This, of course, was in large part created by classical English social anthropology. Gellner suggests that other social sciences are likely to prosper insofar as it becomes generally used. Before describing what is a rather simple approach, it is as well to note a presupposition behind the whole enterprise. This method is based upon a heuristic belief that men are the same everywhere, members of social groups, whose behaviour depends far more on a recognition of necessary social tasks and the division of power than it does on the naive acceptance of a ruling ideology.[55] The fact that men are similar in these respects gives encouragement to those who desire to *explain* social behaviour.

The structural-functional method, not surprisingly in view of Gellner's previous criticism, is not sympathetic to idealism. The great difficulty with idealism is that it would allow, at least logically, any set of concepts to come into existence. Gellner clearly feels that such doctrinal fantasy is not possible, in light of various 'needs', physical and otherwise, that a society must meet.[56] His method is perhaps closer to pure materialism but this too is an insufficient basis, given that similar physical circumstances do not produce societies of a single type. The method in fact offers a type of multi-faceted materialism whereby various social practices are to be explained with reference to their place inside the social structure. Thus belief is examined with a view to the role it may play in the workings of the society. This approach makes it possible to ask about the elective affinity between belief and circumstances, and to investigate whether a belief is fostered by a ruling class, whether it is the property of an underclass and so on. All-in-all, it makes sense not to trust the self-image of society since this can positively mislead, and does not in any case own-up about the social support it needs to operate successfully.

Before looking at some examples of the method in action, it is important to realise that Gellner dissociates himself from functionalism as a theory of society. In particular, he has little time for the functionalist presupposition of social stability. He suggests that it is possible to divorce the method from the theory of society so that the method may then be used to investigate the structural factors making for change and discontinuity. Making this separation allows Gellner to rescue history from an approach that had sought to do without it. Gellner agrees that the structural-functional method is correct to ask for explanations in terms of social structure, and he notes that this militates against historians who have tended to offer explanations in genetic terms. Nevertheless, history offers a mine of information that cannot be ignored, and which can be interpreted in structural terms.[57]

Two examples of the method may be drawn from Gellner's own work. The first of these is that of nationalism. This theory has already been outlined, but its dimensions may be noted once again.

The theory is, first of all, designed to explain in a determinate fashion; it seeks to make sense of a rather confusing diversity. It suggests that nationalism is a modern phenomenon born of particular social circumstances (above all, an educated intelligentsia uses the label to gain the power from which it is excluded on grounds of race or colour). Moreover, as a creed it is concerned with creating a literate population fit to man an industrial society. Thus it can be understood in structural and practical terms. It would, however, be disastrous to proper understanding to take the self-image of nationalism seriously since this would hide its innovative capacity to create a nation where none really existed before.

The second example also exhibits this belief that explanations can be offered that go further than mere self-image. It would be insufficient to explain the egalitarian society of the tribesmen of the High Atlas by saying that they have a great respect for equality, although this happens to be the case. The possibility of holding such a belief can be more fully explained by, ironically, the presence of inegalitarian saintly lineages which mediate between these competing groups:

> ....These inegalitarian, stratified, pacific, 'artificial' outsiders perform functions which enable the feud addicted tribesmen to work their remarkably pure segmentary system. Here a separation of powers is not merely a check on tyranny, as intended in classical political theory, but also a check on inequality. The inegalitarian potential of the society is, as it were, drained by the saints.[58]

Once again, a structural explanation serves instead of one couched in terms of belief or conceptual necessity. Indeed, the immeasurable question of the benefits of the spiritual identification that saints also bring is allotted only a passing reference.[59]

Gellner's comments on method are very much those of a practising social scientist, that is, they do not form part of a treatise on method in their own right. But they are interesting, and I think it useful to try and systematise them in four points, at the same time bearing in mind his philosophy of science. If we seek to explain the world, we therefore involve ourselves in trying to reduce surface phenomena to something else. It is easy to see how this might be applied in the case of physical necessities that a society faces. But in what sense can one 'reduce' belief?

(1) Gellner's occasional comments give the impression that human aims are not so far removed from the picture of the human calculator provided by utilitarianism. I think that there is much to recommend this rather brutal view, although it is by no means

defensible as a complete picture of social behaviour. Gellner has made this clear in a recent essay in which he points out that men in fact spend less time pursuing aims of any sort than in avoiding gaffes.[60]

It is worth stressing that an over vigorous attempt to reduce men's beliefs to self-interest can quickly lapse into the cynical view whereby a belief is seen as a virtually self-conscious front for economic interests. This standpoint does not reduce human behaviour by explaining it, but reduces it in an altogether different sense. So the presumption of the social-anthropological method that 'men are the same everywhere' must not be taken to mean that greed is universal and the only thing of significance. Gellner certainly does not do this, and this makes the second and third points the crux of his sociology of belief. The first point, then, is really not much more than a limitation placed on the more extravagant excesses of hermeneutic understanding: it is as well to start at a low level, but this is not to insist that one stays there.

(2) Gellner's most general point is that belief can be explained. This is not to say that the belief itself is somehow unreal, but only to seek to discover the social circumstances that give it its character and cause it to gain prominence at a particular time. Thus we cannot understand the great ideologies of the modern period unless we realise that they are occasioned by the great transition: men whose lives are completely disrupted who yet feel attracted to the millenarian dreams of traditional society are naturally drawn to socialism, nationalism, Islam, various combinations of the three, and so on.[61] Nationalism (and other modernising creeds to be considered) call for an equalisation of conditions or, more specifically, for the creation of a common citizenry because this is a functional requirement of the modern world. In a nutshell, Gellner offers what I have called a materialist account of ideology and historical change.

Two points may be made about this approach of Gellner's. He avoids falling into errors that would result from taking the tenets of a belief literally. A Winchian sociologist might, for example, tell us that nationalism *is* the awakening of a nation that had been suppressed by imperialism, and thus not realise that much of nationalist creeds is mythical. Here, in other words, the refusal to take belief at face value, i.e. to seek for the circumstances behind it, is essential for proper sociology. Secondly, we can now give some sense to the presumption that 'men are the same everywhere'. This can be interpreted generously so as to allow rational actors ideational as well as instrumental needs. It then becomes possible to understand why circumstances such as depression, disruption and civil war can make large-scale ideologies appear sensible.

(3) Gellner rejects Wittgensteinian Platonism because he feels that it caricatures the character of belief systems. These are not so coherent as really to be able to constrain conceptually; on the contrary, they are often so full of holes that men are forced to stand outside them. More importantly, belief systems offer options that can be taken up by a particular social group in the service of its interests (generously understood) when the moment is right. This view of the nature of belief is plausible and subtle, and deserves serious consideration. Here, again, the sociologist must not take belief at face value since to do so would mean ignoring the way in which various social groups can accentuate one or another part of a ruling ideology.

Some critical comments immediately spring to mind. In what sense does this conception of sociology 'reduce' belief? There are very complex issues at work here, and distinctions must be drawn. This view of method does not reduce belief falsely and cheaply; it does not diminish its reality by seeing it as a mere facade. However, it refuses to accept beliefs at face value, and seeks to relate them to the structure of the society. In a loose sense, this is to follow the dictum of mechanism—to explain a thing in terms of something else. However, I think that it would be a mistake to see this reduction of belief to social structure in strong terms. It seems to me unlikely that a sociological specification of the social factors supporting belief would have the same disenchanting effect as, say, realising that schizophrenia is the result of chemical processes. Gellner essentially admits this is arguing that sociological knowledge is not notably high-powered; we can say something about particular ideologies inside the social world, he argues, but the crucial problem of how we generate a social world in the first place remains well beyond our powers.[62] Putting this another way, Gellner sees men as very actively trying, by working away at the edges of their belief systems, to make the most of their lives. But he insists that we realise that the social structure places limits on what rational social actors can themselves achieve.

I think it just, considering a comment of Gellner's on the Arab-Israeli conflict,[63] to illustrate this last point by means of Tom Nairn's very Gellnerite account of the situation in Northern Ireland.[64] Nairn sensibly realises that an ideational conflict is at work in Northern Ireland, but he does not therefore adopt some sort of Platonist view whereby men are totally encapsulated by their beliefs and unable to calculate their best chances. He explains the force of Orange sectarianism by noting the immense differences that existed between an industrial, urban area in the North and a poor, peasant society to the South. As this structural situation changes, i.e. as the South develops, he argues, we can hope that it may prove possible for the Northern Ireland Protestants to begin to lose, not their identity, but their fear that it would be swamped in a larger and distinct community.

One final point about Gellner's method needs to be highlighted. Although he has a strong sense of social structure and offers us a materialist view of ideology and history, there is nothing dogmatic about his position. Indeed, he even countenances a little Platonism of his own when arguing that Hinduism has no in-built puritanical industrialising option (an idea to be explained later with reference to Islam). Whilst it would, of course, be a terrible mistake to presume that Indian development is held down *only* by Hinduism, it probably remains the case that the lack of rationalising potential in this world tradition has some importance—it might, for example, mean that Indian development depends on general secularisation. There is a reverse side to this same point: that human beings are not always so capable as to create a way of thinking that truly helps them. The development of the cognitive norms of modern science was both fortunate and miraculous.[65]

(4) We must not forget that Gellner's philosophy leads him to say that in modern scientific and rationalised society there is substantially less possibility of creating ideologies that explain the world fully. The price of science must be that loss of faith in our *Lebenswelt* summed up in the disenchantment thesis already examined. Men are, in other words, for the first time going systematically to have to try and live without the symbolic ordering characteristic of historical societies.

The Peculiarity of Liberty

Gellner places a high value on liberty for conventional reasons. The first of these is derived from Raymond Aron for whose sociology Gellner has great regard. Gellner agrees with Aron that Western liberal democracies, whilst not being striking instances of classical democratic theory at work, are worth defending since they allow sufficient pluralism to check the arbitrary exercise of power. In his words:

> ....we cannot but prefer a society in which the rich (i.e. those who control industry) have to bribe, marry, corrupt, bamboozle, persuade, infiltrate, etc., those controlling other crucial positions in society, to one in which they don't need to do any of these

things, because they happen to be identical with them. Similarly, we cannot but prefer a system in which rival cliques of potential power-holders are at least bound to solicit the votes of an electorate possibly bamboozled by mass-media, to one in which the bamboozling is not even necessary to elicit a deluded consent, but only occurs as *l'art pour l'art*.[66]

The second reason that Gellner offers owes much to Popper. Gellner values the 'openness' of liberal societies, meaning by this that such societies are not so constituted as to sabotage absolutely change and social reform. The ability to choose one's future in some measure is judged to be intrinsically worthwhile, but Gellner notes a more important benefit of characterising liberalism in terms of openness. The liberalism of thinkers such as John Stuart Mill had tended to defend liberty in non-social terms; man was judged to be free insofar as he could slough off social interferences of one sort or another. Gellner considers this picture of an ultimate redoubt of selfhood, free from society, unrealistic. The defence of liberalism in terms of openness is judged to be a considerable improvement:

> It allows—as is the case—that even, or especially, the ultimate recesses of our being, are socially formed. It merely requires that it be feasible that sometimes we should be able to tinker with the social organisation and culture which forms us; it defines liberty as an attribute of societies which tolerate and facilitate peaceful reassessments and reforms.[67]

The critical note Gellner uses against classical liberalism may be extended. In his political views, as elsewhere, Gellner operates on puritanical lines; in this case this means that he does not wish to rely on many of the traditional defences of liberalism. He points out that present liberal societies often rest upon archaic principles, and are inclined to tolerate poverty in the midst of affluence. But most importantly, Gellner wishes to abandon the defence of liberalism in terms of laissez-faire. He is quite brutal in his evaluation of laissez-faire dubbing the belief in the beneficence of the hidden hand a straightforward fantasy.[68] His most basic objection is to the silliness of an approach that stresses individual, non-social contribution at a time when modernised societies are responsible for creating and supporting a massive social infrastructure, notably in education, that is entirely collective in character.

This critical note should warn us that Gellner's views on liberty are not completely conventional. He argues, for instance, that liberty only came to characterise Western societies as a result of a series of accidents. Capitalism's stress in separating the market from political rule is seen as a very rare event in human history; the more usual pattern is for those with wealth to choose to turn it into immediate political muscle. This relative restraint is explained on two counts. Firstly, the Protestant ethic supplied an inner compulsion to reinvest and, secondly, Gellner suggests, the industrialisation of Western Europe took place on the basis of a rather low level of technology. This meant that:

> The state tolerated the producers/accumulators partly because it could *afford* to tolerate them, without itself being devoured: they were not so very big or so very destructive. They enjoyed the framework it provided, but they did not smash it or take it over. They rocked the boat a bit—but not so much as to make it unnavigable.[69]

In other words, the piecemeal nature of Western industrialisation made it possible for this 'route to the modern world' to be one that combined industrialisation and democracy.

Both these factors could be summed up by saying that western industrialisation was unplanned. Gellner's unblinkered view of man leads him to hope that the liberal structure of these societies can be maintained now that they are capable of providing affluence. But this same image of man suggests to him that men will put up with authoritarian government so long as it provides a reasonable, that is an industrial, standard of living (This argument is, of course, in striking contrast to Dahrendorf's Warrior Ethic.) Unfortunately, the creation of industrialism by means of central planning, i.e. the method which nearly all the world except the West must use, is such as to undermine the very chance of liberty.[70] This 'creation' of an industrial nation state is so dramatic as to virtually rule out the possibility of democracy gaining much foothold. For the theory of democracy depends on the exercise of 'willing consent'; this becomes a rather useless criterion in a situation of such fundamental change that, literally, new men with new wills are being created. But the problem has deeper roots. The mobilisation and education in a single national language (and thus the elimination of others) of a whole population can most easily, perhaps only, be achieved by directives issued from a centralised power. Once power is centralised it is likely to remain so even after affluence has been achieved. Pace Habermas, technical growth rules out moral development.

Gellner notes an irony of this situation that accords well with his general view of the use that men make of their concepts for particular ends. Those countries which wish to industrialise are likely to be attracted to Marxism rather than to Western notions of laissez-faire since it stresses central direction, and serves well as a Protestant ethic for twentieth century industrialisers. Gellner suggests that the adoption of this creed is to be seen as highly instrumental and rational. This awareness of, as it were, the non-ideological attractions of Marxism means that he has not felt especially threatened by the increasing number of, so-called, Marxist regimes in the Third World.

The process of industrialisation then is likely to be inimical to the spirit of liberty. In particular, this process is one which is likely to pay scant heed to the two major reasons that Gellner offered for his own high valuation of liberalism. Openness and pluralism must be scorned by non-industrialised countries since indoctrination and concentration of power are able to produce more dramatic returns more quickly.

Hopes and Fears

The likelihood that industrialisation and democracy stand in inverse relation is the essential fact limiting the chances of liberty in the modern world. But Gellner is not prepared to leave the question at this point. Much of his recent work has been concerned to investigate the lacunae within this general framework, and he has done so in four ways that have taken him beyond the viewpoint offered by Aron.

Development

Gellner has retained his interest in Third World countries. Most immediately, he suggests that it is a mistake to ignore the differential chances that there are for liberty in various Third World countries. He has, for example, recently visited and written about Nepal. Here the presence of an urban, literate middle class, the Newars, whom the patrimonialist state cannot afford to ignore, holds out the possibility that a measure of pluralism may be retained throughout the modernisation process.[71] He has also drawn a distinction between the pluralism allowed by a short colonial war (for example in Tunisia) and the ascendancy of a single ideology consequent on the destruction of all local institutions in a long one (as in Algeria).[72]

However, his most interesting work has been done on the 'puritan ethic' available as an option in Islam. Islam is archetypically a religion of the book, and it is largely the presence of 'dissident' tribesmen on the periphery of North African societies that has made the disciplinarian injunctions of the book hard to enforce. However, Gellner has described how modern North African nationalism may make use of this central tradition to impose those standards of discipline and literacy inculcated by Protestantism in the West and regarded by Gellner as a necessary part of the infrastructure of

industrial society. This use of Islamic belief as an aid to industrialisation certainly characterises both Algeria and Libya. Unlike
Turkey, these societies have placed no emphasis on foreign
parliamentary traditions but have made most effective use of the
shared religious tradition in the mass mobilisation of their people.[73]
The use of a shared tradition probably makes for speed and
effectiveness, but Gellner is clear that there is so far insufficient
evidence to enable us to judge whether the leaders of these societies
are true believers or merely pragmatists. What evidence there is at
present suggests that the latter may well be the case since the children of
the national leaders still tend to be educated in the West, and in
French.[74]

The fact that Islam is able to offer its own 'Protestant ethic'
clearly amuses Gellner, especially when it is mixed up with the more
celebrated industrialising creed, namely Marxism. He is, once
again, impressed and delighted by the subtlety and ingenuity with
which men are able to manipulate their concepts, although he
suggests that there is some limit to this. Hinduism, for example, has
no similar stress on egality or literacy and thus, despite the attempts
of the Nepalese, probably has no inherent puritan ethic option.

Gellner's reflections on the options available in 'rationalised'
Islam have become rather topical as the result of the revolution in
Iran. In a recent essay, he stresses how extraordinary a revolution
this was: made against an army specifically designed to prevent it,
and in a country that had not recently suffered a defeat in war (the
precipitating factor of most revolutions)[75] But Gellner knows no
better than anyone else exactly how to interpret the ascendancy of
puritanical Islam. Optimistically, one can perhaps hope that a
rationalised local ideology will make the transition period shorter.
But more immediately, as Gellner stresses, the change in terms of
trade due to the reliance of Europe on oil has given Islamic ideology
such bite as to make us realise that the future of the West may no
longer be in its own hands.

Liberalisation

Gellner's basic emphasis on the impossibility of combining liberty
with modernisation has led him to look elsewhere for increased
chances for liberty. Hence he has concentrated on the fate of
societies with authoritarian governments which are, however,
reasonably affluent. He suggests that a concern with liberalisation is
going to occupy our attention far more in the future than the more
traditional concern with revolution which will become less and less
relevant as the number of industrialised societies increases. Liberal-

isation, he says, should be seen in terms of a game, and his interest is in seeing the rules of this game spelled out. Its central rule, he believes, is to proceed with cautious energy, and the dangers of going too fast are only too clear: at worst, one can be branded a traitor to the ideology under which industrialisation was achieved. However, Gellner offers us no set of rules, he just points to the sort of factors that need to be considered:

> Is there a generic difference between Left and Right Liberalization? How much difference does economic centralisation make to the process? Or the existence of a large and indispensable class of technical, or literary, intelligentsia? Or the existence of a precise and codified ideology, with fairly unambiguous sources of scriptural authority, as opposed to loose or even plural ideologies? Or the presence of regional nationalism, available as allies? Or the intrusion of international politics, given that, curiously, the precise degree of internal freedom can serve as a badge of block adherence and loyalty? Is liberalisation favoured by economic success or by failure? Do the groups which crystallised out in a previously centralised state bear any resemblance to the traditional categories of 'class' etc?[76]

These are indeed crucial questions, and one might add to them. Does the memory of civil war account for the extraordinary restraint, and hence success, shown by Spaniards in their current liberalisation? Is the presence of a liberal monarch a crucial ingredient?

Gellner's own most sustained analysis of an attempt at liberalisation takes the form of a review of a work on Czechoslovak society written by Pavel Machonin and others, which appeared only after the Russian invasion of 1968. Gellner is full of praise for the inherent merit of this study of social stratification under socialism, and is particularly interested to note that social stratification does not correspond simply to inequalities of wealth.[77] But he is most impressed with the theorising in favour of liberalisation. Machonin and his colleagues suggest that a useful typology of societies would include capitalism, dictatorship of the proletariat and bureaucratic, egalitarian, technocratic-meritocratic and socialist societies. Czech society, it is argued, has become a curious mixture of bureaucratic and egalitarian types, a mixture consisting, basically, of a great measure of economic equality in combination with absolute political inegalitarianism. Gellner is fascinated by Machonin's advocacy of *greater* social stratification in Czechoslovakia, but is not quite certain as to whether this is needed in the interests of economic efficiency or whether only classes are sufficient to serve as a basis for political pluralism.

Gellner is deeply impressed by the subtlety with which Eastern Europeans can so manipulate Marxism as to find options within it for liberalising behaviour. This self-consciousness accounts, in part, for the fact that he is more optimistic about liberalising societies than about either the Third World or liberal democracy. He has recently written a series of very striking papers on Soviet anthropologists, demonstrating the vigour and ability with which Marxism can sensibly be used to great effect.[78] There is every indication, in other words, that a significant group exists who, unlike the more publicised dissidents, are trying to liberalise from within. The mere presence of such a group would not in itself give much cause for optimism, but Gellner argues that an advanced industrial society comes to depend more and more on the services of a skilled technical intelligentsia. His hope is that the elite will realise that the loyal adherence of this group may so help the regime by increasing the success of the economy as to allow them to liberalise without undermining their position.

I think that there is no doubt that liberalisation is indeed one of the crucial issues of our time and it is refreshing to read Gellner's account of the measure of liberalisation he feels to have been already accomplished in Czechoslovakia.[79] But although we can hope that he is right, it is worrying, as we shall emphasise in the postscript, that the social group mainly interested in liberalisation is intellectual. Is it not likely that the creation of a more inegalitarian, albeit pluralist, socialist society' will meet from opposition on the part of the working class who, as Machonin stresses, have benefited from state socialism?

The Vanity of Human Wishes

In one of his essays on Soviet anthropologists, Gellner noted that:

> .... the visitor from the West is liable to get a surprise—an agreeable one as far as the present writer was concerned. Contemporary Russian Marxism is *intelligible*. To anyone who has the misfortune of acquaintance with Western high-brow Marxist fashions, this comes as a shock indeed. Here in the West, neo-Hegelian, existentialist, phenomenological, *structuraliste*, etc., interpretations of Marx have completed in recent decades the transition characterised (I think by Raymond Aron) as the move from dogmatic to imaginary (and unintelligible) Marxisms.[80]

If one adds to this list the later Wittgenstein, Reich, Freud, ethnomethodology, and idealism in general, one has a fair list of those Gellner considers to be the re-enchanters. This list has obvious similarities to the 'Antinomians' describes by Bell, and those who are posing the motivational crisis according to Habermas. Moreover,

Gellner is close to the analysis of both Bell and Habermas in suggesting that the re-enchanters wish to accord some priority to the 'human' at the expense of the organised structures of society. But he differs from both in arguing the re-enchanters present absolutely no danger to capitalism or to industrial society in general. This is made plain in a comment on Bell's 'cultural contradiction of capitalism' thesis, in which Gellner suggests that the poor quality of 'Antino-main' thought is all too 'functional' in advanced societies:

> A really advanced industrial society does not any longer require cold rationality from its consumers; at most, it may demand it of its producers. But as it gets more advanced, the ratio both of personnel and of their time is tilted progressively more and more in favour of consumption, as against production. More consum-ers, fewer producers; less time at work, more at leisure. And in consumption, all tends towards ease and facility of manipulation rather than rigour and coldness. A modern piece of machinery may be a marvel of sustained, abstract, rigorous engineering thought; but its operating controls must be such that they can easily and rapidly be internalised by the average user, without arduousness or strain. So the user lives in a world in which most things have an air of easy, 'natural', 'spontaneous' manipulabil-ity. And why should not the world itself be conceived in this manner?[81]

Gellner is here implying that the discipline engendered by bourgeois-puritan society had, as its unintended consequence, the creation of a rigorous intellectual culture.[82] Gellner's own allegiance is to this culture, and his extreme hostility to the re-enchanters results from the facile way in which they find themselves a warm identity at a time when serious analysis of our position shows that an element of cold disenchantment is unavoidable.[83] But Gellner's own feelings about the matter should not hide that—sociologically—his criticism of the re-enchanters is that their thought is, as it were, desperately innocuous; its facility mirrors, all too exactly, advanced society and it is thus unlikely to be a danger to the social order.

A few details of Gellner's analysis need to be filled out in order to make our understanding of it complete. He argues that both Kant and Weber, the respective philosophical and sociological exponents of the modern disenchanted world view, were too quick to assume that a rationalised world would necessarily be a cold one. As noted, the more extreme forms of affluence may well allow for new revivalisms, of one sort or another, that once again place man and his meaningful capacities at the centre of the stage. One of the classic strategies in this general approach is that of phenomenology:

> The irony is, we have only come to be aware of [the Lebenswelt] when we no longer live in it, at any rate not exclusively or

predominantly. Phenomenology claims to 'suspend' it, to suspend judgement about its reality-status, to see it simply *as* a Lebenswelt. But that, precisely, is what it no longer is. And by pretending to 'suspend' it, phenomenology in fact covertly fortifies it, it ratifies it by a kind of sleight-of-hand; by seeming to exempt it from even entering and competing in the scientific reality-stakes, it implies that at least simply *qua* Lebenswelt, in its more modest pretentions, its status cannot be in any doubt. *Qua* Lebenswelt at least it is secure and vindicated....[84]

The reason why we do not any longer trust the knowledge of our *Lebenswelt* is straightforward: only impersonal, non-commonsensical scientific knowledge can provide the affluence which is the effective legitimation force in modern society. In the last analysis, Gellner says:

> The new pseudo-cultures continue to rely on this technology for a standard of living to which its members are accustomed and which they are most certainly not seriously prepared to forego. These monks go out to an air-conditioned wilderness. It is all rather like Tolstoy re-enacting peasant life in one part of his house and maintainig his habitual standards in another. So many Tolstoys these days....[85]

The Demise of the Danegeld State

Gellner's declaration that the re-enchanters present no threat to the social order is consonant with his habitual emphasis on more basic structural forces in society. However, his own analysis of the manner in which these are coming to work in liberal democracy seems increasingly to suggest to him that stability is no longer as easily guaranteed as was once generally thought. In a recent piece constrasting the mood of the 1970s with the 're-enchanting' or 'expressivist' 1960s, Gellner suggests that the student demands of 1968 were, finally, unimportant:

> ....a shadow of a shadow, *ersatz* of *ersatz*, it re-enacted 1848, which in turn had re-enacted 1789. But the 1970s scare me stiff. The expressivists never made the *Financial Times* Index tremble. The miners and the oil-sheikhs, who do have that power, are not activated by expressivist yearnings. All they want is a much bigger share of those post-Enlightenment goodies which express-ivism spurns.[86]

This is a revealing passage and it is one that is easily explained. In *Thought and Change* Gellner suggested that discontent inside indust-rial society could be bought off as a result of the plethora of danegeld available to the rulers.

Gellner considered it appropriate to think of Western liberal societies as 'danegeld states' since they are based upon an internal political contradiction that makes the giving of danegeld a necessity for the proper functioning of the system. This political contradiction is simple: the exploited in such societies are possessed of the vote and so can only be made to work through either the 'stick' of unemployment (less acceptable with the rise of Labour parties) or the 'carrot' of increased wages. In contrast, Eastern Europe is not, in general, possessed of sufficient formal freedom to make such societies internally inconsistent, however important wage-bargaining may be below the surface. This said, the explanation for Gellner's fears for liberal society is straightforward, namely that the 1970s have witnessed the cessation of the flow of danegeld or, more simply, a crucial slow-down in economic growth. This scares Gellner since liberal societies are, he feels, consequently in trouble.

Gellner's thoughts on the matter are directed both at a larger and smaller target. He considers that much of the problem of liberal society in general is explained by the continuing demand for higher wages in situations where rises in world prices—especially oil-prices—make this no longer automatically possible, except at the cost of self-destructive inflation. But he is writing more particularly about England. He is unwilling to say whether he considers England a laggard or a forerunner of things to come. Nevertheless, he is quite clear about the characteristics of the English 'crisis'. The English working class, he claims, is characterised by obstinate militancy. Alone amongst European working classes in not suffering a cataclysm in recent memory, the English working class has been able to combine a feeling of the illegitimacy of capitalist organisation with an expectation that affluence was their birthright. Gellner summarises these points by suggesting that, in England, the combination of Marxism feeling with Keynesian demands has resulted in the effective crippling of the economic system:

> It is not an increasingly impoverished proletariat, over-concentration of wealth, and deficient demand . . . . which may be killing capitalism, or what is left of it. The Right is moralistically begging for economic central planning of demand and distribution, the Left howling for untrammelled free bargaining. The Keynesian central manipulation of demand, once intended to be the saviour of capitalism, to be its Counter-Reformation, is now an essential element in its self-destruction through inflation. So is the alleged facade state: its welfare provisions and political liberalism ensure that it is not only possible, but positively comfortable to dig the grave of capitalism.[87]

Gellner's argument is thus of the difficulties of success; continuing demand for the 'goodies' provided by affluence raises central questions of social justice once economic growth slows down.

Gellner considers it a terrible irony that Britain seems fated to base her policies on versions of the two great nineteenth century analyses of industrial society, those of the laissez-faire economists and Marx. He regards both of these of very little use in understanding our current dilemma. Laissez-faire theorists fantasise about the possibility of making governments give up their power to control the economy in order that the market place—in Gellner's eyes not half as fair as its protagonists claim—may work unhindered. Curiously, Marxists share the belief in a kind of anarchist utopia, albeit this utopia is placed very firmly in the future. Both these theories fail to ask the crucial question as to how industrialism, with its inevitable emphasis on the concentration of power, can be made to work democratically.

Interestingly, in accord with the structural and material tone of his sociology, Gellner suggests that there are two ways in which the system as such may be made legitimate—the implication being that this might again allow for greater economic growth, or at least to a diminution of inflation. Firstly, that it may be necessary to buy off, systematically, those sections of the working class capable of disrupting the economic machine. This solution amounts to stating that status and rewards should be dissociated so that those with economic muscle (and occasionally the worst jobs) receive high rewards; those with rewarding jobs are likely to remain loyal in any case. Gellner sees this as a real solution, it must be emphasised, because of Machonin's discovery that Czechoslovakia has divorced status and reward. Secondly, he suggests, en passant, that all liberal democracies may have to try and adopt the Japanese custom of building a career-structure into working-class jobs as much as into those of the middle class.

Gellner's analysis is brilliant but idiosyncratic. His argument that the core of capitalism lay in laissez-faire is certainly useful in highlighting the origins of liberal societies, and in clearly delineating the problems that they face when a 'half-integrated' proletariat has some real, albeit perhaps negative, access to power. But the suggestiveness of the analysis is matched, perhaps not surprisingly, by a lack of detail about some proposals that are implied. If the political market is disastrous, how much and in what way can the economic market be retained? More importantly, what exactly are the implications of refusing to define capitalism in terms of the ability to pass on privileges? Gellner does not adopt this definition since he feels that it is no longer so easy for the rich automatically to gain power and have their way—as the industrial relations crisis evidences. Does this mean as a consequence that, in the West, social democracy can rest simply on the pluralism of a complex society rather than on that resulting from the distinction between capital and labour? Would a state-encouraged divorce between status and wealth abolish class structure or merely complicate it? These are weighty questions touched on below, and we can only hope that Gellner returns to them in the future at much greater length.

Conclusion

Gellner has produced a remarkably fruitful mixture of sociology and philosophy, and he has offered us a conception of our situation that is of very great range and power. Some of the issues he touches on are discussed in chapter eight, but we can conclude here by comparing him very briefly with Raymond Aron. I have loosely paired these thinkers, but the attentive reader will be well aware of substantial differences between them. Gellner's social theory is 'materialist', and considers that all human knowledge must involve reduction and disenchantment; above all, perhaps, he is a strong rationalist. In contrast, Aron has always remained influenced by the *Geisteswissenschaften*—an influence, it must be remembered, encountered at the moment Aron was witnessing 'history on the move' in pre-Nazi Germany. Although personally a rationalist, Aron's experience has left traces of radical relativism in his thought. This difference of temperament between them can be seen in the different solutions they offer to the problems of Western society—Gellner's being much more 'material' than Aron's. And besides temperamental differences, there is an important difference of substance between them to be noted.

Gellner's conception of 'episodes' of human history suggests that we can map the broad contours of human development. This viewpoint in effect spells out clearly the basis of Aron's own work, and it is an advance upon it in specifying the circumstances that led to the age of ideologies. There is agreement between the two thinkers on two further points: that the explanatory scheme of modern science is disenchanting, but that sociological explanation is not of sufficient power to be of this type. However, Aron insists that disenchantment is to be understood, as it were philosophically rather than sociologically.[88] This is not to say that he can produce any number of large-scale beliefs to refute Gellner, but he can produce one, namely that states continue, as in 1914, to be able to rely on the loyalty of their citizens in moments of stress. There are good reasons for this loyalty, perhaps most importantly that circumstances are such that both capital and labour conduct themselves as national rather than transnational phenomena.[89] This should not be understood as saying that new European wars are likely or that national loyalty is of much use in internal politics. But it does mean that the disenchantment thesis is best understood as an a priori truth that has not yet, as it were, become a powerful social reality in its own right. And for Aron this point is of immense potential importance. The caution he shows in refusing to say that history has any pattern can best be understood as being due to his fear that the continuing reality of inter-state rivalry may be such as to make history, in the end, more or less formless.

8 Postscript

The main task of this book—the analysis of six views of our social condition—is now complete. In concluding, however, I propose to follow the practice formally adopted by Brian Barry of offering some more general reflections, to be taken as debating points rather than fixed arguments, that are occasioned by the themes discussed.[1]

The key characteristic of our social life does seem to me to be that of the industrial stage, albeit it must be understood that this 'mode of production' is capable of supporting different political systems; and the transition to industrialism, so heavily marked by the great ideologies, is likely to be made under dictatorial rather than democratic aegis. Given these baselines, i.e. ruling out post-industrialism as a new stage of human history, what may we hope and what should we fear? What options remain for us? Four issues seem to dominate all others; not nearly enough is known about any of them, and this makes it mandatory to avoid two of the vices of intellectuals—prophesying doom or radiating certain hope.

We are well situated with regard to the first point, that of the chances of liberalising regimes, traditional and, above all, state socialist, since Aron and Gellner have recently highlighted the issues involved succinctly. Aron is convinced that liberalisation must proceed so as to prevent a revolution, i.e. the traditional powers must include the people in the society *before* they have time to make a revolution, if democratic society is to remain pluralist and liberal. Accordingly, Aron is deeply impressed by the post-Franco era, and has kind words for the skill of the Greek Leadership. As noted, however, he is very pessimistic about Eastern Europe since he thinks that an ensconced monopolistic party is unlikely, especially when the economy is not working well, to allow its power to be abrogated in any way. Gellner would not, of course, deny the abilities of the Spanish or Greek leaders, and might indeed consider that certain factors present in both cases—memories of a collective disaster, the Common Market—make liberalisation easier. But he differs from Aron about liberalisation in the East:

> The counter-argument to Aron's pessimism seems to me to run as follows: an advanced industrial society requires a large scientific,

technical, administrative, educational stratum, with genuine competence based on prolonged training. In other words, it cannot rely on rigid ideologues and servile classes alone. It is reasonable to assume that this kind of educated middle class, owing its position to technical competence rather than to subservience, and inherently, so to speak professionally, capable of distinguishing reality and thought from verbiage and incantation, will develop or has developed the kind of tastes we associate with its life-style—a need for security, a recognition of competence rather than subservience, a regard for efficiency and integrity rather than patronage and loyalty in professional life... This class is large, and it cannot be penalised effectively without a cost to the economy which may no longer be acceptable. The main body may sacrifice or even disavow its own 'dissident' advance guard, whilst benefiting from its courage, though it may perhaps secure some moderation at least in the price exacted for that courage by the old authorities.

Furthermore, relative economic success, national pride, and the legitimacy conferred on any regime by sheer longevity, may make it easier—because less risky—for the rulers to make concessions to this class. As material resources become more plentiful, competition for them may become less acute. Affluence, if not classlessness, may at least reduce antagonisms and thus, for good Marxist reasons, diminish, though it cannot eliminate, the need for a repressive state. The end of ideology, erroneously predicted in the West, may yet get its second chance in the East. Could it not perish from sheer boredom? So, as the system gains in authority through stability, it may afford to relax without putting itself intolerably at risk.[2]

It would be foolish of me to pretend that I could somehow adjudicate this debate, especially given the very different circumstances of the various state socialist societies. But one point does deserve to be made. Although we can hope that Gellner is right, it is noticeable that his case rests heavily on the intellectual and administrative classes. I wonder if this is a sufficient support for liberalisation: specifically, would not a more dynamic economy mean removing much of the security of the working class in Eastern Europe? Reduced emphasis on security, with greater emphasis on the work ethic, would pay off *in the long run* but, unfortunately, that may not be enough.

If it is possible to hope for liberalisation in the East, it is hard not to have fears for the future of Western societies. These have recently been characterised by Kolakowski in terms of their ability to combine some measure of equality, freedom and democracy, each of which taken singly leads to disaster:

Absolute equality can be set up only within a despotic system of rule which implies privileges, i.e. destroys equality; total freedom means anarchy and anarchy results in the domination of the physically strongest, i.e. total freedom turns into its opposite; efficiency as a supreme value calls again for despotism and despotism is economically inefficient above a certain level of technology.[3]

It is worth stressing that the differences between Western societies, for instance the 'welfare corporatism' of Sweden on the one hand and America on the other, remain great and important. Nevertheless, I have argued that the precarious balance of Western society as a whole is running into difficulties. This is to say that Great Britain is not the exception to the rule (although there are exceptional circumstances at work), but the general pacemaker. The problem of Western societies results from the combination of social inequality and democracy, which creates the rationality crisis of the state, especially in its inflationary aspect. This crisis was brutally exhibited in the winter of 1978/9 in Great Britain when a Labour government was unable to enforce limited wage rises that would, ironically, have been in the interest of everyone, again, *in the long term.* As noted, this sort of conflict does not well accord with Marxist scenarios: working class action is much more 'the capitalism of the proletariat', whilst the state itself, far from 'doing the work of capital' is relatively feeble. This situation has unpleasant historical resonances to it. Between about 1930 and 1933, Carl Schmitt analysed with ruthless logic the inability of the centre to hold in Weimar Germany, and he concluded that only a strengthening of political authority could save society. His arguments appealed to both Left and Right, and he fascinated his contemporaries because nobody was quite sure which side he would come down on (he chose the right).[4] There are many differences between modern liberal democracy and Weimar, but *any* parallel is uncomfortable.

Little comfort, too, is to be found from the two basic recipes designed to make Western societies work more smoothly—especially once it is noted that they are so completely polarised. The Right effectively seeks to discipline the workforce by allowing higher levels of unemployment. It has recently been pointed out that there is perhaps a certain Machiavellian wisdom in this strategy: provided that the young unemployed are looked after, the others out of work are unlikely to disturb the social order given their age and social isolation—for instance, their lack of union backing.[5] But besides being unpleasant this strategy seems to me to depend far too heavily on mysterious changes in psychological mood. More importantly, two institutional facts, the continuing existence of the unions and the electoral pressure to reflate, remain and are likely, as hitherto, to undermine it.

In contrast, the Left is coming to argue that only a democratic and centrally planned economy can now be efficient. It must be said at once that there is no sign of voter demand for such a vision. Perhaps this is not surprising, given that no details are available as to how exactly this mix is to be achieved and to function. There are three major problems here. Whilst state intervention can be organised in a number of ways, there is no reason whatsoever to believe that complete central planning is efficient. A local factor that weighs heavily, at least with me, is the almost certain inability of the Oxbridge-trained English Civil Service to manage industry better than anyone else. Second, full-blooded central planning, i.e. that involved, for example, in an 'industrial regeneration of Great Britain', would seem very likely to run up against union interests. But thirdly—and more fundamentally—are not the comments made so far perhaps too narrowly economic? They *are* economic and, in my opinion, should be so since an efficient industrial economy has done quite as much to raise life-chances as any well-laid human plans. However, the point being made against this is that socialism should be seen as an attempt to abolish class privileges.

On the one hand, class privileges often cannot be abolished without a successful economy, i.e. the sharing of 'cultural capital' in education depends, as Halsey has demonstrated, upon high levels of state expenditure on education.[6] On the other, the belief, highlighted so well by Habermas, that the abolition of privilege will lead to a new consensus that will again give the state room to act is question-begging. Whilst a diminution of class privileges remains desirable in itself, pace Bell and Dahrendorf, and a present task—albeit, regrettably, not one which the 'class war' leading to inflation is aiming at—I am by no means convinced that this would of itself solve the problems of the political economy. For is it not likely that an industrial economy will always depend somehow on unequal reward? Even if this were purely meritocratic, is it not still likely that the combination of social (but not class) inequality and democracy will be unstable?

These rather fallible-looking extremes can only be improved by much more imaginative solutions. I am not in possession of a magic cure-all, but some points seem obvious. A group that has sufficient negative power to disrupt the economy must be more thoroughly integrated into the power structure. The risk here is that such integration might merely encode stalemate at a higher political level.

This is something that we know too little about, but comparative studies of corporatism—for this is what this strategy amounts to—seem likely to suggest that this is by no means inevitable. Secondly, for greater skill could be shown in the politics of industrial relations. For example, Richard Layard has demonstrated that irreparable damage is done through conflating an index of wages designed to avoid leap-frogging with the redistribution of income as such.[7] Finally, I have argued for a Hirschian attempt to break the traditional association between status and reward so as to allow for different sources of reward in society. I am well aware that all three strategies have their difficulties: they might work in the abstract but not if the state is seen to be directing them; or, more generally, they are designed to re-legitimate, but perhaps depend upon some prior sense of legitimacy for their being put into effect. For all that, however, something of this order seems a pressing necessity.

The third and fourth points are at least equally as important, but can be dealt with more cursorily. These comments on the options available inside industrial societies—thirdly—must not let us forget that national rivalry has been powerful enough in the recent past to change our historical condition entirely. The stable duopoly of the nuclear giants remains in force in theory since only the Soviet Union and the United States have complete systems, i.e. first and second strike capacity, and so on. But the spread of nuclear weapons is surely a present reality that cannot be ignored given that different actors might not accept the rules of the nuclear game played hitherto. In these circumstances, should Europe have its own defence, become independent, or what? And just as important here are economic considerations. The Western economic system as a whole has worked well when it has had one state, either Great Britain or America, capable of giving a lead, but very badly in the inter-war years when leadership was disputed. This probably makes some agreement between Europe and America imperative in relation to their changed positions.

However, perhaps the most important question in international relations depends upon the fourth point, namely the fate of the underdeveloped countries. Dahrendorf has distinguished between Third and Fourth world countries, i.e. those about to develop and those without any natural resources to speak of, and he has made much of the necessity for a North-South dialogue.[8] If this is not morally obvious to most people, it certainly is politically, either since the oil crisis of 1973 or, failing that, since the overthrow of the Shah in Iran. The revolution in Iran, moreover, demonstrates that full-blooded ideology, in this case that of militant Shi'ite Islam, continues to appeal to those who are uprooted by the transition from agrarian to industrial eras. This raises the possibility that some of the above discussion of the options *in* industrialism might be proved irrelevant by the simple fact that its fate is not its own. Any investigation of 'our social condition' in the future will need to be done on a world scale.

References and Notes

1. Introduction

1. See P. Anderson, *Passages from Antiquity to Feudalism* and *Lineages of the Absolutist State*, both New Left Books, London, 1974; M. Mann, *Sources of Social Power*, Methuen, London, forthcoming; I. Wallerstein, *The Modern World-System*, Academic Press, New York, 1974.

2. M. Jay, *The Dialectical Imagination*, Heinemann Educational Books, London, 1973, p. 63.

3. M. Hollis, *Models of Man*, Cambridge University Press, Cambridge, 1977.

4. One thinker who has insisted on a generous view of interests, Michael Mann ('Idealism and Materialism in Sociological Theory', in J. Freiburg, ed., *Critical Sociology*, Irvington, New York, 1979) has offered us a very striking piece of historical sociology ('States, Ancient and Modern', *European Journal of Sociology*, vol. 18, 1977) in which he makes the more assumptions: 'That mankind is restless and greedy for more of the good things of life, and that essentially this is a quest for greater material rewards'.

5. See M. Mann, 'Idealism and Materialism in Sociological Theory', in J. Freiburg, ed., op. cit.

6. Hollis, op. cit., chapter 9.

7. I have chronicled the weaknesses of naive Marxism in understanding literature in J. A. Hall, *The Sociology of Literature*, Longmans, Harlow, 1979.

8. L. Kolakowski, *Positivist Philosophy*, Penguin, London, 1972, chapter 1.

2. Herbert Marcuse

1. Marcuse provided these details in an interview with Jürgen Habermas and others in 1978. See Habermas et al., *Gësprache mit Herbert Marcuse*, Suhrkamp, Frankfurt, 1978. The main interview in this volume has since been translated as H. Marcuse, J. Habermas, H. Lubasz and T. Spengler, 'Theory and Politics', *Telos*, no. 38, 1978–9.

2. Marcuse later argued that Social Democrat parties in central Europe were responsible in the immediate post-war years for drawing the teeth from a revolutionary situation. See Marcuse, *Soviet Marxism*, Routledge and Kegan Paul, London, 1958, Penguin ed. 1971, pp. 14–15.

3. Marcuse, *Hegel's Ontologie und die Grundlegung einer Theorie der Geschicht-lichkeit*, Vittorio Klosterman, Frankfurt, 1932, especially section 2.

4. The classic exposition of this is T. Adorno and M. Horkheimer's 1947 study *Dialectic of Enlightenment*, Verso Paperbacks, London, 1978.

5. S. Freud, *Civilisation and Its Discontents*, Hogarth Press, London, 1949, p. 14.

6. Marcuse, 'On the Problem of the Dialectic', (1932), *Telos*, no. 27, Spring 1976, p. 24.

7. Marcuse, 'Contributions to a Phenomenology of Historical Material-ism', (1928), *Telos*, no. 4, 1969, p. 13.
8. Ibid., p. 14.
9. Ibid., p. 22.
10. Marcuse, 'Philosophical Foundations of the Concept of Labour', (1933), *Telos*, no. 16, Summer, 1973, p. 22.
11. Marcuse's essay on 'The Foundations of Historical Materialism' appeared in 1932, and is now part of his essay collection *Studies in Critical Philosophy*, New Left Books, London, 1972, p. 29.
12. Marcuse, 'On the Problem of the Dialectic', op. cit., p. 16.
13. Ibid., pp. 19–21.
14. Marcuse, 'Philosophical Foundations of the Concept of Labour', op. cit., p. 13.
15. Ibid., p. 24.
16. Marcuse, *Reason and Revolution*, 2nd ed., Routledge and Kegan Paul, London, 1969, p. 26.
17. Marcuse, 'The Foundations of Historical Materialism', op. cit., p. 39.
18. Marcuse, 'Philosophical Foundations of the Concept of Labour', op. cit., pp. 33 ff.
19. Adorno's review appeared in *Zeitschrift für Sozialforschung*, vol. I, no. 3, 1932.
20. The interview with Habermas et al. already cited (see ref. 1.) contains some interesting discussion about the internal organisation of the Institute.
21. *Negations*, Penguin, London, 1972, pp. 18–19.
22. Ibid., pp. 26–7.
23. Ibid., pp. 31–42.
24. Ibid., p. 11.
25. The Rumanian case is an outstanding refutation of the received Marxist theory of fascism, and it is insufficiently well-known. A good account of Rumanian fascism is N. M. Nagy-Talavera, *The Green Shirts and the Others*, Stanford, California, 1970.
26. J. Orr, 'German Social Theory and the Hidden Face of Technology', *European Journal of Sociology*, vol. 15, 1974, passim.
27. Marcuse, *Reason and Revolution*, op. cit., p. 113.
28. Ibid., especially 179–80.
29. Ibid., p. 187.
30. Ibid., p. 314.
31. Ibid., p. 256.
32. Ibid., pp. 332–40.
33. Ibid., pp. 350–1.
34. Ibid., p. 355.
35. Marcuse, *Negations*, op. cit., p. 147.
36. Ibid., p. 50.
37. Ibid., p. 60.
38. Ibid., p. 187.
39. Ibid., p. 172.
40. Ibid., 'The Affirmative Character of Culture', passim, especially p. 90.
41. Ibid., especially pp. 108–9. There is a valuable essay on Marcuse's aesthetics by M. Schoolman, 'Marcuse's Aesthetics and the Displace-ment of Critical Theory', *New German Critique*, no. 8, 1976.
42. Marcuse, *Negations*, op. cit., p. 111.

43. Ibid., pp. 129–33.
44. Ibid., p. 136.
45. Ibid., p. 195.
46. Marcuse, *Reason and Revolution*, op. cit., p. 293.
47. T. Adorno and M. Horkheimer, *Dialectic of Enlightenment*, op. cit., M. Jay makes this point forcefully in his *The Dialectical Imagination*, Heinemann Education, London, 1973, p. 75 and passim.
48. Marcuse, *Reason and Revolution*, op. cit., 'The Analysis of the Labour Process', pp. 295–312.
49. M. Jay, *The Dialectical Imagination*, op. cit., chronicles the general move to pessimism well, especially in chapters 6 and 8.
50. See Marcuse's 'Sartre's Existentialism', in *Studies in Critical Philosophy*, op. cit.
51. Marcuse, *Negations*, op. cit., p. xvi. This passage was written for the German republication of the bulk of the Zeitschrift essays in *Kultur und Gesellschaft*, Suhrkamp, Frankfurt, 1965.
52. Marcuse, *Eros and Civilisation*, Vintage Books, New York, 1962, p. 236.
53. Marcuse's discussion of these matters is very unclear, but is contained in ibid., pp. 20–7.
54. Ibid., p. 36.
55. Ibid., p. 63.
56. P. A. Robinson, *The Sexual Radicals*, Paladin Books, London, 1972, p. 156.
57. Marcuse describes the concepts in *Eros and Civilisation*, op. cit., pp. 32 ff.
58. Ibid., p. 76.
59. Ibid., p. 92.
60. Ibid., pp. 77–8.
61. Ibid., pp. 78–9.
62. Ibid., p. 88.
63. Marcuse and R. Aron, 'Can Communism be Liberal?', *New Statesman*, 23.6.72.
64. Marcuse, *Eros and Civilisation*, op. cit., p. 132.
65. The fullest account of the psychological factors at work in art, and of 'stillness' in particular, is contained in a 1967 essay 'Art in the One-Dimensional Society' by L. Baxandall in *Radical Perspectives in the Arts*, Penguin Books, London, 1972.
66. Marcuse, *Eros and Civilisation*, op. cit., pp. 150–1.
67. Ibid., pp. 153–4.
68. Ibid., p. 192.
69. Ibid., p. 185.
70. Ibid., pp. 196–7.
71. Ibid., pp. 205–6.
72. Ibid., p. 215.
73. Ibid., p. 206.
74. Marcuse made this point in the interview with Habermas et al., op. cit., (see ref. 1), p. 136.
75. *Negations*, op. cit., pp. 243–7.
76. This prediction was made in 'On Hedonism', in *Negations*, op. cit., p. 187.
77. See Marcuse, *Eros and Civilisation*, op. cit., 'Preface to the Vintage Edition'.

78. Marcuse, *One-Dimensional Man*, Abacus, London, 1972, p. 59.
79. Ibid., p. 63.
80. Ibid., pp. 64–6.
81. Ibid., pp. 70–4.
82. Ibid., p. 195.
83. Ibid., p. 13.
84. Ibid., p. 16.
85. Ibid., p. 10.
86. Ibid., pp. 42–4.
87. Ibid., pp. 49–51.
88. J. Goldthorpe et al, *The Affluent Worker in the Class Structure*, Cambridge University Press, Cambridge, 1969; M. Mann, 'The Social Cohesion of Liberal Democracy', *American Sociological Review*, vol. 20, 1970; N. Abercrombie and B. S. Turner 'The Dominant Ideology Thesis', *British Journal of Sociology*, vol. 29, 1978.
89. Marcuse and Aron, 'Can Communism be Liberal?', op. cit.
90. J. Orr, 'German Social Theory and the Hidden Face of Technology', op. cit., p. 333.
91. Marcuse, 'On Science and Phenomenology', in A. Giddens, ed., *Positivism and Sociology*, Heinemann Educational Books, 1974, London, pp. 228–9.
92. Marcuse, 'Industrialisation and Capitalism in the Work of Max Weber', in *Negations*, op. cit., pp. 223–4.
93. This neo-Marxist attitude depends in part upon making so much use of C. Wright Mill's *Power Elite*, although the contradiction is clearly present in the earlier 'Some Social Implications of Modern Technology', *Philosophy and Social Science*, vol. 9, 1941. At one point in *One Dimensional Man*, op. cit., (p. 44) Marcuse seems to suggest that the 'vested interests' will advantageously allow themselves to be managed by some sort of pure technology, but this Veblenesque theory is not developed.
94. Marcuse, *One Dimensional Man*, op. cit., p. 182.
95. Ibid., p. 188.
96. Marcuse, *Soviet Marxism*, op. cit., p. 110.
97. Ibid., p. 73.
98. Ibid., p. 45 and passim.
99. M. Kaldor, *The Disintegrating West*, Penguin, London, 1979.
100. Marcuse, *Soviet Marxism*, op. cit., chapter 5, especially p. 93.
101. Ibid., p. 110.
102. Ibid., p. 180.
103. Many examples of Marcuse's early adulation of students could be cited. Two especially clear ones are 'Freedom and Necessity', *Praxis*, vol. 5, 1969 and *An Essay on Liberation*, Penguin Books, 1971, passim.
104. Marcuse, *An Essay on Liberation*, op. cit., chapter 3.
105. Marcuse, 'Art in the One Dimensional Society', op. cit.
106. Marcuse, *An Essay on Liberation*, op. cit., p. 21.
107. Marcuse, *Counter-revolution and Revolt*, Beacon Press, Boston, 1972, p. 71.
108. E. P. Thompson, *Whigs and Hunters*, Allen Lane, London, 1976, conclusion.
109. Marcuse, *An Essay on Liberation*, op. cit., p. 25.
110. Marcuse, 'Murder is not a Political Weapon', *New German Critique*, no. 12, 1977.

111. Marcuse, *The Aesthetic Dimension*, Macmillan, London, p. 29.

3. Jürgen Habermas

1. Some of the early attacks he made in the 1960s on the illusory pretensions of the student movement have been translated in his *Towards a Rational Society*, Heinemann Educational Books, London, 1971. A representative attack on the right is his 'Stumpf gewordene Waffen aus dem Arsenal der Gegenaufklärung', in K. Sontheimer, F. Duve, H. Böll, K. Stroeck, eds. *Briefe zur Verteidigung der Republik*, Reinbek bei Hamburg, Rowolt, 1977.
2. Habermas, *Knowledge and Human Interests*, Heinemann Educational Books, London, 1971, p. 317.
3. Habermas, *Strukturwandel der Öffentlichkeit*, Neuwied, Luchterhand, 1976, see section 9.
4. The clearest statement of the weaknesses, made by Habermas in the 1960s, is 'Between Philosophy and Science: Marxism as Critique', in his *Theory and Practice*, Heinemann Educational Books, London, 1974.
5. Habermas, *Strukturwandel der Öffentlichkeit*, op. cit., p. 188, (my translation).
6. Ibid., see section 18.
7. T. Adorno and M. Horkheimer, 'The Culture Industry', in their *Dialectic of Enlightenment*, New Left Books, London, 1978.
8. Habermas, *Strukturwandel der Öffentlichkeit*, op. cit., p. 226, (my translation).
9. Ibid., pp. 263–78.
10. Habermas, *Towards a Rational Society*, op. cit., p. 111.
11. Ibid., p. 118.
12. Habermas, *Theory and Practice*, op. cit., p. 282.
13. See especially Hannah Arendt, *The Human Condition*, Anchor Books, New York, 1959.
14. Habermas's clearest description of labour and interaction occurs in a discussion of these writings, 'Labour and Interaction: Remarks on Hegel's *Jena Philosophy of Mind*', in *Theory and Practice*, op. cit.
15. Ibid., p. 66.
16. Habermas, *Knowledge and Human Interests*, op. cit., p. 42 and passim chapters 1–3.
17. Habermas, *Towards a Rational Society*, op. cit., p. 58.
18. Ibid., p. 107.
19. Habermas, *Theory and Practice*, op. cit., p. 271.
20. In 1978 Habermas gave a lecture series in Frankfurt largely on Max Weber. It is likely that some of the material of these lectures, especially that offering a conception of the rationality of action that is opposed to Max Weber's, will be included in his next book. It is this material that I am grateful to Habermas for having let me peruse at length.
21. Max Weber, 'Politics as a Vocation', in H. H. Gerth and C. W. Mills, eds., *From Max Weber: Essays in Sociology*, Oxford University Press, New York, 1970.
22. This applies especially to the views of Niklas Luhmann. See Habermas and Luhmann, *Theorie der Gesellschaft oder Sozialtechnologie?* Suhrkamp, Frankfurt, 1971 and Habermas, *Legitimation Crisis*, Heinemann Educational Books, 1976, part 3.
23. The possibility of rationalisation in both realms is mentioned clearly in

'Technology and Science as Ideology', in *Towards a Rational Society*, op. cit.

24. The difference with Marcuse on this matter can be clearly seen in a discussion between Marcuse and Habermas (and some others), now in English as 'Theory and Politics', *Telos*, no. 38, 1978–9.

25. Boris Frankel, 'Habermas Talking: An Interview', *Theory and Society*, vol. 1, 1974, p. 46. Habermas's most considered judgement on Marcuse's work remains his 'Technology and Science as Ideology', in *Towards a Rational Society*, op. cit.

26. T. McCarthy in *The Critical Theory of Jürgen Habermas* (Hutchinson, London, 1978) distinguishes with exceptional clarity between the early and later Habermas and I am indebted to this analysis.

27. Habermas, *Knowledge and Human Interests*, op. cit., p. 87.

28. Ibid., p. 29.

29. Ibid., pp. 196–7.

30. Ibid., p. 121.

31. Ibid., p. 137.

32. This is made especially clear in the unpublished Christian Gauss Lectures given at Princeton in 1971 entitled 'Thoughts on the Foundation of Sociology in the Philosophy of Language'.

33. Habermas, *Zur Logik der Sozialwissenschaften*, Suhrkamp, Frankfurt, 1970, pp. 143–4. This passage is cited by McCarthy (*The Critical Theory of Jürgen Habermas*, op. cit., p. 146) and the translation is his.

34. Habermas, *Knowledge and Human Interests*, op. cit., p. 176.

35. Habermas, *Zur Logik der Sozialwissenschaften*, op. cit., p. 283. The section of his book dealing with Gadamer has been translated by McCarthy and is available as 'A Review of Gadamer's *Truth and Method*', in T. McCarthy and F. Dallmayer, *Understanding and Social Inquiry*, University of Notre Dame Press, London, 1977. I have cited McCarthy's translation, page 357.

36. Habermas, *Knowledge and Human Interests*, op. cit., p. 227.

37. Ibid., p. 276.

38. Ibid., chapter II, especially p. 269.

39. Habermas, 'A Postscript to *Knowledge and Human Interests*', *Philosophy of Social Sciences*, vol 3, 1973, p. 182.

40. Habermas, 'A Postscript to *Knowledge and Human Interests*', p. 176.

41. This is pointed out with great force in 'Habermas's Critique of Hermeneutics' in his *Studies in Social and Political Theory*, Hutchinson, London, 1977.

42. Habermas, 'What is Universal Pragmatics?', in his *Communication and the Evolution of Society*, Heinemann Educational Books, London, 1979, p. 19.

43. Ibid., pp. 27–8.

44. Ibid., p. 16.

45. This is based on the table in ibid., p. 68.

46. Habermas made this clear to me in an interview in Frankfurt in May, 1978.

47. Habermas, 'A Postscript to Knowledge and Human Interests', op. cit., p. 169.

48. There is an excellent construction of what a systematic critique of Popper by Habermas would look like in McCarthy, *The Critical Theory of Jürgen Habermas*, op. cit., chapter 1, section 3. McCarthy's account is

based on occasional comments by Habermas on Popper especially in the essays edited by T. Adorno, *The Positivist Dispute in German Sociology*, (Heinemann Educational Books, London, 1976), as well as on the general spirit of Habermas's argument.

49. Habermas, 'Wahreitstheorien', in *Wirklichkeit und reflexion: Walter Schulz zum 60. Geburtstag*, Neske, Pfullingen, 1973, pp. 226–7. This passage is cited by McCarthy, *The Critical Theory of Jürgen Habermas*, op. cit., p. 311.

50. Habermas, *Legitimation Crisis*, op. cit., p. 89.

51. Habermas, *Communication and the Evolution of Society*, op. cit., pp. 185–6.

52. Habermas, 'Zur Entwicklung der Interaktionscompetenz', unpublished manuscript 1974 cited and translated by McCarthy, *The Critical Theory of Jürgen Habermas*, op. cit., p. 338.

53. This diagram is based on those in Habermas, 'Moral Development and Ego Identity', in *Communication and the Evolution of Society*, op. cit., especially p. 89.

54. Habermas, 'Zur Einführung', in R. Dobert, J. Habermas and C. Nunner-Winkler, eds. *Die Entwicklung des Ichs* (Keipenheuer and Wirsch, Cologne, 1977, p. 27). This passage is cited and translated by McCarthy, *The Critical Theory of Jürgen Habermas*, op. cit., p. 335.

55. Habermas, *Legitimation Crisis*, op. cit., p. 7.

56. Habermas, *Communication and the Evolution of Society*, op. cit., p. 136.

57. Ibid., p. 139.

58. Ibid., p. 140.

59. Ibid., pp. 153–4.

60. Habermas, *Legitimation Crisis*, op. cit., chapter 3.

61. Habermas, *Communication and the Evolution of Society*, op. cit., p. 143.

62. Ibid., pp. 167–9.

63. Ibid., p. 146.

64. Ibid., pp. 147–8.

65. Ibid., p. 154.

66. Habermas, *Zur Rekonstruktion des Historischen Materialismus*, Suhrkamp, Frankfurt, 1976, pp. 260–70.

67. Habermas, *Communication and the Evolution of Society*, op. cit., p. 120.

68. Ibid., p. 125.

69. See Wallerstein, *The Modern World System*, Academic Press, New York, 1974.

70. M. Mann, 'A Sociological Critique of Historical Materialism', in *Sources of Social Power*, forthcoming.

71. Habermas, *Legitimation Crisis*, op. cit., p. 45.

72. This paragraph draws on ibid., pp. 50–60.

73. Ibid., p. 64.

74. Ibid., p. 71.

75. Ibid., p. 73.

76. This is slightly simplifying the account offered by Habermas in ibid., pp. 75–92.

77. Ibid., p. 85.

78. Ibid., p. 89.

79. Ibid., p. 90.

80. Habermas confirmed this point for me in an interview in Frankfurt in June, 1978.

81. See Habermas, *Legitimation Crisis*, op. cit., especially pp. 117–30.

82. McCarthy, *The Critical Theory of Jürgen Habermas*, op. cit., chapter 5, passim.
83. Cole admitted that his theory of participatory democracy (always changing, but most fully stated in his *Guild Socialism Restated*, Leonard Parsons, London, 1921) was defective in *The Next Ten Years*, Macmillan, London, 1929, especially p. 161.
84. Marcuse, Habermas et al., 'Theory and Politics', op. cit., p. 139.
85. Habermas, *Communication and the Evolution of Society*, op. cit., p. 224.
86. For a brilliant account of Hobhouse, see L. T. Collini, *Liberalism and Sociology*, Cambridge University Press, Cambridge, 1979.
87. Habermas, 'Conservatism and Capitalist Crisis', *New Left Review*, no. 115, 1979, p. 74.

4. Daniel Bell

1. Bell gave me this information in an interview, 19.12.1976.
2. Bell, 'The Return of the Sacred? The Argument on the Future of Religion', *British Journal of Sociology*, vol. 28, 1977, p. 428.
3. Bell, 'The Grass Roots of American Jew-Hatred', *Jewish Frontier*, June, 1944, p. 15.
4. Bell, 'Notes on Authoritarian and Democratic Leadership', in A. Gouldner, ed., *Studies in Leadership*, Free Press, New York, 1950, p. 407.
5. R. Hofstader, The *Paranoid Style in American Politics*, Vintage Books, New York, 1965.
6. Bell, 'Interpretations of American Politics', in Bell, ed., *The Radical Right*, Anchor Books, New York, 1964, pp. 61–2.
7. Ibid., p. 64.
8. Ibid., p. 47.
9. Bell, 'The Dispossessed', in ibid., p. 24.
10. Ibid., p. 42.
11. Ibid., pp. 42–3.
12. For a fully-fledged argument along these lines see D. Martin's magnificent *A General Theory of Secularisation*, Blackwell, Oxford, 1978.
13. Bell, 'The End of American Exceptionalism', *The Public Interest*, no. 40, Fall, 1975.
14. Ibid., p. 206.
15. Ibid., p. 211.
16. Bell, 'Crime as an American Way of Life: A Queer Ladder of Social Mobility', in his *The End of Ideology*, revised edition, Collier Books, New York, 1962.
17. Bell, 'The Breakup of Family Capitalism', in ibid., p. 45.
18. Bell, 'Interpretations of American Politics', op. cit., p. 73.
19. Bell, *Marxian Socialism in the United States*, Princeton University Press, Princeton, 1967, passim.
20. Ibid., p. 16.
21. C. Vann Woodward, *The Burden of Southern History*, Vintage Books, New York, 1960, p. 157.
22. M. P. Rogin, *The Intellectuals and McCarthy: The Radical Specter*, MIT Press, Cambridge Mass., 1969, p. 280.
23. For this theory of anti-semitism, see H. Arendt, *Anti-semitism*, Viking Books, New York, 1968; for some comments on the agricultural roots of fascism, see B. Moore, *The Social Origins of Dictatorship and Democracy*, Penguin Books, London, 1969.

24. Rogin, op. cit., p. 277.
25. C. Vann Woodward, *The Burden of Southern History*, op. cit., p. 153.
26. This is Rogin's thesis, op. cit.
27. For England and Wales, see J. H. Goldthorpe (with the assistance of C. Llewellyn and G. Payne), *Social Mobility and Class Structure*, Oxford University Press, Oxford, 1980.
28. The American evidence is summarised by D. W. Rossides, *The American Class System*, Houghton Mifflin, Boston, 1976.
29. The fullest review (drawing on material from the United States and Australia, as well as Western Europe) is J. Scott, *Corporations, Classes and Capitalism*, Hutchinson, London, 1979. But see also P. H. Burch, *The Managerial Revolution Reassessed*, Lexington Books, New Haven, 1972.
30. For a clear statement in the matter see Jean Floud, 'A Critique of Bell', *Survey*, Winter, 1971, vol. 16. The most authoritative recent study of the English and Welsh situation is that of A. H. Halsey, A. Heath and J. M. Ridge, *Origins and Destinations*, Oxford University Press, Oxford, 1980: for America, see S. Bowles and H. Gintis, *Schooling in Capitalist America*, Basic Books, New York, 1976.
31. M. Mann, 'The Social Cohesion of Liberal Democracy', *American Sociological Review*, vol. 35, 1970; also relevant is the criticism of the Marxist view inspired variously by Gramsci and Althusser which sees capitalism held together by a dominant ideology: for a criticism of this see N. Abercrombie and B. S. Turner 'The dominant ideology thesis', *British Journal of Sociology*, vol. 29, 1979.
32. C. Lasch, *The Agony of the American Left*, Vintage Books, New York, 1968, pp. 111−2.
33. J. A. Hall, 'The Roles and Influence of Political Intellectuals: Tawney vs Sidney Webb', *British Journal of Sociology*, vol. 28, 1977.
34. J. Higgins, *The Poverty Business*, Blackwell, Oxford, 1978.
35. Bell, *The End of Ideology*, op. cit., pp. 400−1.
36. For a good account of these two, and of Stirner, see J. Carroll, *Break out from the Crystal Place*, Routledge and Kegan Paul, London, 1972.
37. Bell, 'The Return of the Sacred?', op. cit., p. 421.
38. Ibid., p. 432.
39. See, for example, the description of Nazism in 'The Grass Roots of American Jew-Hatred', op. cit.
40. Bell, 'The Return of the Sacred?', op. cit., pp. 432−8, and his *The Cultural Contradictions of Capitalism*, Heinemann Educational Books, London, 1978.
41. Bell told me in an interview, 19.12.1976, that his next book would be on modernism.
42. I have made this argument at greater length in 'Sincerity and Politics: the "Existentialists" vs Goffman and Proust', *Sociological Review*, vol. 25, 1977.
43. Bell, 'The return of the sacred?', op. cit., pp. 435−8.
44. Bell, *The End of Ideology*, op. cit., pp. 402−3.
45. Bell has written only occasional essays on Eastern Europe, for example, 'The Soviet Union: Ideology in Retreat', in M. Rejai, ed., *The Decline of Ideology*, Aldine Alderton, Chicago, 1971.
46. D. Wrong, 'Reflections on the End of Ideology', in C. I. Waxman, ed., *The End of Ideology Debate*, Fink and Wagnalls, New York, 1968, p. 123.

47. Bell, *The End of Ideology*, op. cit., pp. 404–5.
48. For an important statement along these lines distinguishing the American from the European versions of the thesis, see R. Aron 'On the Proper Use of Ideologies', in J. Ben-David and T. N. Clark, eds., *Culture and Its Creators*, University of Chicago Press, Chicago, 1977.
49. Bell's Commission on the Year 2000 published some of its discussion as: Bell, ed., *Toward the Year 2000: Work in Progress*, Beacon Press, New York, 1969. Much about Bell's position in American life can be learnt from a specialist report he produced on 'general education' for Columbia University: see *The Reforming of General Education*, Columbia University Press, New York, 1966.
50. Bell, *The Coming of Post-Industrial Society*, Penguin Books, London, 1976, p. xi.
51. For the detailed analysis of this, see Bell 'The End of American Exceptionalism', op. cit.
52. Bell, *The Cultural Contradictions of Capitalism*, op. cit., pp. 11–14.
53. Bell, 'Forward: 1978', in ibid.
54. Ibid., p. 21.
55. On this point see the works cited in ref. 31, and also chapter 7 of this work.
56. The most considered discussion is that of K. Kumar, *Prophecy and Progress*, Penguin, London, 1978. But also see the critical papers of Floud, Wiles, Bourricaud, Sartori, and Tominaga in *Survey*, vol. 16, Winter, 1971.
57. Bell, *The Coming of Post-Industrial Society*, op. cit., p. 349.
58. Ibid., p. 79.
59. Ibid., pp. 126–9.
60. Ibid., p. 157.
61. Ibid., p. 164.
62. Ibid., p. 297.
63. Ibid., chapter 4.
64. Ibid., p. 296.
65. Bell, *The Cultural Contradictions of Capitalism*, op. cit., p. 202.
66. Bell, *The Coming of Post-Industrial Society*, op. cit., chapter 1.
67. A. Giddens, *The Class Structure of the Advanced Societies*, Hutchinson, London, 1973, pp. 255–6.
68. P. Stearns, 'Is there a Post-industrial Society?', *Society* vol. 11, 1974, p. 14.
69. Kumar, *Property and Progress*, op. cit., chapters 4 and 6.
70. J. Gershuny, *After Industrial Society?* Macmillan, London, 1978, p. 69.
71. Ibid., especially pp. 105–13.
72. See Scott, *Classes, Corporations and Capitalism*, op. cit.
73. Bell, *The End of Ideology*, op. cit., p. 257.
74. Bell in an interview with Alain Clement of *Le Monde*, reprinted in *Times Europa Supplement*, January 1975, p. 5.
75. Bell, *The Coming of Post Industrial Society*, op. cit., pp. 391–402.
76. Bell, 'Veblen and the New Class', in T. Veblen, *The Engineers and the Price System*, Harbinger Edition, New York, 1965.
77. Bell, *The Cultural Contradictions of Capitalism*, op. cit., p. 83.
78. Lionel Trilling, *Beyond Culture*, Penguin, London, 1966, p. 15.
79. Bell, 'Beyond Modernism, Beyond Self', in Q. Anderson, S. Donadio

and S. Marcuse, eds, *Art, Politics and Will*, Basic Books, New York, 1977, pp. 229–30.

80. Bell, 'The Return of the Sacred?', op. cit., p. 434.
81. Bell, *The Cultural Contradictions of Capitalism*, op. cit., pp. 108–19.
82. Bell, 'The Return of the Sacred?', op. cit., pp. 435–8.
83. Bell, 'Beyond Modernism, Beyond Self', op. cit., p. 232.
84. Ibid., p. 248.
85. Bell, *The Cultural Contradictions of Capitalism*, op. cit., p. 169.
86. Bell, 'The Return of the Sacred?', op. cit., p. 444.
87. For a review of the evidence on popular literature see J. A. Hall, *The Sociology of Literature*, Longmans, Harlow, 1979, chapter 5.
88. Bell, *The Cultural Contradictions of Capitalism*, op. cit., p. 82.
89. Hall, *The Sociology of Literature*, op. cit., chapter 8. See also chapter 7 of this book.
90. This criticism is made very strikingly by Raymond Aron in his *Main Currents in Sociological Thought*, vol. 2, Weidenfeld and Nicolson, London, 1968, pp. 56–8.
91. This comment is recorded by S. Lukes in a footnote in his *Emile Durkheim*, Penguin, London, 1975, p. 339.
92. Bell, *The Cultural Contradictions of Capitalism*, op. cit., p. 259.
93. Bell, 'Ethnicity and Social Change', in D. P. Moynihan and N. Glazer, eds., *Ethnicity*, Harvard University Press, Cambridge Mass., 1976, pp. 172–3.
94. 'Potentially prosperous' is designed to cover the cases where the discovery of rich mineral rights—for example 'Scottish' oil—fuels separatist demands. On this see T. Nairn, *The Breakup of Britain*, New Left Books, London, 1977.
95. Bell, *The Cultural Contradictions of Capitalism*, op. cit., p. 240.
96. Bell, 'Ethnicity and Social Change', op. cit., pp. 173–4.
97. Bell, *The Coming of Post-Industrial Society*, op. cit., p. 469.
98. Ibid., p. 424.
99. Ibid., p. 419.
100. Bell, *The Cultural Contradictions of Capitalism*, op. cit., pp. 272–3.

5. Ralf Dahrendorf

1. Dahrendorf, *The New Liberty*, Routledge and Kegan Paul, London, 1975, pp. 3–4.
2. Dahrendorf, *Marx in Perspektive*, Dietz, Hanover, 1953.
3. Dahrendorf, *The New Liberty*, op. cit., p. 4.
4. Dahrendorf, *Class and Class Conflict in Industrial Society*, (German 1955: English revised edition 1957), Routledge and Kegan Paul, London, 1972.
5. Dahrendorf, *Society and Democracy in Germany*, (German 1965: English revised edition 1967), New York, 1967.
6. Whilst in the Commission he wrote an interesting book on Europe—*Pladoyer für die Europäische Union*, Piper, Munich, 1973.
7. Dahrendorf, *Class and Class Conflict in Industrial Society*, op. cit., pp. 30–31.
8. Ibid., p. 161.
9. Ibid., p. 162.
10. M. Mann, 'States, Ancient and Modern', *European Journal of Sociology*, vol. 18, 1977.

11. J. Goody, *Technology, Tradition and the State in Africa*, Oxford University Press, London, 1971.
12. E. Gellner, *Legitimation of Belief*, Cambridge University Press, Cambridge, 1974, p. 171.
13. Dahrendorf, *The New Liberty*, op. cit., p. 32.
14. A typical example of this criticism, usually Marxist or marxisant in tone, is that of David Binns (*Beyond the Sociology of Conflict*, Macmillan, London, 1977, p. 93):

> Dahrendorf's ... conception of class ... is myopic to the way in which the authority relationships he examines are circumscribed and, in the last analysis, determined by wider socio-economic patterns of structured influence and constraint. By abandoning the analysis of the range of *types* of authority which reinforce and legitimise *modes* of production relations, Dahrendorf abandons the theoretical problem of the roots of authority in social power and, as a consequence, the source of that power itself. The key to this mystification is the reification of *authority* as a sociological category.

15. Dahrendorf, *Essays in the Theory of Society*, Routledge and Kegan Paul, London, 1968, p. 172.
16. Ibid., pp. 172–3.
17. C. G. A. Bryant, *Sociology in Action*, Allen and Unwin, London, 1976, p. 277.
18. Dahrendorf, *Essays in the Theory of Society*, op. cit., p. 173.
19. One such critic is J. H. Turner, 'From Utopia to Where? A Strategy for Reformulating the Dahrendorf Conflict Model', *Social Forces*, vol. 52, 1973, p. 173.
20. For example, C. G. A. Bryant, *Sociology in Action*, op. cit., p. 272.
21. Dahrendorf, *Class and Class Conflict*, op. cit., especially p. 193.
22. Dahrendorf, *Essays in the Theory of Society*, op. cit., p. 240.
23. Dahrendorf, *Class and Class Conflict*, op. cit., p. 186.
24. Ibid., p. 187.
25. R. McKibbin, *The Evolution of the Labour Party 1910–24*, Oxford University Press, Oxford, 1974, p. 241.
26. Dahrendorf, *Class and Class Conflict*, op. cit., p. 60.
27. Ibid., p. 225.
28. Ibid., pp. 314–8.
29. Ibid., p. 55.
30. Ibid., p. 300.
31. For some historical evidence on the matter see the first essay in H. Pelling, *Popular Politics and Society in Late Victorian Britain*, Macmillan, London, 1968.
32. Dahrendorf, *Society and Democracy*, op. cit., p. 169.
33. Ibid., pp. 180–1.
34. Dahrendorf told me this in an interview in March, 1978.
35. Most of these points are made by B. Moore, *Social Origins of Dictatorship and Democracy*, Penguin, London, 1969, especially chapter 1; but see also G. Poggi, *The Development of the Modern State*, Hutchinson, London, 1978.
36. M. Mann, 'States, Ancient and Modern', op. cit., p. 279–84.
37. Dahrendorf, *Life Chances*, Weidenfeld and Nicolson, London, 1979, p. 61.

38. K. Popper, 'Reason or Revolution?', in T. W. Adorno et al., *The Positivist Dispute in German Sociology*, Heinemann Educational Books, London, 1976, p. 295.
39. Ibid., p. 292.
40. Gellner, *Legitimation of Belief*, op. cit., chapter 9.
41. Dahrendorf, *Society and Democracy*, op. cit., p. 201.
42. Ibid., p. 220.
43. Ibid., pp. 260–1.
44. Ibid., chapter 24.
45. Ibid., chapter 18.
46. He thus cites approvingly a famous study by Lipset, 'Working Class Authoritarianism', in ibid., p. 177.
47. Dahrendorf, *Class and Class Conflict*, op. cit., p. 46.
48. Ibid., p. 218.
49. Ibid., p. 268.
50. Ibid., p. 57.
51. Ibid., pp. 58–9.
52. Ibid., pp. 61–4.
53. A. Giddens, *The Class Structure of the Advanced Societies*, Hutchinson, London, 1973, p. 73.
54. This is cited on several occasions in *Society and Democracy*, op. cit.
55. Dahrendorf, 'Conflict After Class', Noel Buxton Memorial Lecture 3, Longmans (for the University of Essex), 1967, pp. 13–14.
56. Ibid., p. 20.
57. Dahrendorf, 'Recent Changes in the Class Structure of European Societies', *Daedalus*, no. 93, 1964, p. 263–5.
58. *Professor Ralf Dahrendorf in Australia*, Australian Broadcasting Commission, Sydney, 1978, p. 19 and passim.
59. Dahrendorf, *Essays in the Theory of Society*, op. cit., p. 198.
60. Ibid., p. 201.
61. Ibid., p. 224.
62. Dahrendorf, *Society and Democracy*, op. cit., p. 103.
63. The most recent survey of evidence on ownership and control is in J. Scott, *Corporations, Classes and Capitalism*, Hutchinson, London, 1979.
64. For the most recent evidence see J. H. Goldthorpe (with the assistance of C. Llewellyn and G. Payne), *Social Mobility and Class Structure*, Oxford University Press, Oxford, 1980 and A. H. Halsey, A. Heath and J. K. Ridge, *Origins and Destinations*, Oxford University Press, Oxford, 1980.
65. F. Parkin, *Marxism and Class Theory*, 10th ed., Methuen, 1979, p. 80.
66. Dahrendorf, *Society and Democracy*, op. cit., p. 70.
67. Dahrendorf, *Die angewandte Aufklärung*, Piper, Munich, 1963.
68. Dahrendorf, *Essays in the Theory of Society*, op. cit., p. 58.
69. For an elaboration see J. A. Hall, 'Sincerity and Politics: the "Existentialists" vs Goffman and Proust', *Sociological Review*, vol. 25, 1977.
70. Dahrendorf, *Essays in the Theory of Society*, op. cit., p. 19.
71. Ibid., pp. 80–1.
72. Dahrendorf, *Society and Democracy*, op. cit., pp. 286–7.
73. Ibid., chapter 19.
74. Ibid., chapter 21.
75. Ibid., chapter 22.

76. Dahrendorf, 'European Sociology and the American Self-Image', *European Journal of Sociology*, vol. 2, 1961, p. 361.
77. Dahrendorf, 'Democracy without Liberty: An Essay on the Politics of the Other-Directed Man', in S. M. Lipset and L. Lowenthal, eds., *Culture and Social Character*, The Free Press, Glencoe, 1961, p. 188.
78. This is not spelled out by Dahrendorf, but it seems to me a fair conclusion.
79. Dahrendorf, 'Sociology and the Sociologists', in *Essays in the Theory of Society*, op. cit., passim.
80. Ibid., p. 265.
81. Dahrendorf, *The New Liberty*, op. cit., pp. 46–7.
82. Dahrendorf, *Life Chances*, op. cit., p. 128.
83. Dahrendorf, 'The Limits of Equality; Some Thoughts on Fred Hirsch', *Journal of the Royal Society of Arts*, June 1980.
84. Ibid.
85. Dahrendorf, *The New Liberty*, op. cit., p. 41.
86. Dahrendorf, *Life Chances*, op. cit., pp. 40–43, and passim. Habermas has noted the distinction between option and ligatures used by Dahrendorf; it is not unfair to say that it represents something like his own distinction between labour and interaction. See Habermas, 'Einleitung', *Stichworte zur 'Geistigen Situation der Zeit'*, ed., J. Habermas, Suhrkamp, Frankfurt, 1979, p. 31.
87. Dahrendorf, *The New Liberty*, op. cit., pp. 31–3.
88. Dahrendorf, 'After Social Democracy', Unservile State Papers, no. 25, Liberal Publications, London, 1980.
89. 'Participation: Notes on a Very Confused Issue', *Bank of New South Wales Review*, December, 1977, pp. 12–13.
90. Dahrendorf, 'The Limits of Equality', op. cit.; This point was made especially clearly when this paper was delivered as the Peter Le Foster Neve Lecture for 1980.
91. Dahrendorf, *The New Liberty*, op. cit., chapter 5.
92. Dahrendorf, *Conflict and Contract*, Leverhulme Memorial Lecture, University of Liverpool Press, Liverpool, 1975.
93. Dahrendorf, *The New Liberty*, op. cit., p. 92.
94. *Professor Ralf Dahrendorf in Australia*, op. cit., passim.
95. Dahrendorf, 'Not the Westminster Model', *Third World Foundation Monographs*, no. 2, London, 1980, p. 4.
96. Ibid., p. 7.
97. Dahrendorf, 'Science, Policy and Science Policy', *Proceedings of the Royal Irish Academy*, vol. 75, Dublin, 1975.
98. Dahrendorf, *Life Chances*, op. cit., p. 160.
99. Dahrendorf, *The New Liberty*, op. cit., pp. 26–7.
100. J. Gershuny, *After Industrial Society?*, Macmillan, London, 1978, p. 54.

6. Raymond Aron

1. Aron, *History and Politics*, ed., M. B. Conant, The Free Press, New York, 1978, p. 65.
2. On this point see two essays included in Aron's Festchrift: Gaston Fessard 'Raymond Aron, philosophe de l'histoire et de la politique' and Henri Marrou, 'Introduction à la philosophie de l'histoire: le point de vue d'un historien', in *Science et Conscience de la Société*, ed., Jean Claude Casanova, Calmann-Lévy, Paris, 1971.

3. I owe this point to Professor Joseph Frankel who in turn owed it to a friend of Aron's, René Cassin.

4. A book deserves to be written about this. The three most important Aronien texts are probably *Introduction to the Philosophy of History* (Weidenfeld and Nicolson, London, 1961), *Marxism and the Existentialists* (Harper and Row, New York, 1969) and *History and the Dialectic of Violence* (Blackwell, Oxford, 1975).

5. See especially *La Tragédie algérienne*, Plon, Paris, 1957.

6. Aron, *The Elusive Revolution*, Pall Mall, London, 1969.

7. Aron, *Le Grand Schisme*, Gallimard, Paris, 1948 and *The Century of Total War*, Derek Verschoyle, London, 1954.

8. Aron, *Penser la guerre, Clausewitz: Vol. 2, L'Âge Planétaire*, Gallimard Paris, 1976. This is hereafter cited as *Clausewitz, Vol. 2*.

9. Aron's most comprehensive review of a subject he has treated on many occasions is his recent 'De L'impérialisme sans empire', in his *Plaidoyer pour L'Europe Décadente*, Laffont, Paris, 1977.

10. Aron, *The Century of Total War*, op. cit., p. 16.

11. Ibid., p., 60.

12. Aron, *Imperial Republic*, Weidenfeld and Nicolson, London, 1974, pp. 220–85.

13. Ibid., Part 1, and *Clausewitz, Vol. 2*, op. cit., especially, pp. 147–58.

14. Aron, 'The Dawn of Universal History', now in *History and Politics*, op. cit., passim.

15. Aron's analysis of the loss of control by politicians is most easily available in *Clausewitz, Vol. 2*, op. cit., chapter 1.

16. Ibid., pp. 19–27.

17. Aron, 'Reason, Passion and Power in the Thought of Clausewitz', *Social Research*, vol. 39, 1972, pp. 607–8.

18. Aron, *Clausewitz, Vol. 2*, op. cit., chapter 1.

19. Aron, *Main Currents in Sociological Thoughts*, vol. 1, Weidenfeld and Nicolson, London, 1965, p. 258.

20. On this point, see A. J. P. Taylor, *The Origins of the Second World War*, Penguin, London, 1972, chapter 2 and passim.

21. His treatment of fascism is most easily available in *The Century of Total War* (op. cit., chapter 14), *Democracy and Totalitarianism* (Weidenfeld and Nicolson, London, 1968, chapter 12) and 'Etats democratiques et états totalitaires' (*Bulletin de la Société française de philosophie*, vol. 40, 1945).

22. The most important of these were collected in *De l'armistice à l'insurrection nationale* (Gallimard, Paris, 1945), *L'homme contre les tyrans* (Gallimard, Paris, 1945), and *L'âge des empires et l'avenir de la France* (Défense de la France, Paris, 1945).

23. Aron, *Imperial Republic*, op. cit., chapter 1.

24. See especially his contribution to a debate about Eastern Europe initiated by Bauman that was aired in the *European Journal of Sociology*, 'Remarques sur un débat', *European Journal of Sociology*, vol. 13, 1972.

25. Simone de Beauvoir, *Force of Circumstance*, Penguin, London, 1968, is interesting on this post-war climate.

26. Aron, *Marxism and the Existentialists*, op. cit., p. 2.

27. M. Mann, 'A Sociological Critique of Historical Materialism', forming part of *Sources of Social Power*, forthcoming.

28. Hobbes, *Leviathan*, Part I, chapter 13, cited by Aron in 'La guerre est une caméléon', *Contrepoint*, no. 15, 1974.

29. Aron, *Clausewitz, Vol. 2*, op. cit., p. 255 (my translation).
30. Montesquieu, *L'Esprit des Lois*, 1, 3 cited by Aron in *Peace and War*, Weidenfeld and Nicolson, London, 1966, p. vii.
31. Aron, 'Reason, Passion and Power in the Thought of Clausewitz', op. cit., p. 621.
32. Aron, 'What is a Theory of International Relations? *History and Politics*, op. cit., p. 174.
33. Aron, *Clausewitz: Vol. 1 L'Age Européen*, Gallimard, Paris, 1976, passim and especially note xxxviii.
34. Aron, *France—Steadfast and Changing*, Oxford University Press, Oxford, 1960, chapter 1.
35. Aron, *Peace and War*, op. cit., p. 91.
36. Aron, 'War and Industrial Society: A Reappraisal', *Millenium*, vol. 7, 1978/9.
37. Aron, *War and Industrial Society*, Oxford University Press, Oxford, 1958, pp. 20–2.
38. Aron, *Clausewitz, Vol. 2*, op. cit., chapter 4.
39. Aron, *Progress and Disillusion*, Praeger, New York, 1970, p. 83.
40. This is yet another of the themes that Aron has treated on many occasions. The clearest statement of the issues involved is his book *The Great Debate*, Doubleday, New York, 1965, chapter 4.
41. Aron, *Peace and War*, op. cit., chapter 18.
42. Aron, *Clausewitz, Vol. 2*, op. cit., pp. 147–57.
43. 'An Interview with Raymond Aron', *Encounter*, vol. 35, 1970, p. 70.
44. Aron, *Clausewitz, Vol. 2*, op. cit., pp. 165–73.
45. Aron, *De Gaulle, Israel and the Jews*, André Deutsch, London, 1969, p. 86.
46. Aron, *Clausewitz, Vol. 2*, pp. 199–210.
47. Ibid., chapter 6, 'La Politique ou l'intelligence de l'État personnifié'.
48. Aron, *Imperial Republic*, op. cit., passim.
49. Aron, *Clausewitz, Vol. 2*, op. cit., p. 286 (my translation).
50. Aron, *Introduction to the Philosophy of History*, op. cit., p. 9.
51. Ibid., p. 80.
52. Ibid., p. 71.
53. Ibid., p. 76.
54. Ibid., p. 74.
55. Ibid., p. 114.
56. Ibid., p. 93.
57. This is made especially clear in Aron's 'Max Weber and Michael Polányi', in *The Logic of Personal Knowledge*, Routledge and Kegan Paul, London, 1964.
58. Aron, *Introduction to the Philosophy of History*, op. cit., pp. 166–73.
59. Ibid., p. 177.
60. Ibid., p. 202.
61. Aron makes this point most clearly in his chapter on Durkheim in *Main Currents in Sociological Thought*, vol. 2, Weidenfeld and Nicolson, London, 1968.
62. Aron, *Introduction to the Philosophy of History*, op. cit., p. 253.
63. Ibid., pp. 290–1.
64. Ibid., p. 300.
65. Ibid., p. 345.

66. Ibid., p. 346.
67. Ibid., p. 333.
68. Aron, *Clausewitz, Vol. 2*, op. cit., pp. 116–26.
69. Aron, *History and the Dialectic of Violence*, op. cit., p. 186.
70. Ibid., p. 195.
71. Aron, 'Science et Conscience de la Société, in his *Études Politiques*, Gallimard, Paris, 1972.
72. Aron, *Introduction to the Philosophy of History*, op. cit., p. 74.
73. Aron made this comment in discussion at a conference at Rheinfelden: see Aron (ed.), *World Technology and Human Destiny*, University of Michigan Press, Ann Arbor, 1963, pp. 234–5.
74. Aron, *Eighteen Lectures on Industrial Society*, Weidenfeld and Nicolson, London, 1967; see also Aron's *The Industrial Society*, Weidenfeld and Nicolson, London, 1967.
75. Aron, *Eighteen Lectures on Industrial Society*, op. cit., p. 41.
76. Ibid., p. 163.
77. His most recent statement on the matter is one of his most lucid and shows him as aware of complexities as ever: 'L'Idéocratie, ou Le Marxisme Idéologie d'Etat', in his *Plaidoyer pour l'Europe Décadente*, op. cit.
78. Aron, *Eighteen Lectures on Industrial Society*, op. cit., pp. 161–2.
79. Aron, *Democracy and Totalitarianism*, op. cit., pp. 154–61.
80. Aron, *Eighteen Lectures on Industrial Society*, op. cit., pp. 94–5.
81. Aron, *Democracy and Totalitarianism*, op. cit., p. 63.
82. Aron, 'On Liberalisation', *Government and Opposition*, vol. 14, 1979.
83. Aron, *Eighteen Lectures on Industrial Society*, op. cit., p. 103.
84. Ibid., p. 83.
85. Aron, *Plaidoyer pour l'Europe Décadente*, op. cit., chapter 7.
86. Aron, *Eighteen Lectures on Industrial Society*, op. cit., chapters 13 and 14.
87. Aron, *La Lutte de Classes*, Gallimard, Paris, 1964, p. 107 (my translation).
88. Ibid., p. 227 (my translation).
89. Ibid., chapter 15.
90. Ibid., p. 175 (my translation).
91. Aron, *Democracy and Totalitarianism*, op. cit., p. 23.
92. Ibid., p. 91.
93. Aron, *Eighteen Lectures on Industrial Society*, op. cit., p. 202.
94. Aron, *An Essay on Freedom*, Harper and Row, New York, 1970, p. 71.
95. Aron, 'On Liberalisation', op. cit., passim.
96. Aron, *Plaidoyer Pour l'Europe Décadente*, op. cit., p. 249 and passim.
97. F. Parkin, *Marxism and Class Theory*, 10th ed., Methuen, London, 1979.
98. The argument is made in *Plaidoyer Pour l'Europe Décadente*, op. cit., pp. 393–407. For a critique see J. Gershuny, *After Industrial Society?* Macmillan, 1978, pp. 105–113.
99. Aron, *The Elusive Revolution*, op. cit., passim.
100. Aron, 'On the Proper Use of Ideologies', in J. Ben David and T. N. Clark, eds., *Culture and Its Creators*, Chicago University Press, Chicago, 1977.
101. Aron, *Imperial Republic*, op. cit., p. 321 and passim.
102. F. S. Fitzgerald, *The Crack Up with Other Pieces and Stories*, Penguin, London, 1971, p. 39.

7. Ernest Gellner

1. E. Gellner, *Thought and Change*, Weidenfeld and Nicolson, London, 1964, pp. 33–4.
2. Ibid, p. 145.
3. For Gellner's relation to his predecessors, see his review of Ginsberg's *On the Diversity of Morals* in *Universities Quarterly* 12, no. 1, November 1957, pp. 83–91.
4. Gellner, *Thought and Change*, op. cit., p. 168.
5. Ibid., p. 154.
6. Ibid., p. 155.
7. This is to say that the emergence of the nation state in Western Europe is more of a home-grown phenomenon. But I believe that some of the factors in Gellner's theory—especially the blocked mobility of the intelligentsia—apply here as well.
8. Gellner, *Thought and Change*, op. cit., p. 171.
9. Ibid., op. cit., p. 177.
10. Gellner told me about his 'trinitarianism' in an interview, 13.1.77.
11. R. Descartes, *Discourse on Method and Meditations*, Penguin, London, 1972, p. 95.
12. There is a very clear exposition of the Crusoe tradition in Gellner's *Thought and Change*, op. cit., especially pp. 105–10. For the general predicament, however, see his *Legitimation of Belief*, Cambridge University Press, Cambridge, 1974, chapter 1.
13. For an explanation along these lines see J. W. Burrow, *Evolution and Society*, Cambridge University Press, Cambridge, 1966, passim.
14. Gellner, *Thought and Change*, op. cit., chapter 1.
15. Ibid.
16. Gellner's views on Pragmatism are contained in two essays in his *Spectacles and Predicaments*, Cambridge University Press, Cambridge, 1979. His views on Popper are in *Legitimation of Belief*, op. cit., especially chapter 9.
17. Gellner, *Legitimation of Belief*, op. cit., p. 48.
18. Ibid., p. 49.
19. Ibid., p. 53.
20. It is the main theme of *Legitimation of Belief*, op. cit., especially chapters 4–6.
21. Ibid., especially pp. 83–99.
22. Ibid., p. 118.
23. Gellner, 'An Ethic of Cognition', in his *Spectacles and Predicaments*, op. cit., p. 164.
24. Gellner, *Legitimation of Belief*, op. cit., p. 163.
25. Ibid., p. 122.
26. Ibid., p. 111.
27. Ibid., p. 127.
28. Gellner, 'Positivism Against Hegelianism', an unpublished paper on the positivist dispute in German sociology.
29. Gellner, *Legitimation of Belief*, op. cit., p. 172 and chapter 9 passim.
30. Ibid., p. 179 and chapter 9 passim.
31. Gellner, 'An Ethic of Cognition', in *Spectacles and Predicaments*, op. cit., p. 179.
32. Ibid., p. 176.
33. Gellner, *Legitimation of Belief*, op. cit., p. 99.

34. B. Dylan, 'The Man in Me', *New Morning*, CBS Records, 1970.
35. Gellner, *Legitimation of Belief*, op. cit., pp. 101–2.
36. Ibid., pp. 183–8.
37. Ibid., pp. 191–202.
38. The comment in the paragraph on the Nietzschean tradition is based on an unpublished manuscript by Gellner on the Nietzsche/Freud tradition entitled 'The Cunning of Unreason'.
39. Gellner, *Words and Things* (1959), republished with a new introduction, Routledge and Kegan Paul, London, 1979, p. vii.
40. Gellner, *Legitimation of Belief*, op. cit., chapter 7.
41. Gellner has commented on the similarity between the projects of Durkheim and Wittgenstein on a number of occasions. See, for example, *Legitimation of Belief*, op. cit., p. 93 and *Thought and Change*, op. cit., pp. 183–4.
42. The locus classicus of the new idealism in social science is, of course, P. Winch, *The Idea of a Social Science*, Routledge and Kegan Paul, London, 1958.
43. Gellner, 'The New Idealism', in his *Cause and Meaning in the Social Sciences*, Routledge and Kegan Paul, London, 1973.
44. The question of human rationality is one of Gellner's underlying concerns but rationality is not discussed as such; however it is plain that the attempt in *Legitimation of Belief* to specify non-context-bound standards of truth is, in effect, nothing other than a specification of standards of rationality.
45. Gellner, 'The New Idealism', In his *Cause and Meaning in the Social Sciences*, op. cit., pp. 60–1.
46. E. Evans-Pritchard, *The Position of Women in Primitive Society and Other Essays in Social Anthropology*, cited in *Legitimation of Belief*, op. cit., p. 143.
47. Ibid., p. 156.
48. I. C. Jarvie, *Concepts and Society*, Routledge and Kegan Paul, London, 1972, p. 48.
49. Gellner, 'Concepts and Society', in his *Cause and Meaning in the Social Sciences*, op. cit., p. 39.
50. The key papers in this debate were: E. Gellner, 'Ideal Language and Kinship Structure', in his *Cause and Meaning in the Social Sciences*, op. cit.; R. Needham, 'Descent Systems and Ideal Language', *Philosophy of Science*, vol. 27, 1960; E. Gellner, 'The Concept of Kinship', in his *Cause and Meaning in the Social Sciences*, op. cit.; J. A. Barnes, 'Physical and Social Kinship', *Philosophy of Science*, vol. 28, 1961; E. Gellner, Nature and Society in Social Anthropology', in his *Cause and Meaning in the Social Sciences*, op. cit.
51. Gellner, *Saints of the Atlas*, Weidenfeld and Nicolson, London, 1969, p. 125.
52. Ibid., p. 38.
53. Gellner, 'Concepts and Society', in his *Cause and Meaning in the Social Sciences*, op. cit., p. 44.
54. Gellner, 'A Wittgensteinian Philosophy of (or against) the Social Sciences', in *Spectacles and Predicaments*, op. cit., p. 69.
55. Gellner's clearest statement of his views on method is in 'Sociology and Social Anthropology', in his *Cause and Meaning in the Social Sciences*, op. cit.
56. Ibid., p. 123.

57. This is one of the arguments of 'Sociology and Social Anthropology' in *Cause and Meaning in the Social Sciences*, op. cit., and it was stressed by Gellner in an interview on 13.1.77.

58. *Saints of the Atlas*, op. cit., p. 64.

59. Ibid., especially chapter 11.

60. Gellner, 'A Bundle of Hypotheses, of the Gaffe-Avoiding Animal', unpublished paper.

61. Gellner, 'From the Revolution to Liberalisation', in *Spectacles and Predicaments*, op. cit.

62. Gellner, 'Notes towards a theory of ideology', in ibid.

63. Gellner made this point in an interview 13.1.77.

64. T. Nairn, *The Breakup of Britain*, New Left Books, London, 1977, especially chapter 5.

65. Gellner's analysis of the puritan option in Islam and its absence in Hinduism was made in the Millenium Chase Lecture for 1979. Gellner has a forthcoming book *Muslim Society* from the Cambridge University Press.

66. Gellner, *Thought and Change*, op. cit., p. 119.

67. Ibid., p. 112.

68. Gellner, 'A Social Contract in Search of an Idiom: The Demise of the Danegeld State?', in his *Spectacles and Predicaments*, op. cit.

69. Ibid., pp. 287–8.

70. Gellner, 'Democracy and Industrialisation', in his *Contemporary Thought and Politics*, Routledge and Kegan Paul, London, 1974, especially pp. 26–7.

71. Gellner, 'The Kathmandu Option' in his *Spectacles and Predicaments*, op cit.

72. Gellner made this point in an interview, 13.1.77.

73. Gellner, 'The Unknown Apollo of Biskra: The Social Base of Algerian Puritanism', *Government and Opposition*, vol. 9, 1974.

74. Gellner made this point in an interview, 13.1.77.

75. Gellner, 'Recollection in Anxiety: *Thought and Change* Revisited', *Government and Opposition*, vol. 15, 1980.

76. Gellner, 'From the Revolution to Liberalisation', in his *Spectacles and Predicaments*, op. cit., p. 333.

77. Gellner 'The Pluralist Anti-Levellers of Prague', in his *Contemporary Thought and Politics*, op. cit., especially pp. 166–7.

78. Two papers are as yet unpublished; those that are available are: 'The Soviet and the Savage', *Current Anthropology*, vol. 16, 1975; 'Ethnicity and Anthropology in the Soviet Union', *European Journal of Sociology*, vol. 18, 1977; 'State before Class: the Soviet Treatment of African Feudalism', *European Journal of Sociology*, vol. 18, 1977.

79. Gellner, 'Getting Along in Czechoslavakia', *New York Review of Books*, vol. 25, no. 17, 1978.

80. Gellner, 'The Soviet and the Savage', op. cit., p. 596.

81. Gellner, 'The Re-Enchantment Industry, or the Californian Way of Subjectivity', in his *Spectacles and Predicaments*, op. cit., pp. 61–2.

82. For an analysis of bourgeois culture along these lines see the concluding chapter of my *The Sociology of Literature*, Longmans, 1979.

83. Gellner made this point in an interview, 13.1.77.

84. Gellner, 'The Re-Enchantment Industry, or the Californian Way to Subjectivity', op. cit., pp. 60–1.

85. Gellner, *Legitimation of Belief*, op cit., pp. 192–3.

86. Gellner, 'The Absolute in Braces', in his *Spectacles and Predicaments*, op. cit., p. 39.

87. Gellner, 'A Social Contract in Search of an Idiom: The Demise of the Danegeld State', in ibid., p. 294. The remaining paragraph of this section draws on this essay.

88. R. Aron, *History and Politics*, ed. M. B. Conant, Free Press, New York, 1978, p. 76.

89. M. Mann, 'A Sociological Critique of Historical Materialism', in his *Sources of Social Power*, Methuen forthcoming.

8. Postscript

1. B. Barry, *The Liberal Theory of Justice*, Oxford University Press, Oxford, 1973, epilogue.

2. Gellner, *Spectacles and Predicaments*, Cambridge University Press, Cambridge, 1979, pp. 339–40. The debate was occasioned by Gellner's 'From the Revolution to Liberalisation' in ibid., and appeared in *Government and Opposition*, vol. 14, 1979.

3. L. Kolakowski, 'My Correct Views on Everything', *Socialist Register 1974*, Merlin Press, London, 1974, p. 20.

4. I am indebted for this information to Edgar Feuchtwanger whose family knew Schmitt at this time in their capacity as publishers.

5. K. Bradley and A. Gelb, 'The radical potential of cash nexus breaks?', *British Journal of Sociology*, vol. 31, 1980.

6. A. H. Halsey, A. Heath, and J. M Ridge, *Origins and Destinations*, Oxford University Press, Oxford, 1980, chapter 11.

7. R. Layard, 'Wages Policy and the Distribution of Income', Centre for Labour Economics, London School of Economics, Discussion Paper 47, 1979.

8. R. Dahrendorf, 'International Affairs: A European Perspective', *International Affairs*, vol. 13, 1977. See also D. Bell, 'The Future World Disorder: the Structural Context of Crisis', *Foreign Policy*, no. 27, 1977.

Select Bibliography

Only the major works of the authors discussed are included. Complete bibilographies of Habermas (up to 1979), Gellner (up to 1978) and Marcuse (up to 1967) are available elsewhere: see respectively R. Görtzen and F. Van Gelder, 'The Complete Bibliography of the Works of Jürgen Habermas', *Human Context*, Volume 2, 1979; Gellner, *The Devil in Modern Philosophy*, ed. I. C. Jarvie and J. Agassi, Routledge and Kegan Paul, London, 1974 and Gellner, *Spectacles and Predicaments*, ed. I. C. Jarvie and J. Agassi, Cambridge University Press, Cambridge, 1979: and K. Wolff and B. Moore, eds., *The Critical Spirit*, Beacon Press, Boston, 1967. Aron is an incredibly prolific writer, but a longer list of his more important pieces is in his Festchrift, *Science et Conscience de la Société*, ed. J. C. Casanova, Calmann-Lévy, 1971. The first date of publication of works by these authors is given where appropriate. The secondary material listed is selective, including only main criticisms of the authors, and works cited or others of obvious importance.

Abercrombie, N. and B. S. Turner, 'The Dominant Ideology Thesis', *British Journal of Sociology*, vol. 29, 1979.

Adorno, T. and M. Horkheimer, *Dialectic of Enlightenment*, New Left Books, London, 1978.

Adorno, T. et al., *The Positivist Dispute in German Sociology*, Heinemann Educational Books, London, 1976.

Anderson, P., *Passages from Antiquity to Feudalism*, New Left Books, London, 1974.

Lineages of the Absolutist State, New Left Books, London, 1974.

Ardagh, J., *The New France*, 3rd ed., Penguin, London, 1977.

Arendt, H., *The Human Condition*, Anchor Books, New York, 1959.

Antisemitism, Viking Press, New York, 1968.

Aron, R., *German Sociology* (1935), 2nd ed., Heinemann Educational Books, London, 1957.

La Philosophie Critique de l'Histoire, Vrin, Paris, 1938.

Introduction to the Philosophy of History (1938), Weidenfeld and Nicolson, London, 1961.

'États démocratiques et états totalitaires', *Bulletin de la Société française de philosophie*, vol. 40, 1945.

De l'armistice à l'insurrection nationale, Gallimard, Paris, 1945.

L'Homme contre les tyrans, Gallimard, Paris, 1945.

Le Grand Schisme, Gallimard, Paris, 1948.

The Century of Total War, Derek Verschoyle, London, 1954.

Polémiques, Gallimard, Paris, 1955.

Éspoir et peur du siècle, Calmann-Lévy, Paris, 1957.

La Tragédie algérienne, Plon, Paris, 1957.

Aron, R., *The Opium of the Intellectuals* (1957), Norton, New York, 1962.
War and Industrial Society, Oxford University Press, Oxford, 1958.
France—Steadfast and Changing, Oxford University Press, Oxford, 1960.
ed., *World Technology and Human Destiny*, University of Michigan Press, Michigan, 1963.
'Max Weber and Michael Polyáni', *The Logic of Personal Knowledge*, Routledge and Kegan Paul, London, 1964.
Peace and War, Weidenfeld and Nicolson, London, 1966.
La Lutte de Classes, Gallimard, Paris, 1964.
The Great Debate, Doubleday, New York, 1965.
Eighteen Lectures on Industrial Society, Weidenfeld and Nicolson, London, 1967.
The Industrial Society, Weidenfeld and Nicolson, London, 1967.
Main Currents in Sociological Thought, 2 vols., Weidenfeld and Nicolson, London, 1965 and 1968.
Democracy and Totalitarianism, Weidenfeld and Nicolson, London, 1968.
Marxism and the Existentialists, Harper and Row, New York, 1969.
De Gaulle, Israel and the Jews, Deutsch, London, 1969.
The Elusive Revolution, Pall Mall, London, 1969.
D'une Saint Famille à l'Autre, Gallimard, Paris, 1969.
'An Interview with Raymond Aron', *Encounter*, vol. 35, 1970.
An Essay on Freedom, Harper and Row, New York, 1970.
'Remarques sur un débat', *European Journal of Sociology*, vol. 13, 1972.
Progress and Disillusion, Praeger, New York, 1970.
Études Politiques, Gallimard, Paris, 1972.
'Reason, Passion and Power in the Thought of Clausewitz', *Social Research*, vol. 39, 1972.
'La guerre est un caméléon', *Contrepoint*, no. 15, 1974.
Imperial Republic, Weidenfeld and Nicolson, London, 1974.
History and the Dialectic of Violence, Blackwells, Oxford, 1975.
Penser la guerre, Clausewitz, vol. 1: *L'Age Européen*; vol. 2: *L'Age Planétaire*, Gallimard, Paris, 1976.
'The Crisis of the European Idea', *Government and Opposition*, vol. 11, 1976.
'On the Proper Use of Ideologies', in J. Ben-David and T. N. Clark, eds., *Culture and Its Creators*, Chicago University Press, Chicago, 1977.
Plaidoyer pour l'Europe Décadente, Laffont, Paris, 1977.
History and Politics, ed., M. B. Conant, Free Press, New York, 1978.
'War and Industrial Society: A Reappraisal', *Millenium*, vol. 7, 1978/9.
'On Liberalisation', *Government and Opposition*, Vol. 14, 1979.

Barnes, J., 'Physical and Social Kinship', *Philosophy of Science*, vol. 28, 1961.
Barry, B., *Sociologists, Economists, and Democracy*, Collier Macmillan, London, 1970.
The Liberal Theory of Justice, Oxford University Press, Oxford, 1973.
Bauman, Z., *Critical Sociology*, Routledge and Kegan Paul, London, 1976.
de Beauvoir, S., *Force of Circumstance*, Penguin, London, 1968.
Bell, D., 'Grass Roots of American Jew-Hatred', *Jewish Frontier*, June 1944.
'Notes on Authoritarian and Democratic Leadership', in A. Gouldner, ed., *Studies in Leadership*, Free Press, New York, 1950.
Marxism, Socialism in the United States (1952), Princeton University Press, Princeton, New Jersey, 1967.

Bell, D., *The End of Ideology*, revised edition, Collier Books, New York, 1962.

ed., *The Radical Right*, Anchor Books, New York, 1964.

'Veblen and the New Class', in T. Veblen, *The Engineers and the Price System*, Harbinger, New York, 1965.

'Marxism-Leninism: A Doctrine on the Defensive', in M. M. Drachovitch, ed., *The Appeals and Paradoxes of Contemporary Marxism*, Praeger, New York, 1966

The Reforming of General Education, Columbia University Press, New York, 1966.

'Socialism', *International Encyclopedia of Social Sciences*, Free Press, New York, 1968.

'Charles Fourier', *American Scholar*, vol. 38, 1968/9.

with Irving Kristol, ed., *Confrontation*, Basic Books, New York, 1969.

'The Soviet Union: Ideology in Retreat', in M. Rejai, ed., *The Decline of Ideology*, Aldine Atherton, Chicago, 1971.

The Coming of the Post-Industrial Society (1973), Penguin, London, 1976.

'The End of American Exceptionalism', *The Public Interest*, no. 40, 1975, and Alain Clement, 'Interview', *Times Europa Supplement*, January 1975.

'Ethnicity and Social Change', in N. Glazer and D. P. Moynihan, eds., *Ethnicity*, Harvard University Press, Cambridge, Mass., 1976.

'The Return of the Sacred? The Argument over the Future of Religion', *British Journal of Sociology*, vol. 28, 1977.

'Beyond Modernism, Beyond Self', in Q. Anderson, S. Donadio, and S. Marcus, eds., *Art, Politics and Will*, Basic Books, New York, 1977.

The Culture Contradictions of Capitalism (1976), Heinemann Educational Books, London, 1978.

'The Future that Never Was', *The Public Interest*, no. 51, 1978.

'The Future World Disorder: the Structural Context of Crisis', *Foreign Policy*, no. 27, 1977.

'Teletext and Technology', *Encounter*, vol. 48, 1977.

Benton, T., *Philosophical Foundations of the Three Sociologies*, Routledge and Kegan Paul, London, 1977.

Bernstein, R., *The Restructuring of Social and Political Theory*, Blackwell, Oxford, 1977.

Binns, D., *Beyond the Sociology of Conflict*, Macmillan, 1977.

Bottomore, T., *Elites and Society*, Penguin, London, 1966.

Bourdieu, P., *La Distinction*, Éditions de Minuit, Paris, 1979.

Bowles, S., and H. Gintis, *Schooling in Capitalist America*, Basic Books, New York, 1976.

Bradley, K. and A. Gelb, 'The radical potential of cash nexus breaks', *British Journal of Sociology*, vol. 31, 1980.

Breines, P., ed., *Critical Interruptions*, Herder and Herder, New York, 1970.

Bryant, C. G. A., *Sociology in Action*, Allen and Unwin, London, 1976.

Burch, P. H., *The Managerial Revolution Assessed*, Lexington Books, New Haven, 1972.

Burrow, J. W., *Evolution and Society*, Cambridge University Press, Cambridge, 1966.

Carroll, J., *Break Out from the Crystal Palace*, Routledge and Kegan Paul, London, 1972.

Casanova, J. C. ed., *Science et Conscience de la Société*, Calmann-Lévy, Paris, 1971.

Cohen, G. A., 'The Philosophy of Marcuse', *New Left Review*, no. 57, 1969.

Cole, G. D. H., *Guild Socialism Restated*, Leonard Parsons, London, 1921.
The Next Ten Years, Macmillan, London, 1929.

Collini, S., *Liberalism and Sociology*, Cambridge University Press, Cambridge, 1979.

Connerton, P., *The Tragedy of Enlightenment*, Cambridge University Press, Cambridge, 1980.

Crespigny, A. de, and K. Minogue, eds., *Contemporary Political Philosophers*, Methuen, London, 1976.

Dahrendorf, R., *Marx in Perspektive*, Dietz, Hanover, 1953.
Class and Class Conflict in Industrial Society (German 1955: English revised edition 1957), Routledge and Kegan Paul, London, 1972.
Gesellschaft und Freiheit, Piper, Munich, 1961.
'European Sociology and the American Self-Image', *European Journal of Sociology*, vol. 2, 1961.
'The Politics of the Other-Directed Man', in S. M. Lipset and L. Lowenthal, eds., *Culture and Social Character*, Free Press, Glencoe, 1961.
Die angewandte Aufklärung, Piper, Munich, 1963.
'Recent Changes in the Class Structure of European Societies', *Daedalus*, no. 93, 1964.
Das Mitbestimmungsproblem in der deutschen Sozialforschung, 2nd ed., Piper, Munich, 1965.
Society and Democracy in Germany (German 1965: English revised edition 1967), Doubleday, New York, 1967.
Bildung ist Burgerrecht, Die Zeit Books, Oznabruck, 1966.
'Conflict after Class', Noel Buxton Memorial Lecture, Longmans for the University of Essex, 1967.
Pfade aus Utopia, Piper, Munich, 1967.
Für eine Erneuerung der Demokratie in der Bundesrepublik, Piper, Munich, 1968.
Essays in the Theory of Society, Routledge and Kegan Paul, London, 1968.
Konflikt und Freiheit, Piper, Munich, 1972.
Plaidoyer für die Europäische Union, Piper, Munich, 1973.
'Towards a European Science Policy', Fawley Lecture, Southampton University Press, Southampton, 1974.
'Citizenship and Beyond: The Social Dynamics of an Idea', *Social Research*, vol. 41, 1974.
The New Liberty, Routledge and Kegan Paul, London, 1975.
'Conflict and Contract', Leverhulme Memorial Lecture, Liverpool University Press, Liverpool, 1975.
'Science, Policy and Science Policy', *Proceedings of the Royal Irish Academy*, vol. 75, 1975.
'International Affairs: A European Perspective', *International Affairs*, vol. 13, 1977.
'A Confusion of Powers: Politics and the Rule of Law', *The Modern Law Review*, vol. 40, 1977.
Participation: Notes on a Very Confused Issue', *Bank of New South Wales Review*, December, 1977.

Dahrendorf, R., *Professor Ralf Dahrendorf in Australia*, Australian Broadcasting Corporation, Sydney, 1978.
'Europe and America: A Reassessment', *West European Politics*, vol. 1, 1978.
Life Chances, Weidenfeld and Nicolson, London, 1979.
'Abwarten und Teetrinken', *Stern*, 15.2.1979.
'Towards the Hegemony of Post-Modern Values', *New Society*, vol. 50, 1979.
'After Social Democracy', Unservile State Papers, no. 25, Liberal Publications, London, 1980.
'Not the Westminster Model', *Third World Foundation Monographs*, no. 2, London, 1980.
'The Limits of Equality: Some Comments on Fred Hirsch', The Peter Le Neve Foster Lecture, *Journal of the Royal Society of Arts*, June, 1980.
'Social Policy', *London Review of Books*, vol. 2, 1980.
Descartes, R., *Discourse on Method and Meditations*, Penguin, London, 1972.
Dunn, J., *Western Political Theory in the Face of the Future*, Cambridge University Press, 1979.

Floud, J., 'A Critique of Bell', *Survey*, vol. 16, 1971.
Freud, S., *Civilisation and Its Discontents*, Hogarth Press, London, 1949.
Fry, J., *Marcuse*, Harvester Press, Brighton, 1974.

Gallie, W. B., *Philosophers of War and Peace*, Cambridge University Press, Cambridge, 1978.
Gellner, E., 'Use and Meaning', *Cambridge Journal*, vol. 4, 1951.
'Review of Morris Ginsberg, *On the Diversity of Morals*', *Universities Quarterly*, vol. 12, 1957.
Words and Things (1959), Routledge and Kegan Paul, London, 1979.
Thought and Change, Weidenfeld and Nicolson, London, 1964.
Saints of the Atlas, Weidenfeld and Nicolson, London, 1969.
Cause and Meaning in the Social Sciences, I. C. Jarvie and J. Agassi, eds., Routledge and Kegan Paul, London, 1973.
Contemporary Thought and Politics, I. C. Jarvie and J. Agassi, eds., Routledge and Kegan Paul, London, 1974.
The Devil in Modern Philosophy, I. C. Jarvie and J. Agassi, eds., Routledge and Kegan Paul, London, 1974.
Legitimation of Belief, Cambridge University Press, Cambridge, 1974.
'The Unknown Apollo of Biskra: the Social Base of Algerian Puritanism', *Government and Opposition*, vol. 9, 1974.
'The Soviet and the Savage', *Current Anthropology*, vol. 16, 1974.
'Ethnicity and Anthropology in the Soviet Union', *European Journal of Sociology*, vol. 18, 1977.
'State before Class: the Soviet Treatment of African Feudalism', *European Journal of Sociology*, vol. 18, 1977.
'Getting along in Czechoslovakia', *New York Review of Books*, vol. 25, 1978.
Spectacles and Predicaments, I. C. Jarvie and J. Agassi, eds., Cambridge University Press, Cambridge, 1979.
'Recollection in Anxiety: *Thought and Change* Revisited', *Government and Opposition*, vol. 15, 1980.

Gellner, E., *Muslim Society*, Cambridge University Press, Cambridge, forthcoming.

Gershuny, J., *After Industrial Society?*, Macmillan, London, 1978.

Giddens, A., *The Class Structure of the Advanced Societies*, Hutchinson, London, 1973.

Studies in Social and Political Theory, Hutchinson, London, 1977.

Goldthorpe, J. H., D. Lockwood, F. Bechhofer, and J. Platt, *The Affluent Worker in the Class Structure*, Cambridge University Press, Cambridge, 1969.

Goldthorpe, J. H. (with the assistance of C. Llewelyn and G. Payne) *Social Mobility and Class Structure*, Oxford University Press, Oxford, 1980.

Goody, J., *Technology, Tradition and the State in Africa*, Oxford University Press, Oxford, 1971.

Gouldner, A., *The Dialectic of Ideology and Technology*, Macmillan, London, 1976.

Habermas, J., *Strukturwandel der Öffentlichkeit* (1962), Neuwied, Luchterhand, 1976.

Theory and Practice (1963), Heinemann Educational Books, London, 1974.

Zur Logik der Sozialwissenschaften (1967), Suhrkamp, Frankfurt, 1970.

Knowledge and Human Interests (1968), Heinemann Educational Books, London, 1971.

Towards a Rational Society, Heinemann Educational Books, London, 1970.

'On Systematically Distorted Communication, *Inquiry*, vol. 13, 1970.

'Towards a Theory of Communicative Competence', *Inquiry*, vol. 13, 1970.

and N. Luhmann, *Theorie der Gesellschaft oder Sozialtechnologie?* Suhrkamp, Frankfurt, 1971.

Thoughts on the Foundation of Sociology in the Philosophy of Language, Christian Gauss Lectures, Princeton, 1971, unpublished.

'Why More Philosophy?', *Social Research*, vol. 38, 1971.

Philosophisch-politische Profile, Suhrkamp, Frankfurt, 1971.

Legitimation Crisis (1973), Heinemann Educational Books, London, 1976.

'Wahreitstheorien', in *Wirklichkeit und Reflexion: Walter Schulz zum 60. Geburtstag*, Neske, Pfullingen, 1973.

'On Social Identity', *Telos*, no. 19, 1974.

and B. Frankel, 'Habermas Talking', *Theory and Society*, vol. 1, 1974.

'A Postscript to *Knowledge and Human Interests*', *Philosophy of Social Science*, vol. 3, 1975.

'Hannah Arendt's Communications Concept of Power', *Social Research*, vol. 44, 1977.

'Stumpf gewordene Waffen aus dem Arsenal der Gegenaufklärung', in K. Sontheimer, F. Duve, H. Böll and K. Streck, eds., *Briefe zur Verteidigung der Republik*, Rowolt, Reinbek bei Hamburg, 1977.

Communication and the Evolution of Society, Heinemann Educational Books, London, 1979.

'Conservatism and Capitalist Crisis', *New Left Review*, no. 115, 1979.

ed., *Stichworte zur 'Geistigen Situation der Zeit'*, 2 vols, Suhrkamp, Frankfurt, 1979.

Hall, J. A., 'Sincerity and Politics: the "Existentialists" vs Goffman and Proust', *The Sociological Review*, vol. 25, 1977.
'The Roles and Influence of Political Intellectuals: Tawney vs Sidney Webb', *British Journal of Sociology*, vol. 28, 1977.
The Sociology of Literature, Longmans, Harlow, 1979.
Halsey, A. H., A. Heath and J. M. Ridge, *Origins and Destinations*, Oxford University Press, Oxford, 1980.
Higgins, J. M., *The Poverty Business*, Blackwell, Oxford, 1978.
Hofstader, R., *The Paranoid Style in American Politics*, Vintage Books, New York, 1965.
Hollis, M., *Models of Man*, Cambridge University Press, Cambridge, 1977.
Hookway, C. and Pettit, eds., *Action and Interpretation*, Cambridge University Press, Cambridge, 1978.
Howard, D., *The Marxian Legacy*, Macmillan, London, 1977.

Jarvie, I. C., *Concepts and Society*, Routledge and Kegan Paul, London, 1972.
Jay, M., 'The Metapolitics of Utopianism', *Dissent*, vol. 17, 1970.
The Dialectical Imagination, Heinemann Educational Books, London, 1973.

Kaldor, M., *The Disintegrating West*, Penguin Books, London, 1979.
Kolakowski, L., *Positivist Philosophy*, Penguin, London, 1972.
'My Correct Views on Everything', *Socialist Register 1974*, Merlin Press, London, 1974.
Kolko, G., *The Triumph of Conservatism*, Free Press, Glencoe, 1963.
Kortrian, G., *Métacritique*, Éditions de Minuit, Paris, 1979.
Kumar, K., *Prophecy and Progress*, Penguin, London, 1978.

Layard, R., 'Wages Policy and the Distribution of Income', Centre for Labour Economics, London School of Economics, Discussion Paper 47, 1979.
Lasch, C., *The Agony of the American Left*, Vintage Books, New York, 1968.
Leiss, W., *The Domination of Nature*, Beacon Press, Boston, 1974.
Lenin, V. I., *Imperialism, the Highest Stage of Capitalism*, Lawrence, London, 1933.
Libera, A. de., 'La critique de Hegel', *La Nef*, January–March, 1969.
Lukes, S., *Emile Durkheim*, Penguin, London, 1973.

McCarthy, T., *The Critical Theory of Jürgen Habermas*, Hutchinson, London, 1978.
and F. Dallmayr, eds., *Understanding and Social Inquiry*, University of Notre Dame Press, London, 1977.
McIntrye, A., *Marcuse*, Viking Books, New York, 1970.
McKibbin, R., *The Evolution of the Labour Party 1910–24*, Oxford University Press, Oxford, 1974.
MacPherson, C. B., *The Life and Times of Liberal Democracy*, Oxford University Press, Oxford, 1977.
Mann, M., 'The Social Cohesion of Liberal Democracy', *American Sociological Review*, vol. 35, 1970.
'States, Ancient and Modern', *European Journal of Sociology*, vol. 18, 1977.

Mann, M., 'Idealism and Materialism in Sociological Theory', in J. Freiburg, ed., *Critical Sociology*, Irvington Publishers, New York, 1979.

'A Sociological Critique of Historical Materialism', in *Sources of Social Power*, Methuen, forthcoming.

Maravall, J. M., 'The Limits of Reformism', *British Journal of Sociology*, vol. 30, 1979.

Marcuse, H., 'Contributions to a Phenomenology of Historical Materialism' (1928), *Telos*, no. 4, 1969.

'On the Problem of the Dialectic' (1930/1), *Telos*, no. 27, 1977.

Hegel's Ontologie und die Grundlegung einer Theorie der Geschichtlichkeit, V. Klostermann, Frankfurt, 1932.

'On the Philosophical Foundations of the Concept of Labour' (1933), *Telos*, no. 16, 1973.

Reason and Revolution (1941), 2nd ed., Routledge and Kegan Paul, London, 1969.

Eros and Civilization (1955), Vintage Books, New York, 1962.

Soviet Marxism, Routledge and Kegan Paul, London, 1958.

'The Ideology of Death', in H. Feifel, ed., *The Meaning of Death*, McGraw Hill, New York, 1959.

'The Problem of Social Change in Technological Societies', lecture presented to a UNESCO Symposium on Social Development. Printed for limited distribution under the auspices of Raymond Aron and Bert Hoselitz.

One-Dimensional Man (1964), Abacus, London, 1972.

'Socialism in the Developed Countries', *International Socialist Journal*, vol. 2, 1965.

'Remarks on a Redefinition of Culture', *Daedalus*, vol. 94, 1965.

'Repressive Tolerance', in *Critique of Pure Tolerance* by H. Marcuse, B. Moore and R. P. Wolff, Beacon Press, Boston, 1965.

'On Science and Phenomenology' (1965), in A. Giddens, ed., *Positivism and Sociology*, Heinemann Educational Books, London, 1974.

'The Obsolescence of Marxism', in N. Lobkowicz, ed., *Marx and the Western World*, University of Notre Dame Press, Notre Dame, Indiana, 1967.

Negations (1968), Penguin, London, 1972.

An Essay on Liberation (1969), Penguin, London, 1971.

Five Lectures, Beacon Press, Boston, 1970.

Studies in Critical Philosophy, New Left Books, London, 1972.

Counter-Revolution and Revolt, Beacon Press, Boston, 1972.

and Raymond Aron, 'Can Communism by Liberal?', *New Statesman*, 23.6.1972.

'Art in the One-Dimensional Society', in L. Baxandall, ed., *Perspectives on the Arts*, Penguin, London, 1972.

'Art as a Form of Reality', *New Left Review*, no. 74, 1974.

and F. Olafsen, 'Heidegger's Politics: An Interview', *Graduate Faculty Philosophy Journal*, vol. 6, 1977.

'Murder is not a Political Weapon', *New German Critique*, no. 12, 1977.

and J. Habermas, H. Lubasz and T. Spengler, 'Theory and Politics', *Telos*, no. 38, 1978/9.

The Aesthetic Dimension, Macmillan, London, 1979.

Martin, D., *A General Theory of Secularisation*, Blackwell, Oxford, 1978.

Miller, D. B., *Social Justice*, Oxford University Press, Oxford, 1976.
Moore, B., *Social Origins of Dictatorship and Democracy*, Penguin, London, 1969.
    Injustice, Macmillan, London, 1978.

Nagy-Talavera, N. M., *The Green Shirts and Others*, Stanford, California, 1970.
Nairn, T., *The Breakup of Britain*, New Left Books, London, 1977.
Needham, R., 'Descent Systems and Ideal Language', *Philosophy of Science*, vol. 27, 1960.

O'Neill, J., ed., *On Critical Theory*, Heinemann Educational Books, London, 1977.
Orr, J., 'German Social Theory and the Hidden Face of Technology', *European Journal of Sociology*, vol. 15, 1974.

Parkin, F., *Class Inequality and Political Order*, Paladin, London, 1972.
    Marxism and Class Theory, 10th ed., Methuen, London, 1979.
Pelling, H. M., *Popular Politics and Society in Late Victorian Britain*, Macmillan, London, 1968.
Philosophy of Social Science, 'Review Symposium on Habermas', vol. 2, 1972.
Piccone, P. and A. Delfini, 'Marcuse's Heideggerian Marxism', *Telos*, no. 6, 1971.
Pierce, R., *Contemporary French Political Theory*, Oxford University Press, Oxford, 1966.
Poggi, G., *The Development of the Modern State*, Hutchinson, London, 1978.

Reich, W., *The Function of the Orgasm*, Panther, London, 1968.
Robinson, P. A., *The Sexual Radicals*, Paladin, 1970.
Rogin, M. P., *The Intellectuals and McCarthy: The Radical Specter*, MIT Press, Cambridge, Mass., 1969.
Rossides, D.W., *The American Class System*, Houghton Mifflin, Boston, 1976.

Scott, J., *Corporations, Classes and Capitalism*, Hutchinson, London, 1979.
Schmidt, A. and H. Marcuse, *Existentialistische Marx-Interpretation*, Europäische Verlaganstalt, Frankfurt, 1973.
Schoolman, M., 'Marcuse's Aesthetics and the Displacement of Critical Theory', *New German Critique*, no. 8, 1976.
Schumpeter, J., *Capitalism, Socialism and Democracy*, Allen and Unwin, London, 1976.
Stearns, P., 'Is there a post-industrial society?', *Society*, vol. 11, 1974.

Taylor, A. J. P., *The Origins of the Second World War*, Penguin, London, 1972.
Thompson, E. P., *Whigs and Hunters*, Allen Lane, London, 1976.
Trilling, L., *Beyond Culture*, Penguin, London, 1966.
Turner, J. H., 'From Utopia to Where? A Strategy for Reformulating the Dahrendorf Conflict Model', *Social Forces*, vol. 52, 1973.

Veblen, T., *Imperial Germany and the Industrial Revolution*, Viking Press, New York, 1939.

Wallerstein, I., *The Modern World-System*, Academic Press, New York, 1974.
Waxman, C., ed., *The End of Ideology Debate*, Fink and Wagnalls, New York, 1968.
Weber, M., *From Max Weber*, ed., H. H. Gerth and C. W. Mills, Oxford University Press, New York, 1970.
Weinstein, J., *The Corporate Ideal in the Liberal State*, Beacon Press, Boston, 1968.
Wellmer, A., *The Critical Theory of Society*, Herder and Herder, New York, 1971.
Wolff, K. H. and B. Moore, eds., *The Critical Spirit*, Beacon Press, Boston, 1967.
Woodward, C. V., *The Burden of Southern History*, Vintage Books, New York, 1960.
Wiles, P. J. D., *Economic Systems Compared*, Blackwell, Oxford, 1977.
Winch, P., *The Idea of a Social Science*, Routledge and Kegan Paul, London, 1958.

Index